the daily
WRITER

WRITER'S DIGEST BOOKS
Cincinnati, Ohio
www.writersdigest.com

the daily
WRITER

FRED WHITE

----

366 meditations to cultivate
a productive and meaningful
writing life

For more resources for writers, visit www.writersdigest.com/books.

To receive a free weekly e-mail newsletter delivering tips and updates about writing and about Writer's Digest products, register directly at http://newsletters.fwpublications.com.

12 11 10 09 08   5 4 3 2

Distributed in Canada by Fraser Direct
100 Armstrong Avenue
Georgetown, Ontario, Canada L7G 5S4
Tel: (905) 877-4411

Distributed in the U.K. and Europe by David & Charles
Brunel House, Newton Abbot, Devon, TQ12 4PU, England
Tel: (+44) 1626-323200, Fax: (+44) 1626-323319
E-mail: postmaster@davidandcharles.co.uk

Distributed in Australia by Capricorn Link
P.O. Box 704, Windsor, NSW 2756 Australia
Tel: (02) 4577-3555

Library of Congress Cataloging-in-Publication Data

White, Fred D.
 The daily writer : 366 meditations to cultivate a productive and meaningful writing life / Fred White. -- 1st ed.
    p. cm.
 Includes index.
 ISBN 978-1-58297-529-0 (pbk. : alk. paper)
 1. Authorship. 2. Calendars. I. Title.
 PN145.W445 2008
 808--dc22   2008021448

Edited by KELLY NICKELL
Designed by TERRI WOESNER
Illustrations by KATE QUINBY
Production coordinated by MARK GRIFFIN

fw
F+W PUBLICATIONS, INC.

For Therese
Daily Devotion

introduction

Writing can be a deeply fulfilling spiritual experience, as well as an intellectual and artistic one. Consider: You are using words to convey your deepest thoughts and feelings, either to yourself by way of a diary, to your loved ones through letters, or to the whole world through poems, stories, essays, reportage, plays. Regardless of genre, you are wielding that most powerful, mind- and spirit-enhancing tool that civilization has ever invented, the tool of language, and you are doing so in ways that illuminate people's lives, sometimes improving their lives in practical ways, while at the same time aesthetically delighting them.

Whether you are working on a collection of poems that provides fresh insight into human nature or the natural world, or a memoir that shows how one person has endured and overcome misfortune, or a novel that takes readers on a thrilling adventure or illuminates a dark corner of the human condition or the vagaries of the human heart, you are practicing a wonderful kind of mind-alchemy: the transformation of ideas into stories, private thoughts into public discourse. To think about writing in this manner is ennobling, soul-satisfying—but it can also be intimidating, sometimes to the point where you dare not attempt such alchemy yourself. What can I contribute to the world of letters that Homer and Shakespeare, Tolstoy and Emily Dickinson, have not already contributed? It's the oldest not-to-write excuse in the world: Nobody can criticize my writing if I don't write!

The Daily Writer is designed to help awaken and nurture the spiritual side of writing through daily meditation and practice throughout the calendar year. A writer needs to acquire a certain degree of mental readiness, of deep concentration and attentiveness, necessary for embarking on a daunting writing task and then staying on course. Daily meditations are an effective way of reminding you of the care and quality that must go into a writing project. Singular flashes of inspiration do not do the trick; instead, a writer needs to sustain a heightened awareness that must be nurtured from day to day. People write not just because they "get ideas" but because they have immersed themselves in a life of thought and emotional involvement with the world.

HOW TO USE THIS BOOK

There are at least four ways in which this collection of 366 meditations and the writing tasks that accompany each one of them can help you reach your goal of becoming a successful writer:

1. **It can help you integrate writing into your life.** Writing is a way of thinking, a way of seeing and interacting with the world; hence, you must give yourself time to make writing as much a part of your life as eating. Tending to your writing on a daily basis will ensure that the writing habit takes hold.

2. **It can help you get your writing day off to an effective start.** Daily reflection on any of the topics represented in this book will help place you in the frame of mind needed for literary creativity.

3. **It can help you break through writer's block.** It is easy to become immobilized. Concentrating on a topic in this book can help you to take a fresh look at your settings, characters, or story progression.

4. **It can help you gain insight into one of the many aspects of the writing craft.** Do you have trouble with openings, narrative progression, conflict, specific details, or character development? This book includes entries on these and many other aspects of the craft.

THE IMPORTANCE OF WRITING IN DAILY DOSES

One morning while gulping down my daily dose of vitamins and wonder drugs, I suddenly found myself wishing: If I could write as regularly as I take my pills, I would have completed a gazillion books by now. Then the writing teacher in me spoke up: *Well, what's keeping you from writing as regularly as you take your pills?* Writing, after all, is the best medicine for a writer—not dreaming about writing, not talking about the books you plan to write "one of these days, as soon as I find the time," not grinding your cognitive wheels, convinced that you must map everything out in your head before committing a word to paper or screen—but old-fashioned, intense, tongue-between-the-teeth writing … every day. Those last two words are the tricky part. How does one keep up a daily writing regimen? The answer is simple: The same way one keeps up the regimen of taking pills daily, by simply *doing* it, knowing that not doing it will adversely affect your health—in the case of writing, the health of your novel or memoir.

As your project takes shape, you may become more selective in which tasks to work on. This book's index is oragnized by subject and can help you decide which tasks will be most productive for you, given the present circumstance.

One final note: *The Daily Writer* is ideal for writers on the move, whether traveling or driving to work every day or running errands of one sort or another or hiking in the wilderness. You can keep this book in your purse or backpack—or on your bedside table. You might have carved out a special time of day for writing, but the thoughts about what you're writing arrive at all hours.

Here's to a fulfilling literary year and to your long-term writing success.

JANUARY 1
USES OF ALLEGORY

Every aspiring writer should read an allegory now and then because it illustrates, in a vivid, compact way, the essence of storytelling. An allegory is a narrative in which abstract principles are represented by persons, places, objects. Thus gluttony might be represented by a foul-smelling swamp or by a grotesquely obese character named Gluttony.

One of the finest allegories ever written is John Bunyan's *The Pilgrim's Progress*. The hero, Christian (allegories are supposed to be explicit), journeys from the City of Destruction to the Celestial City—but the journey is fraught with nearly overwhelming obstacles like the Slough of Despond into which he sinks because of his heavy burden of sin (think of the Ghost of Marley's chains in Dickens' *A Christmas Carol*), or the Worldly Wiseman, who tries to talk Christian out of his dangerous journey.

In an allegorical story, then, worthy goals are fraught with obstacles the hero must triumph over. Like parables (stories that teach a religious or moral lesson) and fables (stories in which the characters are animals whose actions reveal their wisdom or stupidity), allegories convey wisdom by translating abstract principles into dramatic incidents. We all learn best through example.

FOR FURTHER REFLECTION

Think about the way facets of your life can be represented allegorically. To see how allegory can serve as a guide, read Louisa May Alcott's *Little Women*. In this novel, all four of the March girls—Meg, Jo, Amy, and Beth—turn to Bunyan's *Pilgrim's Progress* to guide them through difficult times as they struggle to support their family while their father is away.

..................................TRY THIS....................................

Compose an allegory, keeping in mind that each of your characters represents an abstract trait. Give your main character a goal she struggles against powerful obstacles to attain. For example, imagine that your main character is Compassion, who struggles to reach the Land of Honor by helping impoverished people in Third World countries. In order to get to the Land of Honor, however, she must escape from Fear (who saps her spirit by describing the deadly dangers she must face).

JANUARY 2
CONTEMPLATING ART

A great painting, drawing, photograph, sculpture, or tapestry can profoundly stir our emotions, heighten our perceptions, and stimulate our imagination—often inspiring us to create our own works of art. Contemplating works of art, then, is an excellent way for writers to pique their aesthetic perceptions. Images powerfully rendered—think of Michelangelo's Sistine Chapel ceiling fresco, "The Creation of Adam," or Edvard Munch's "The Scream"—seize our attention, heighten our fascination with the subject that so fascinated the artist. For Michelangelo it was God's paradoxical nature as both transcendent power and a compassionate parent, not just to Adam but to all humankind: the mortal hand *almost* touches the Almighty one; actual contact would have constituted idolatry. For Munch, the distinction between subjective and objective reality collapses in this moment of primal, nightmarish fear: Reality is what our minds—awake or asleep or somewhere in-between—make of it.

FOR FURTHER REFLECTION

A work of art presents a vision of nature or a statement of the human condition. A painter or sculptor uses images to embody ideas and experiences much as a writer uses words for the same purpose. Art—whether it employs paint or clay, sounds or words—transforms the abstractions of human experience into shapes that can be readily apprehended by the senses.

.....................................TRY THIS....................................

Spend several moments contemplating a work of art of your choice, and then write a one-page story in which you enter that work of art. Describe how you interact with your surroundings. Remember the scene from *Mary Poppins* when Mary and Bert and the children leap into one of Bert's sidewalk paintings? Try something similar with your story.

ACTING UPON YOUR NEW YEAR'S RESOLUTIONS

It's easy to make resolutions but tough to follow through on them. Before you make yours, think about the psychology behind wanting to do so in the first place. We look upon the beginning of a new year as a chance to renew our lives. Our resolutions are promises to ourselves that we're going to accomplish what we've been dreaming to accomplish but "just haven't gotten around to." The only problem is that, all too soon, the sense of commitment begins to fade. Why is that?

For writers, New Year's resolutions are motivational prods that actually can work, *if* you set up a means of fulfilling the resolution along with the resolution itself.

For this new year, resolve not only to succeed at writing, but to write every day. To make the resolution stick, get into a routine; make writing a *habit*. This means carving out a set time for writing and adhering to it.

FOR FURTHER REFLECTION

Resolutions are best enforced through a daily routine. Eventually, the routine becomes habitual; writing will become an integral part of your life, no different from sitting down to dinner or shopping for groceries—except, of course, that writing involves uninterrupted concentration. It's a good idea, before committing to a writing routine, to "test the waters" for a few days just to see how well you can handle four or five hours of writing at one sitting. You may discover that spending only two hours a day would work best for you.

..............................TRY THIS......................................

To ensure that you write every day, set aside a realistic chunk of time relative to the demands on your workday. Approach your writing time as you do eating: as something you *must* do. Decide ahead of time what kind of writing you're going to do (work on an outline for a novel, profile a character, describe a setting, and so forth) and *do* it.

THINKING ABOUT YOUR READERS

In *Leaves of Grass*, Walt Whitman sought to erase the boundary between art and life. "Camerado, this is no book," he proclaims in "Song of Myself," "Who touches this touches a man." Poetry, for Whitman, was not to be confined to the page, but infused with living, an extension of himself—a human being addressing fellow human beings, reminding them what it meant to be alive in America.

When you sit down to write, think of yourself not so much as "a Writer," but as a man or woman reaching out to an audience, entering the conversation of humanity, enriching that conversation with a new voice, a new way of thinking about important matters. Whitman is sometimes mistaken as egotistical or narcissistic, with proclamations such as "I celebrate myself and sing myself, / And what I assume you shall assume"—but I would argue that this is a gesture more of *humility* than of egotism. An egotist wishes to be perceived apart from others; Whitman wishes to merge his soul with all humanity.

FOR FURTHER REFLECTION

How do you see yourself in relationship to your readers? Answering that question will shed light on your reasons for wanting to be a writer. Perhaps you see yourself as a teacher, motivated to share your knowledge with others. Perhaps you see yourself as an entertainer, motivated to delight your audience with a captivating story. Perhaps you see yourself like Walt Whitman, as a participant in the drama of life, one whose voice serves as a catalyst for a multitude of voices.

...................................TRY THIS...................................

Draft a poem or letter addressed to your fellow citizens in which you share one idea for making the world a better place. Is it the importance of individual citizens exercising civic responsibility? Is it having faith in a higher power? Perhaps you have a vision for education reform? Be as detailed as you can about the program you propose.

JANUARY 5
REVERENCE FOR BOOKS AND READING

One cannot become a good writer without being a good reader. After all, since writers *create* reading, they learn to appreciate the range of quality and content that makes reading so rewarding. In order to develop such appreciation, writers must read widely and deeply. The pleasures and possibilities of the written word should stir the soul of every aspiring writer.

Perhaps you can recall a time when a reading experience changed your thinking about the world. As a child, the philosopher, novelist, and playwright Jean-Paul Sartre revered books to such a degree that he regarded the library as a temple: "Though I did not yet know how to read," he tells us in his autobiography, *The Words*, "I already revered those standing stones, upright or leaning over. ... I felt that our family's prosperity depended on them. [Their] permanence guaranteed me a future as calm as the past." *Permanence* is the special word to reflect upon here. Sartre grew up appreciating the way good books contribute permanent values and insights into the collective human experience.

FOR FURTHER REFLECTION

What kinds of books do you enjoy reading most? Science fiction? Historical fiction? Memoirs? Books about nature? Folktales from different cultures? Spy thrillers? Maybe you're an omnivore and enjoy almost everything. Describe your favorite kinds of books and what it is about the genre that you enjoy. For example, if you enjoy mysteries set in the Middle Ages, like those of Ellis Peters, perhaps it's because you love to get a taste of daily life in the tenth century, especially if you can learn about it in the context of enjoying a suspenseful murder mystery.

......................................TRY THIS....................................

Think back to a childhood experience with one special book. How did it affect you? Which characters were the most memorable? What did you learn? What long-term influence has it had on your life? Read the book again so that you may be reminded of its magical effect on you.

BRAINSTORMING FOR EFFECTIVE TITLES

What's in a title? Lots of things! Titles have a way of helping writers focus on what is essential to their work in progress and of helping to keep writers on track. Even though you will most likely change your title by the time you finish, a working title (or series of working titles) serves as a prod to keep your premise, or central idea, in mind. Titles even have the potential to get the writing going by conjuring up a particular scene or character trait. Tennessee Williams once started work on a play with the title *Poker Night* in mind. It was just the catalyst he needed to help envision his characters. Soon, the play evolved into one of the great achievements in American theater. Williams eventually settled on a more intriguing title: *A Streetcar Named Desire*.

Titles for nonfiction ought to be both informative and engaging. You may have noticed that most nonfiction book titles have two parts: an engaging main title and a more informative subtitle. Here are a few examples:

- *Dinosaur in a Haystack: Reflections in Natural History* (Stephen Jay Gould)

- *The Passion of the Western Mind: Understanding the Ideas That Have Shaped Our World View* (Richard Tarnas)

- *Will in the World: How Shakespeare Became Shakespeare* (Stephen Greenblatt)

- *Eats, Shoots & Leaves: The Zero Tolerance Approach to Punctuation* (Lynne Truss)

FOR FURTHER REFLECTION

Titles are important because they're the first things readers encounter in a publication. Bookstore patrons often browse titles, so it stands to reason that titles should be both clever and informative. The same holds true for the titles of stories and articles in a magazine's table of contents. It is often the cleverly worded title that helps you decide whether to read the piece.

....TRY THIS......................................

Brainstorm for the title of a short story or magazine article you've recently begun. Be inventive! Come up with several possible titles; circle those that best arouse curiosity. For fiction titles, try hinting at the storyline, as Poe does with "A Descent Into the Maelstrom" or "The Premature Burial." For nonfiction titles, use a main title + subtitle approach as described above.

CREATING REALISTIC CHARACTERS

The great Jazz Age novelist F. Scott Fitzgerald once scribbled in his notebook for *The Last Tycoon* (the Hollywood novel he never lived to finish), "action is character." In other words, incidents occur because of people who cause them. We can also better understand incidents when we learn about the people involved. Think of the Civil Rights Movement: It sounds like a disembodied concept. But now imagine Rosa Parks refusing to give up her seat to a white man one afternoon in Selma, Alabama; or think of Martin Luther King, Jr. standing on the steps of the Lincoln Memorial, facing an audience of a quarter-million people, proclaiming, "I have a dream!" Action, indeed, is character.

As you think about the people you plan to put into your novel or memoir, think about their behavior—on the job, in a crisis, with their friends and family—how they affect others. Keep in mind that even extreme personality types are complex and capable of a wide range of actions.

FOR FURTHER REFLECTION
Think about the people you know best—members of your family, perhaps: What are their dominant behavioral characteristics? What common features do they share? How is each person distinctive? Such analyzing of loved ones may seem a bit cold-blooded, but it is necessary writer's work.

...................................TRY THIS...................................

First, prepare a one- or two-page "bio sheet" of a character you'd like to include (or have already included) in your memoir or novel. Include the following attributes:

- physical and behavioral characteristics
- temperament (impulsive? cautious? paranoid? reflective?)
- habits of speech
- beliefs (spiritual, ideological)
- eccentricities
- fears, anxieties
- likes and dislikes

Next, write a scene consisting of narration, dialogue, and action, in which your viewpoint character interacts with another character, and in which you capture as many of the above character attributes as you can.

To create realistic characters, you need to pay attention to all of their attributes, even if you wind up using only a few of them explicitly.

MAGIC IN THE DETAILS

Samuel Johnson, the eighteenth-century lexicographer and critic, once explained to his biographer, James Boswell, that if a biographer truly wished to capture his subject's life, close attention should be paid to the "little" details—for those contribute to the subject's distinctiveness. "Nothing is too little for so little a creature as man," Johnson quipped. Boswell took the advice; his *Life of Johnson* is one of the world's great biographies. In the following excerpt, Boswell captures Johnson's playful side, surprising in light of his formidable personality.

> One night when Beauclerk and Langton [Johnson's friends] had supped at a tavern in London, and sat till about three in the morning, it came into their heads to [fetch] Johnson, and … prevail on him to join them in a ramble. They rapped violently at the door … till at last he appeared in his shirt, with his little black wig on the top of his head … and a poker in his hand, imagining, probably, that some ruffians were coming to attack him. When he discovered who they were, and was told their errand, he smiled, and with great good humour agreed to their proposal: "What, is it you, you dogs! I'll have a frisk with you." He was soon drest, and they sallied forth together into Covent-Garden, where the greengrocers and fruiterers were beginning to arrange their hampers.

Notice how those details—the black wig slapped onto his head, the dialogue, the bustling Covent-Garden merchants (at 3 A.M.!)—conjure up a vivid picture of eighteenth-century life, together with a vivid picture of Johnson.

FOR FURTHER REFLECTION
The illusion of reality that fiction creates has mainly to do with the concrete and sensory details writers are able to concoct. Exacting details awaken the senses, just like the objects and sensations themselves, and contribute to a memorable reading experience.

......................................TRY THIS..................................

Imagine being inside a scary place, such as the unlit cellar of a haunted house or an abandoned graveyard late at night. Use specific sensory descriptions—of smells, sounds, images (insofar as they are discernable in weak light), and physical sensations.

THE ART OF REVISING

"Writing is rewriting," asserted the late Pulitzer Prize-winning journalist and professor of English, Donald M. Murray. To put it another way, rewriting is an inevitable stage in the writing process, unless you are one of those rare prodigies who can revise in your head and not put a word to paper until you have it just right.

Nothing freezes up writers more than worrying about the words not coming out right. What if it sounds dumb? What if my facts are wrong? What if my sentence structure is awkward or my paragraphs do not progress in a logical manner? Such worry often can be traced to high school teachers who "corrected" with stern red abbreviations such as FRAG, DICT, WEAK, AWK—like the squawking of a crazed parrot. Such impersonal feedback can dampen the spirit of any aspiring writer.

Good writers often are their own harshest critics. The philosopher and novelist William H. Gass once said that he must revise several times just to achieve mediocrity. It took Leo Tolstoy seven drafts before he was satisfied with *War and Peace*.

"My first draft," Susan Sontag writes, "has only a few elements worth keeping." Experienced writers take for granted that much of what comes out as rough draft will have to be revamped, even discarded—but that does not mean the writing was a waste of time. On the contrary, without that rough draft, nothing productive could have followed.

FOR FURTHER REFLECTION

Conveying our ideas in writing is a complex task; hence, revising is inevitable. Once we acknowledge that fact, we can better approach revision not as a chore but as an integral part of the art of writing.

....................................TRY THIS....................................

Write a one-page description of an object that is familiar to you but not to others—your vintage-model car, your aunt Bertha's crazy quilt, your uncle Sylvester's collection of clipper ships in bottles. Over the next few days, tinker with the sketch: Add new details, and take out boring, verbose passages. Then, as a last step, proofread your draft for GR, DICT, SP, MECH, FRAG, AWK, and all that.

DREAMS: A WRITER'S RESOURCE

The wisdom behind the poet William Butler Yeats's oft-quoted adage, "In dreams begin responsibility," is perhaps best appreciated when applied to writers. Our dreams, however fragmentary and irrational, represent our subconscious mind's efforts to resolve anxieties we haven't consciously been able to confront. One does not need to be a psychoanalyst to interpret one's own dreams, provided you do a little background reading beforehand. Freud's *Interpretation of Dreams* or Carl Jung's book *Dreams* (a collection of eight papers on the subject) can be helpful. But even without this background knowledge, you can gain insight into your own dreams simply by trying to write them out. Of course, you'll need to keep a notepad—or better yet, a dream journal—close by, and scribble them down the moment you wake up; otherwise, likelier than not, they will dissipate like smoke (see the entry for November 15). In your effort to translate your dream images into words, the dreams will begin to make more sense to you.

FOR FURTHER REFLECTION

Dreaming delivers us out from the rational surface of life and into its murkier depths, the root cellars of our minds. Here, we can explore the hidden world of human behaviors, fears, and desires in order to gain a deeper understanding of—and sympathy for—the complexities of being human. Do not fear to enter these lower depths: They are the wellsprings of life itself and offer writers a wealth of insights for character-driven stories.

..................................TRY THIS..................................

Choose an entry from your dream journal and build it into an episode that is comprehensible without sacrificing its dreamlike qualities. If scenes shifted without any logical connection, then try to emulate those scene shifts in your episode. Also, pay attention to irrational juxtapositions of objects. The idea here is to allow objects which, in the waking world, have no logical connection with each other—a timepiece with a rabbit, for example—to suggest a whimsical or uncanny connection: say, the White Rabbit in *Alice in Wonderland*, holding his pocket watch and exclaiming, "I'm late! I'm late!"

DRAWING FROM EXPERIENCE

Aspiring writers are sometimes pessimistic about success because they haven't had the kind of experiences they think writers should have. The truth of the matter is that, yes, extraordinary first-hand experiences can prove to be a writer's cash cow, but they're not essential. Thorough research, together with a vigorous imagination, can take you far. You might find it hard to believe, if you've read *The Red Badge of Courage*, that Stephen Crane never fought in the Civil War, having been born six years after the war ended. How do you suppose a novelist like Steven Saylor captures the authentic milieu of ancient Rome in novels like *The Venus Throw*? Saylor has intimate historical knowledge of that period—not only the result of his majoring in history at the University of Texas, but of his deep reading into primary sources, such as ancient law documents.

Novelist Flannery O'Connor once noted that anyone who survives his childhood has enough story material for a lifetime.

FOR FURTHER REFLECTION

Your own life experiences, however "ordinary" you think they might be, have equipped you for becoming a writer. Remember that "experience" can mean a lot of things. You don't have to rob a bank to write about someone who does; our imagination allows us to extrapolate from stories we've read about bank heists and our own familiarity with banks. Better to have a little experience and a lot of imagination than vice versa.

..................................TRY THIS....................................

List ten events from childhood. Don't pass up any just because they seem "ordinary." Possibilities might include being frightened by an animal or by some adult; getting lost; getting a crush; being treated unfairly by a teacher. Next, write a page or so in which you capture one of these experiences as vividly as you can. Avoid merely summarizing the experience. Project yourself back into to the child you were when the experience occurred, and dramatize the event (that is, use dialogue and a narrative line that gives the impression that the scene is unfolding before the reader's eyes).

GIVING AND RECEIVING FEEDBACK

Even the most experienced writers value feedback on work in progress (whether an outline, partial draft, or completed draft) for four reasons. First, there are so many things to keep track of—story or idea development, clarity, coherence, accuracy, and so on; it is all too easy to overlook things. Second, feedback helps writers think more about audience expectations and reactions—always important because, after all, one writes not only for publication in order to be read, but for posterity. Third, feedback—giving as well as receiving—is always a way of learning additional strategies for storytelling and language-use. The fourth reason may be the most important: Feedback helps you to become a better critic of your own work. This is not to say that you'll eventually outgrow your need for feedback—rare is the writer who does—but it does mean that you will become better able to identify problems before they get out of hand.

FOR FURTHER REFLECTION

If you're just starting out as a writer, you might feel queasy about showing a draft of your work to others. You may feel as if your privacy is invaded, and in a sense it is: You are laying out your innermost thoughts, and that in itself can be embarrassing, let alone having someone tell you that there are problems with it. But if you want to publish your work, this is an initiation rite you need to go through.

......................................TRY THIS....................................

Give a draft of your short story in progress to a not-too-close friend or relative (the closer he is, the less likely he can be objective), and ask for specific feedback: Are the characters realistic? Is the writing fresh and alive? Does the narrative progress in an engaging and (if appropriate) suspenseful manner? Is the outcome satisfying? If your reader is also a writer, then invite her to show you a story for your feedback.

FOOD FOR THOUGHT

Food must come first, playwright Bertolt Brecht reminds us through the gangster Macheath in *The Threepenny Opera*:

> Now all you gentlemen who wish to lead us
> Who teach us to desist from mortal sin
> Your prior obligation is to feed us:
> When we've had lunch, your preaching can begin.
> —Translation by Eric Bentley

Before we can do good work and think good thoughts and hold fast to our ideals, bread must be on the table (and, by extension, we must do what we must to earn enough money to put bread on the table). Food manifests itself in so many ways: as a shaper of family and social life, as entertainment and celebration, as ritual, as a rich source of aesthetic pleasure, and, of course, as the basis for strife between the haves and have-nots. It is not surprising, therefore, that food finds its way into literature. It helps define characters (Leopold Bloom's kidneys, the Cratchit family's Christmas goose; Algernon's muffins from Oscar Wilde's *The Importance of Being Earnest*; Mr. Wonka's strawberry-flavored chocolate-coated fudge from Roald Dahl's *Charlie and the Chocolate Factory*).

FOR FURTHER REFLECTION

Because food is such a basic necessity, we want to make it more than that. We have raised food preparation to the level of art and culture; we have made it a prominent part of our special occasions—birthday parties, reunions, holiday celebrations, wedding receptions, even funeral receptions. Think about some of your fondest food-related experiences: What is the larger social or cultural context for those experiences?

..................................TRY THIS..................................

Write a scene involving two or more individuals meeting over dinner to discuss serious business or to celebrate a special occasion. Work in detailed descriptions of the food and the way it has been prepared together with the particulars of the get-together.

RESEARCHING AS SEARCHING

The very word "research" can intimidate many a would-be writer, conjuring up, as it does, not-too pleasurable hours in the college library working on research papers. But research can be an adventure when there's no grade anxiety interfering with your concentration. Research, after all, is *searching*—not merely sleuthing through the library stacks or surfing the Internet for information, but talking to experts, going on field trips, getting yourself behind the scenes, examining unpublished documents and observing unreported activities. Before you know it, your research is taking you into areas you've never anticipated.

Novelist Jean Auel, author of the Earth's Children series set in prehistoric times, thinks of research as a Pied Piper: "It just leads you on." When embarking on an information-gathering venture, try to determine ahead of time what information you need to uncover, but also be ready for surprises.

FOR FURTHER REFLECTION

Think back on your experiences conducting research—for example, in your high school and college courses; also, in job-related contexts: researching court cases if you're a lawyer, reading up on clinical case histories if you're a psychologist or nutritionist. Homemakers too need to do research of one sort or another: locating an ideal low-carbohydrate or low-sodium recipe for dinner, reading up on how to entertain guests for your upcoming party. What research projects have you most enjoyed? Perhaps the answer will suggest your next writing project!

......................................TRY THIS...................................

Put Jean Auel's Pied Piper metaphor to the test by choosing a topic you'd like to explore in depth and write about. Now, using your favorite Internet search engine, gather preliminary information. If you love sailing, for example, use the search engine to find Web sites relating to the basics of sailing, the history of sailboats, or of sailboat races. If you're planning to write a novel about country and western singers, then find information on the Web about the origins of C & W music and about Nashville, Tennessee—the industry's capital. Summarize in one or two pages the new knowledge you've gained from this preliminary research.

KEEPING A JOURNAL

If you do not yet keep a journal (writer's notebook, daybook, diary—call it what you will), then start one now. I mean now—this minute. It is a fundamental writer's tool for several important reasons:

- for jotting down ideas (for new works or works already underway), observations, sensory impressions of unusual experiences, descriptions of people, places visited, recollected or overheard conversations (writers are inveterate eavesdroppers, and that's perfectly okay—just be inconspicuous about it), trial sketches for scenes you might develop, even dreams (keep it next to your bed for that occasion)

- for keeping you in a state of "writer-readiness," much like the way photographers are always, in effect, composing photographs

- for cultivating the habit of writing

- for flashes of insight (so much of what we think about and observe we immediately forget)

A journal is by definition unfinished writing, meant for the writer's eyes only; hence, you're going to jot things down in it without concern for sentence structure, word choice, spelling, or grammar. Journal writing is writing that you refer back to in order to mine the raw ore of first-hand observations and flash-in-the-pan insights.

FOR FURTHER REFLECTION

The journals/diaries/notebooks of many authors have been published—those of Albert Camus, Ralph Waldo Emerson, F. Scott Fitzgerald, Nathaniel Hawthorne, Henry James, Franz Kafka, Anaïs Nin, Henry David Thoreau, and Dorothy Wordsworth are among the most interesting. Study the journals of several authors and decide which approach you would like to try for your own journal.

...............................TRY THIS...............................

If this is your first journaling experience, begin your journal with a fun-to-write entry, completely nonserious—a bit of writing for the sheer fun of writing *without* a purpose. For example, describe a wild fantasy of yours: becoming an eagle for one full day and flying over mountains and forests or becoming one of your favorite characters, the way Captain Jean-Luc Picard (from *Star Trek: The Next Generation*) becomes private eye Dixon Hill on the *Enterprise*'s holodeck.

ON DEFINITIONS

Definitions help us understand the nature of things; but, paradoxically, definitions can also interfere with that understanding. "Every definition is dangerous," warned Desiderius Erasmus, the Renaissance Dutch scholar and author of *In Praise of Folly*. Erasmus's warning is implicit in the very origin of the word *definition*: It is derived from the Latin, *definire*, "to set limits, to restrict." Of course, dictionaries are the standard-bearers of definitions, but language is a vast, continually evolving organism (which is why dictionaries regularly need updating).

Writers play a major role in the way definitions evolve. They will write popular articles about, say, schizophrenia or relativity or global warming, and the once-specialized terms will acquire more commonplace—and less precise—definitions. Suddenly, anyone with a mood change is "schizophrenic"; suddenly, everything is "relative" in the sense of having no standard value or meaning; suddenly, a local heat wave will be attributed to global warming. As writers, we need to be cautious about the way we define terms, always keeping in mind the ease with which precision is lost when a once-specialized concept enters popular parlance.

FOR FURTHER REFLECTION

Definitions are tools for shaping knowledge. They are classification systems for concepts and for designating relationships among objects. The great eighteenth-century Swedish biologist Linnaeus created the genus/species classification system for all organisms.

However, like any tool, definitions (or classification systems) can be misused. An imprecise definition—that is, one that fails to recognize the complexity of the grouping—can lead to confusion and injustice.

..................................TRY THIS....................................

Think of the conventional definitions of commonplace concepts such as "ethical," "liberal," or "conservative," and stipulate your own definitions, taking care to avoid imprecision. Describe the context that would justify your definitions. For example, consider describing "ethical" in the context of advertising. What kinds of advertising practices would you judge to be ethical, or unethical, and why?

LISTENING HOLISTICALLY

We sometimes listen with half a mind; the other half gets distracted by the surroundings, by our compulsions to editorialize prematurely, or simply by our inadequate ability to pay close attention. If we would simply remind ourselves that listening holistically, without being judgmental, is an opportunity to widen our understanding of the issue at hand, we would become better thinkers as well as better writers. Listening holistically contributes to our capacity for seeing a given issue from multiple perspectives, not just from one or even two. (That cliché, "There are two sides to every story" is an over-simplification: There often are *many* sides to every story.) Of course, to listen holistically is easier said than done. Most of us need to consciously practice it. You'd be amazed by how easy it can be to filter out views at the first hint that they differ from our own.

The next time you are engaged in conversation, make a special effort to listen holistically—that is, to pay as close attention to the views of others, *especially* if they clash with your own, as if they were your own views.

FOR FURTHER REFLECTION

Listening well is an art, and like all arts, it must be deliberately cultivated. How good a listener are you? How closely do you pay attention to what people say? Asking yourself these questions is an important first step toward improving your ability to listen well.

......................................TRY THIS....................................

1. Host a debate with friends on a controversial issue. After each person speaks, write a summary of that person's views. Afterward, ask each person to check your summaries for accuracy.

2. Initiate a conversation with a friend on a topic you have strong opinions about. After your friend leaves, summarize your friend's views and what you've learned from those views, whether or not you disagree with them.

3. Write a short story in which you satirize characters who get into trouble because they fail to listen carefully.

THE ART OF CONCENTRATION

"Concentration is the secret of strength in politics, in war, in trade," wrote Emerson in his *The Conduct of Life*. Applied to writing, concentration should be regarded in both of its principal meanings: as thinking *intensely* about a subject and as thinking about the *essential aspects* of a subject—the former because writing requires undivided attention to its subject; the latter because the writer must dig deeply in order to convey what readers don't already know about the subject.

Is it possible to strengthen your ability to concentrate? Resist the impulsive solution. Be skeptical of solutions that leap into mind before you've had a chance to think about them in detail.

FOR FURTHER REFLECTION

Great ideas, great scientific and artistic achievements, memorable storytelling—these are the fruits of concentration. If you aspire to literary success, take stock of your habit of concentration. Are you easily distracted? Do you lose patience with yourself for thinking too long about something? Extend your powers of concentration by allotting thirty minutes on a problem (such as figuring out the details of an action scene) you would normally allot only ten minutes for.

......................................TRY THIS....................................

Focus your attention on a problem you are facing with one of your writing projects. Perhaps it's a plot detail you haven't yet worked out or an incident in your life you want to incorporate into your memoir but are not sure how to do it. Keep your journal handy in case you need to take notes. Now concentrate in three stages:

- First stage: Describe the event in general terms. X must drive fifty miles through a violent thunderstorm to reach his disabled mother.

- Second stage: Make a list of complications. What obstacles will X face along the way? Go ahead and list more things than you will actually include.

- Third stage: Write out a rough draft of the scene. Don't stop for revisions, and don't think about anything else except that one situation.

SCRAPBOOKING

Just as journals serve as repositories for ideas, fleeting thoughts, observations, mental inventories and such, scrapbooks serve as repositories for documents associated with special events: programs from plays and concerts; souvenirs from cruises; menus from classy restaurants; photographs from innumerable get-togethers, vacations, and special occasions; postcards; and placemats. In addition to mounting these items in the scrapbook, set aside enough space for a paragraph or so in which you describe the experience in question. That way, if you ever wanted to work the experience into a novel or memoir, the photograph-explanation combo will give you a good head start. You might also write a more elaborate entry in your journal to establish a clearer context for each item in the scrapbook. Include cross-referencing information when you do so. For memorabilia you haven't written up, a few sentences in your journal recalling the event should do the trick.

FOR FURTHER REFLECTION

Memories are like tinder boxes: one tiny spark of recollection can set off a firestorm of recollections. That is why memorabilia are important to anyone, especially to writers. Resolve never to toss out anything that could have value to you as a writer. Many memorabilia include important data, such as playbills or catalogues for art exhibitions. If these items are too bulky to mount in a scrapbook, organize them in hanging files or on a bookshelf.

..................................TRY THIS....................................

Go through old, forgotten boxes in your closets, attic, or garage and pluck out anything that kindles a memory. Once a day, write at least a few sentences about the experience. If the memory is too blurry, then speculate on what might have taken place (but make sure you note that you're speculating; you won't want to pass off anything as certain when it isn't).

ON MOTIVATION

What drives us writers to devote countless hours, arduous more than easy-going, to fashioning stories and essays and poems? Some of the motives for doing so are noble: Rebecca West said she wrote books in order to find out about things. In other words, regardless of how much you knew about your subject beforehand, writing a book about it will soon make you realize how relatively little you actually knew. Other motives include wanting to heighten awareness about the dangers of falling victim to one's compulsions, such as gambling or drinking excessively or losing one's temper too easily.

On the other hand, one needn't be Sigmund Freud to realize that motives for writing may also be ignoble. Maybe you've been treated unjustly one time too many and see writing as a way of meting out revenge. Maybe you hate your day job and long to write books that will make you financially self-sufficient, free to travel the world, sleep until noon. Does it really matter what motives us, so long as we get the writing done? Maybe not, but it can be useful to think about the energies (demons?) that make us do what we do; facing them might even help us overcome psychological obstacles.

FOR FURTHER REFLECTION

Gaining insight into what motivates you to become successful may help you better understand how to strengthen or adapt those motives. Do you write in order to show how helping others will be likelier to lead to greater happiness than exploiting others? If so, then you may suddenly realize that you must learn more about the lives of missionaries, homeless-shelter volunteers, and the like, and compare them to the loan sharks and embezzlers.

......................................TRY THIS....................................

Begin a journal entry with the words: "The *real* reason I want to be a writer is as follows ..." Try to give specific reasons (e.g., "I want to create a witty, shrewd, tough-yet-sensitive private detective novels like Robert Parker's Spenser series."), and try to be as honest with yourself as you can.

STRIVING FOR ORIGINALITY

Good writing is paradoxical. To be appreciated, it needs to fulfill basic expectations of idea-development, clarity, grammatical correctness. At the same time, readers crave distinctiveness: a new way of regarding a topic, expressing a thought. Fortunately, each of us perceives the world differently; we just need to feel confident that our distinctive voices would be appreciated. It's tricky, though: Innovation is most appreciated when it doesn't totally do away with existing conventions. True, there may be compelling reasons for changing the conventions themselves: Virginia Woolf and James Joyce used an innovative mode of narrative, stream-of-consciousness, but the public was more-or-less ready for it because of advances in psychoanalysis—a case of art following in the footsteps of science. But dismantling convention for its own sake is likely to yield contrived or unreadable results.

Your best bet is to become familiar with the conventions as well as the innovations, and then to add to the conversation—concentrating first on the idea, then on the manner of expression. Become alert to the way you sound on paper. Readers love distinctive voices. Poet James Merrill once said, "The words that come first are anybody's, a froth of phrases. ... You have to make them your own."

FOR FURTHER REFLECTION

Instead of telling ourselves we must "be original," it would be better to begin at the other end: "Don't be derivative." Instead of writing your own Harry Potter-esque school-for-wizards fantasy, create a fantasy world from scratch. It can still be filled with magic and sorcerers (if you try to be too original in terms of basic genre expectations, you risk losing your audience), but you can still populate this familiar milieu with refreshingly unusual characters.

..................................TRY THIS....................................

Take a typical setting for a horror or fantasy novel—a creepy old house, a castle—and jot down ideas for atypical characters and situations that might take place in that typical setting. For example, instead of ghosts haunting the creepy old house, make it a hold-out for discarded, genetically engineered creatures—half human, half something else.

THOUGHTS ABOUT PLOT

The word "plot" chills the blood of many fiction writers. The main reason stems from two misconceptions about plotting: (1) that it must be completely worked out before the drafting process; and (2) that it has to follow a formula. Partly to blame for these misconceptions are writing teachers who compare a story's plot with an architect's blueprint. It's a faulty comparison because, unlike a blueprint, a plot often evolves as the drafting evolves. House builders do not revise as they go along. Writing stories involves interactions of character and circumstance that are difficult to anticipate. When novelists say that their characters take on lives of their own, they mean it literally. Some writers actually thrive on the pleasures of discovery while drafting; it's what keeps them going. Their creative energies might diminish if they worked out all the plot details in advance.

FOR FURTHER REFLECTION

Writing a story is not unlike reading one: You're not entirely sure how things are going to turn out from one moment to the next. Imagine that you're writing a story about a treasure hunt. Your protagonist is working with a long-hidden map, but it proves to be full of false leads. Like your protagonist, you study the map for subtle clues, maybe including new clues that match up with the sudden new thoughts you had about the terrain over which your protagonist is canvassing. Like a cook who slowly adds a new ingredient to a simmering concoction, you work your new plot ingredient into the evolving story so as not to interrupt the energy flow.

. . . . TRY THIS . . . .

Resume work on an unfinished story by adding plot elements as you go along. Maybe they will send your main character down a blind alley, maybe not. But this is an exercise in adding story elements as they occur to you, not in plot architecture. Let your storytelling imagination take the reins and go, assuming that you'll be revising extensively later on.

THOUGHT AS ACTION

We are the authors of our own lives as much as we are of the stories we write. Our lives are steadily unfolding narratives which would generally make for rather tedious reading. But the more we do with our lives, the more we enrich them, and the more substantive our stories become. Of course what we "do" with our lives need not be overt adventure. A powerful insight, communicated well, can improve lives, enhance beauty, and even change history. Marcus Aurelius (121–180 C.E.), one of the Stoic philosophers as well as Emperor of Rome during a time of invasions and social upheaval, knew this first-hand when he wrote, "One's life is what one's thoughts make it." Henry David Thoreau, similarly, advises us in *Walden* to live our lives "as deliberately as nature"—that is, to plan activities that harmonize with our inner natures, with our personal aspirations and needs—to "follow the sound of our own distant drummer" instead of slavishly adhering to someone else's notions of how to live.

FOR FURTHER REFLECTION

Thought leads to action; one could say that thought is embryonic action, or action in stasis. If you list tasks you wish to accomplish over a given period, then those tasks are in the process of becoming accomplished. Perhaps your thoughts about the connection between improving your social life and embarking on a recreational activity have led to your forming a nature-hiking group. Or perhaps your notion that the city you live in could do more to protect and restore old buildings has led you to become active in a nonprofit organization that helped save that century-old train depot from the wrecking ball and turn it into a museum.

......................................TRY THIS....................................

Take one of your newest ideas or insights—one of those New Year's resolutions you never followed through on, for example—and work up the idea into a step-by-step action plan. Then write an essay in which you describe what actually took place when you put your ideas to work. Don't leave out the missteps or the unforeseen snags.

HONESTY AND AUTHENTICITY

Writing represents carefully directed thought, the fruit of hours of reflection, of searching for the most exact language to convey the veracity of an experience or the complexity of an idea. If your thinking is half-baked or insincere, you may not even realize it until you've begun writing it down. Seeing our thoughts exposed on the naked page or screen in stark letters helps us to discern their authenticity more readily. Often transcribed in haste, our thoughts suddenly stand still for us, poised for scrutiny, as if posing for a photograph. Did you really mean what you just wrote about the way your mother treated you when you were nine? Is that description of your Aunt Mildred's obsession with cleanliness accurate? Did that Halloween prank take place exactly the way you said it did? Fiction writers also must tend scrupulously to honesty and authenticity, or else the characters or the story they are unfolding will not seem genuine. The discipline of writing, as John Steinbeck asserted, punishes both stupidity and dishonesty. In a very real sense, then, writing is one of the most ethical activities we can engage in.

FOR FURTHER REFLECTION

Think about the way you talk about your life to others. Do you "stretch the truth" a bit, as Mark Twain would say? Do you leave out certain negative details or replace them with more positive ones? More importantly, does this tendency transfer to your memoir writing as well? If so, you may want to set some authenticity ground rules for yourself before embarking on your next writing project, or revising an existing one.

......................................TRY THIS....................................

Pull out a draft of one of your unpublished or unfinished short stories, essays, or poems, and begin writing a critical evaluation of its authenticity. Question every detail, every assertion, either in your own voice or that of a persona. Offer yourself suggestions for revision. Get feedback from a friend or family member. Wait a couple of days, and then revise the piece, incorporating this feedback if warranted.

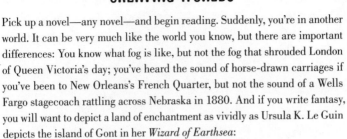

CREATING WORLDS

Pick up a novel—any novel—and begin reading. Suddenly, you're in another world. It can be very much like the world you know, but there are important differences: You know what fog is like, but not the fog that shrouded London of Queen Victoria's day; you've heard the sound of horse-drawn carriages if you've been to New Orleans's French Quarter, but not the sound of a Wells Fargo stagecoach rattling across Nebraska in 1880. And if you write fantasy, you will want to depict a land of enchantment as vividly as Ursula K. Le Guin depicts the island of Gont in her *Wizard of Earthsea*:

> The island of Gont, a single mountain that lifts its peak a mile
> above the storm-racked Northeast Sea, is a land famous for
> wizards. From the towns in its high valleys and the ports on its
> dark narrow bays many a Gontishman has gone forth to serve
> the Lords of the Archipelago in their cities as wizard or mage,
> or, looking for adventure.

As you work at creating your fictional world, *visualize* the setting, using words as pigments. Be generous with details. Keep in mind John Gardner's point, in *The Art of Fiction*: "A scene will not be vivid if the writer gives too few details to stir and guide the reader's imagination."

FOR FURTHER REFLECTION

One of the pleasures of fiction is entering another world: Chicago during Prohibition, ancient England when Druids were constructing Stonehenge; a dusty town in west Texas where rival cattle ranchers confront each other over a land dispute; or another world in the literal sense: a group of pioneering astronauts trekking through a newly discovered Martian cave. Whether the world you create is familiar or strange, you are wielding magic in your world-building.

...................................TRY THIS...................................

Begin creating a world on a single page. Choose any setting you wish—a sublime nature setting like the Yosemite Valley; a twisting dark road in Romania where vampires are said to be lurking; a village in Uganda where medical missionaries are trying to save the lives of malnourished children.

ON CONFESSION

Confession is not only good for the soul, it is good for writing. The impulse to share our innermost troubles, fears, transgressions, and triumphs with others—indeed, with the whole world via publication—is a powerful and vital one: For the impulse to confess is at one with the impulse to be uncompromisingly truthful, and without uncompromising truthfulness, the art will suffer. Confessing does not mean "letting it all hang out"! It is possible to convey disturbing experiences with decorum (not the same thing as censorship) as well as with candor. One need not use ugly language, for example, to describe an ugly experience.

Confessions have an honorable place in literature. Think of St. Augustine's *Confessions*, or Thomas De Quincey's *Confessions of an English Opium-Eater*, or the twelve-volume autobiography of the great political philosopher Jean-Jacques Rousseau, which he titled *Confessions*. Of course, all autobiographies are confessional to some extent, but to use the word explicitly is to say, in effect: *I am going to divulge even my most intimate, embarrassing, heretical thoughts and deeds.* The reason is that the truth of who we are, and what we represent to the world and to God, hangs in the balance.

FOR FURTHER REFLECTION

Admitting our faults and transgressions fulfills a psychological as well as spiritual need regardless of our particular religious convictions. Confession heals. It also discloses the truth of ourselves to ourselves. The habit of confession is important to us writers because it strengthens our capacity for truth-telling. Over the next week, think about your ability to tell the truth about yourself— your temperament, impulses, habits, moral lapses: Do you repress them? Do you obsess over them but do nothing? Take firm steps toward recognizing and acting upon your faults.

....................................TRY THIS....................................

In your journal, confess a secret, a sin, or a regrettable incident. This is for your eyes only (you may change your mind about it later, but for now, you do not want anything constraining your self honesty). Also keep a record of faults you've overcome.

JANUARY 27
ADVENTURE

"Adventure" is synonymous with roller-coaster-like excitement for readers. Fast-paced, danger-filled plots for your adventure novel, or adventure episodes for your memoir, promise exciting reading. In this regard, memoirs are like novels in that your readers want to experience vicariously what you have experienced. The difference, of course, is that adventures in novels are fictitious; in memoirs they actually happened.

There are several types of adventures, which we may categorize as follows:

- the search (e.g., for a missing person or document)
- the quest (a search for what promises to bring spiritual reward)
- the escape (from being trapped or held against one's will)
- the conquest (overcoming a great natural or human obstacle)
- the exploit (embarking on an adventure for the sake of adventure)

Of course, your memoir or novel can include more than one type of adventure, or one type of adventure—say, a quest—can consist of smaller adventures: searches for clues that contribute to the quest, for example.

FOR FURTHER REFLECTION

What constitutes adventure for you? Maybe it's hiking and camping in the wilderness or harbor sailing or exploring the ancient Mayan pyramids in the Yucatán. Maybe it is hot-air ballooning or traveling the back roads of rural and small-town America, as William Least Heat Moon has done, eloquently chronicled in his travel memoir, *Blue Highways*. But adventures can be experienced indoors (or semi-indoors) too: in circuses and theme parks, in museums, even in antique shops. Now think about the characters you plan to put into a short story or novel: What sorts of adventures do they enjoy?

............................TRY THIS....................................

1. Jot down three or four adventure scenarios (one paragraph for each will do) that you've experienced—either as a child or as an adult. Use one of the prompts from the For Further Reflection section as a springboard.

2. Develop one of the paragraphs you wrote for number one into a short story.

CULTIVATING A DISTINCTIVE VOICE

Novice writers sometimes are insufficiently confident of their own voices. Consciously or unconsciously, they try to sound like the writers they most admire. Perhaps you had your Hemingway phase or Jane Austen phase? Actually, it's not a bad idea to imitate an author's style in order to get a feel for how she fashions sentences or unfolds a narrative. Ultimately, though, you should find your own voice, which sounds funny because you already *have* a voice—"voice" meaning your own manner of phrasing, of emphasis. But in order for your writing voice to sound natural you need to use it often. Novices sometimes assume they need to sound a certain way on paper, which can make them sound artificial and insincere.

In a world where language and communication, alas, are often used to deceive, we cannot value authenticity and sincerity too highly. Aristotle asserts in his *Rhetoric* that naturalness is persuasive and that artificiality is not. Work toward cultivating your own voice and vow never to disguise or distort it once you do.

FOR FURTHER REFLECTION

We must be careful about how we cultivate our writer's voice. If we try too hard to sound natural, unaffected, we might wind up sounding more unnatural than writers who yearn to cultivate a distinctive voice.

....TRY THIS.....................................

How can you help yourself uncover your natural voice? Write a page in which you describe, in a relaxed, informal manner, without groping for impressive words, how you feel about one of the front page stories appearing in this morning's newspaper. After you finish the page, read it aloud. If it doesn't sound like you, circle the phrases or sentences that seem artificial or forced. Then keep revising the paragraph until it seems to capture your natural voice.

Now apply the voice test to your current work in progress. Turn to any page, read it aloud, and if sounds artificial, get busy revising it.

SYMBOLS AND REALITY

The real world is what we make of it. Yes, of course, there's a reality "out there," independent of our perception of it, but it is not the reality we inhabit. The universe is a human universe. Everything we experience, from distant galaxies to mountains and cities to microbes, must first filter through our minds, which color all that we perceive. Mountains are not simply vast assemblages of granite and limestone slabs: Mountains possess a grand symmetry, are majestic; they're spiritual abodes, places to which prophets ascend. J.E. Cirlot notes in his *Dictionary of Symbols* (a book that should be on every writer's shelf) that the mountain peak "is the point of contact between heaven and earth." Thus, when a story about struggling to find one's spiritual center includes characters struggling to scale a mountain, we may say that the mountain—and the mountain climbing—symbolize that larger truth. Symbols codify human reality, and in a spiritual sense *become* reality.

FOR FURTHER REFLECTION

Symbols are not just ornaments or ingredients to add to a story like so much butter or salt to a recipe, but embodiments of complex experiences, the abstract rendered concrete. Thus, a bird in flight can symbolize freedom; an egg, fertility; a snake, evil. In fact, we can all too easily get carried away with symbolism—and therein superstition lies. Snakes can be made to symbolize evil (thanks in large part to the Old Testament association of the snake with Satan), but snakes can also represent sorcery and even healing (think of the medical caduceus with its twin snakes coiled around the staff of a pair of wings).

..............................TRY THIS....................................

Make a list of commonplace objects and then free-associate on their symbolic possibilities. Afterwards, compare your associations with those presented in a dictionary of symbols. Here is a sample list:

- window
- bed
- hanger
- mirror
- garden (or individual flowers in a garden)
- door

CONFRONTING WRITER'S BLOCK

Writer's block is an occupational hazard of the writing profession. No matter how prolific you are, or how methodically you follow a set of procedures for completing a writing task, sooner or later, you will find yourself staring at a blank screen, your brain a cipher. What to do?

First, know about the different kinds of writer's block:

1. **Procedural blocks:** The "What do I do now?" syndrome. For example, you've come up against a brick wall in your plot and can't figure out what should happen next.

2. **Creativity blocks:** The idea well seems to have run dry. This might be the toughest block to overcome. See the entry for July 30.

3. **Psychological blocks:** Your inner demon is telling you that you're not good enough to succeed, that the work-in-progress isn't good enough to be published.

4. **Distraction blocks:** Mundane tasks prevent you from concentrating on your writing—friends keep calling, chores need completing.

5. **Procrastination blocks:** You've got more important things to do right now; when they're taken care of, you'll return to your writing.

Regardless of the type of writer's block, you can find a way to overcome it. If you're suffering from procedural blocks, give your subconscious time to digest the material, or play out a scene more extensively, or do more research. There's more to writing than writing! In fact, many writers spend more time gathering information than they do drafting.

FOR FURTHER REFLECTION

Whatever the cause of the writer's block you've been experiencing, it can be overcome, often more easily than you may realize. The thought processes that go into writing are demanding, so you shouldn't be surprised when your brain rebels by going offline for a while. All you need to remember is that *you're* in charge of your brain.

......................................TRY THIS......................................

The next time you get blocked, for whatever reason, promise yourself to write just one more sentence. And when you finish, promise yourself to write one more sentence. Keep doing this until your fingers freeze up.

CULTIVATING THE WRITING HABIT

Is it possible to generate a powerful desire to write? Yes, and quite easily, actually. Erasmus, the prolific Renaissance thinker, author of *In Praise of Folly*, put it simply: "The desire to write grows with writing." For many beginners, few activities seem more unnatural than filling pages with words day after day, year after year. But that is exactly what an aspiring writer must learn to feel comfortable doing. Whatever you learn to do on a regular basis eventually *becomes* natural. If you want to become a prolific writer, you must write out of habit. The longer you keep writing, the easier it will be to make writing a habit.

FOR FURTHER REFLECTION

Good habits take time to catch on, but they do catch on, provided you don't lose patience. Think about the kind of writing habit you want to establish for yourself: maybe an hour of writing every day after your morning coffee. Maybe all you realistically can allot is a half hour. Be honest with yourself. Perhaps you'd enjoy writing more late at night, when the world is a quieter place. Weigh all of these factors before committing.

......................................TRY THIS......................................

1. After determining the kind of writing habit you want to establish, spend the next three weeks writing every day at a designated time. During each session, write one page in addition to any brainstorming or outlining or research.

2. Write a paragraph in your journal during each writing period. Begin your first paragraph like this: "I've decided to write twenty-one paragraphs—a paragraph a day for the next three weeks—on topics relating to my next writing project." If you're writing a novel, then write twenty-one paragraphs about possible situations your characters might find themselves in, or combine that with possible themes you would like your novel to convey. If you're writing a memoir, write a paragraph about twenty-one different experiences in your life. It isn't necessary to write more than a paragraph a day: The object is not to complete this task as soon as possible, but to cultivate a permanent writing habit.

FEBRUARY 1
THE POWER OF ANCIENT MYTHS

The myths of ancient peoples fascinate us because they are stories in which gods and mortals interact. Myths remind us that the gods involve themselves in human affairs; they also remind us that we are not helpless pawns before the brute forces of nature, that those forces are manifestations of divinity and that we can influence them. Thus, myths should not be dismissed as irrelevant, as quaint examples of a primitive age. Wordsworth, in his sonnet "The World Is Too Much With Us," anguishes,

> Great God! I'd rather be a Pagan, suckled in a creed outworn
> So might I, standing on this pleasant lea,
> Have glimpses that would make me less forlorn;
> Have sight of Proteus rising from the sea
> Or hear old Triton blow his wreathed horn.

Writing at the dawn of the Industrial Revolution, Wordsworth beheld the assault of technology on nature and could sense the demise of the spiritual. Better to possess the Pagan's awe of nature's animated power than to domesticate that power with pollution-spewing factories.

FOR FURTHER REFLECTION

The truths embedded in myths continue to shed light on human nature today. Consider the story of Pygmalion, the Cyprian king and sculptor who fell in love with a statue he created. George Bernard Shaw turned it into one of his most famous plays by that name; Lerner and Lowe, in turn, transformed Shaw's play into one of the best-loved musicals of the twentieth century, *My Fair Lady*.

As J.E. Zimmerman, the classical scholar and author of the *Dictionary of Classical Mythology*, points out, "we ... can learn much from the stories of the ancient gods and the Greek and Roman heroes, much that is applicable to our life today."

..................................TRY THIS....................................

Write a paragraph describing how you would transform one of the ancient myths into a modern-day situation. For example, trying creating a modern-day Sisyphus, who is fated to complete a task only to end in futility (the real-world counterpart of rolling a rock up a hill, only to have it roll back down again).

FEBRUARY 2
RENOIR: "LUNCHEON OF THE BOATING PARTY"

Renoir's impressionist painting "Luncheon of the Boating Party" depicts a leisurely and mirthful get-together among friends. It *radiates* the delight that everyone in the scene seems to be experiencing; it also beautifully conveys the harmonious interaction the occasion has generated. With his magical combination of color and form, Renoir gives us a keen sense of the pleasure derived from the company of others—a painterly demonstration of late spring or summer *joie de vivre*. Renoir's subtext is clear: how much happier we would be if we devoted more time to the simplest of life's pleasures, like sharing good food and drink in a relaxed setting.

FOR FURTHER REFLECTION

"Luncheon of the Boating Party" is a study in harmonies: the harmony of social interaction, the harmony of people and nature, the harmony generated by play and the simple pleasures of food and drink, laughter, and conversation. After viewing the painting at www.renoir.org.yu, consider the following questions: What associations and feelings does the painting generate for you? What delights you most about the painting? What kinds of social gatherings do you enjoy that seem to bring out the best in people?

....................................TRY THIS....................................

After studying the painting, write down three or four associations it triggers as you contemplate it. Later, expand one of these associations into a dramatic scene that you might later be able to incorporate into a short story or poem.

FEBRUARY 3
THE VALUE OF ASSERTIVENESS

Let's face it: Writing—speaking your mind—is an audacious act. You are asserting your ideas and values, your peculiar way of looking at the world. In effect, you are saying to the world, *Take time out of your busy lives to listen to what I have to say.* No wonder writing can be intimidating. Our self-confident inner voice begins to quaver—a good thing, actually; otherwise, we may become overconfident in our assertions, insisting that people heed our words when those words do not rise above the mediocre. Or we may become over-confident that our views are the correct ones and not bother to consider alternative views. A balanced attitude—confidence in our views, and understanding that challenging views need to be acknowledged—is the goal. The most informed among us have gaps in our knowledge and must take steps to eliminate them.

Whatever you do, avoid false modesty, and do not heed the alter ego that diffidently whispers, "You're still not good enough"; or, "You can never be good enough."

Assertiveness is the hallmark of freedom, the foundation for advancement. Each of us has something special to offer the human community. Thus, we must cultivate, not repress, our will to assert ourselves by shaping our thoughts and feelings on paper.

FOR FURTHER REFLECTION

We can be assertive without being arrogant, provided our aims are honorable. If we have important ideas to share with the world, and if we do not harbor a Napoleon complex or some self-centered desire to manipulate others, we should be willing to share our views. It could even be argued that writers—those who are experts at communicating ideas clearly and forcefully—have a moral obligation to present their ideas (and the reasoning underlying them) to the world.

..................................TRY THIS....................................

Which of your views on current issues are you most motivated to share with the world? List each view and write a paragraph describing it in detail and then another paragraph explaining your reasons for wanting to share your view with the public.

FEBRUARY 4

CLARIFYING YOUR GOALS: STEP ONE IN WRITING FOR AN AUDIENCE

It may seem like the most obvious thing in the world, woven into the very definition of "writer," that a writer is one who writes for readers. Nevertheless, many beginning writers do not reflect upon what that entails.

Writing is a tug-of-war between innovation and tradition. The more innovative one is with language, story content, or style, the tougher it will be to engage your readers—unless they realize that the discomfort or extra work involved will prove rewarding. This is the case with James Joyce's *Ulysses*, with its brilliant language play, stream of consciousness, and innumerable allusions to works of art, literature, theology, and history. At the other end of the spectrum, traditional works like murder mysteries that adhere solidly to genre expectations can be comforting—but the downside is that even the best of them will seem formulaic.

FOR FURTHER REFLECTION

When it comes to writing, do you see yourself as a traditionalist, an experimentalist, or somewhere in between? In other words, are you inclined to use conventional, "popular" modes of storytelling—modes with which audiences are comfortable—or are you inclined to try new techniques with which audiences would learn to feel comfortable, but might unsettle them initially? If you're serious about writing, you want to be true to your goals, whatever they may be. Do you aspire to write primarily to entertain—i.e., to write tightly-plotted mysteries, espionage thrillers, or bodice-ripping romances? A memoir about your harrowing childhood or your dysfunctional dog? Or do you aspire to write more "serious" fiction that probes perennial issues like the disintegrating family or recovery from psychological trauma or the plight of minorities in the United States? Maybe you'd enjoy writing humor or satire or self-help books. Whatever genre you wish to work in, read thoroughly in it.

............................TRY THIS....................................

Write a memorandum to yourself beginning with "My goal as a writer is to ..." Go into as much detail as you can about the kinds of writing you want to master and what you expect of your readers.

FEBRUARY 5

READING AS WRITING / WRITING AS READING

Reading and writing are two sides of the same coin. When we read a book we assimilate its worldview—its ideas, insights into human nature and other ways of life—into our own worldview. A teenager growing up in rural Missouri, for example, will experience *Huckleberry Finn* differently from one growing up in Los Angeles or Bangkok. When we read a book, we are, in effect, rewriting a part of our own lives; we become, in some small way, a different person. This is what people mean when they claim that such-and-such book has changed their lives.

And when we write a book, we are also reading it—both during and after composition. Like filmmakers who observe "rushes"—a single day's filming—we writers need to get a quick sense of the way our work in progress holds together, if it conveys its intended meaning as clearly and coherently as we want it to. It is important for writers always to be conscious of this readability factor. By reading our writing we continuously monitor its publish-ability.

FOR FURTHER REFLECTION

Think about the last book you enjoyed reading. What was it about the story that most "spoke" to you, that you were able to identify with or appreciate on a deeply personal level? Did it have anything to do with specific events of persons in your life? As a writer, you will be drawing from your own deepest personal experiences as well. Think about how you might convey these experiences through the story you want to tell.

...............................TRY THIS...................................

Write a paragraph or two in which you describe how a certain novel—or particular event in a novel—reawakened a long-forgotten or dormant experience. Perhaps W. Somerset Maugham's *Of Human Bondage* reminded you of a romantic relationship in which the romance flowed in one direction only? Maybe Michael Chabon's *The Amazing Adventures of Kavalier & Clay* reminded you of your love of comic book superheroes?

In describing your experience, try to capture the state of mind of your younger self.

FEBRUARY 6
GENERATING CONTENT FROM MAXIMS

A good dictionary of quotations, like the *The Oxford Dictionary of Quotations*, should be on every writer's bookshelf. Maxims represent thousands of potential launchings for stories, essays, and poems. A good maxim is like a super-condensed parable. Take, for example, these musings of Prospero from Shakespeare's *The Tempest*:

> We are such stuff
> As dreams are made on, and our little life
> Is rounded with a sleep.

The lines not only suggest the rather clichéd notion that life is but a dream, but that we build our lives out of dreams. It's a startling insight into the nature of reality—and one that could suggest all kinds of story scenarios.

Keep works by authors who are famous for their maxims nearby: Emerson, La Rochefoucauld, Shakespeare, and Thoreau are just a few such writers whose pithy sayings you should get to know. And of course, the Bible, the Qur'an, and wisdom writings such as the Upanishads and the Sayings of Buddha, Confucius, and Lao Tse provide an unending resource for spiritual wisdom.

FOR FURTHER REFLECTION

Reading maxims is an effective way to generate story ideas. It is also a delightful way to exercise our imagination and to remind ourselves of all the wisdom that awaits us, stored in the words of great writers through the ages. We writers cannot expose ourselves to too much wisdom!

...................................TRY THIS....................................

1. Open a dictionary of quotations at random, choose a quotation, and use it as a springboard for a short story. For example, write a story inspired by Bertrand Russell's adage that "Of all forms of caution, caution in love is perhaps the most fatal to true happiness."

2. Choose two quotations with contrasting messages and use them to embody the views of two characters pitted against each other. For example, pit a character who agrees with Oscar Wilde, that "nothing that is worth knowing can be taught," against a character who agrees with Henry Adams that "a teacher affects eternity; he can never tell where his influence stops."

FEBRUARY 7
EXPLORING HUMAN NATURE

Writing a novel, biography, or memoir enables you to explore human nature in depth. Readers are fascinated by the way people behave, by the range of personalities and capabilities of people, and the way people change over time (from year to year, even from moment to moment). When we say that characters "come alive," we mean that their individual behavioral attributes (even more than their physical ones) are depicted in detail—and don't assume that just because you're writing fiction you can go lax on precision. Novelist Susan Isaacs compares writing a novel to "fashioning an intimate biography" for each of the principal characters.

How does an aspiring novelist capture human behavior? One method is to maintain, in a notebook, a biographical profile of each character. Don't limit the information to what you think you can use—include everything you consider to be relevant to that individual—that way, you'll acquire a greater sense of the characters as real people, as well as keep track of their attributes as the novel progresses in order to avoid inconsistencies.

FOR FURTHER REFLECTION

Consider the most memorable characters you've encountered in fiction: Rhett Butler from Margaret Mitchell's *Gone With the Wind*? Tiny Tim from Charles Dickens's *A Christmas Carol*? Iago, Falstaff, or any of Shakespeare's other memorable characters? What makes them memorable? Is it their distinctive personalities? Their flaws? Their capacity for experiencing powerful emotions? Recognizing the qualities that make characters memorable will help you create memorable characters of your own.

......................................TRY THIS....................................

Write a two-page biographical sketch for each of three principal characters for your novel. These individuals should be at least partially based on persons you know well. You won't be able to think of everything at one sitting, of course, so allow the character to evolve over time. Keep returning to these initial profiles and add or modify them if needed.

CONJURING UP SENSORY DETAILS

An excellent way to get your readers to experience vicariously the world you are creating with your poem or story is to include sensory details—descriptions that involve one or more of the five senses. Sensory details transform the ordinary into the extraordinary. Memorable poems have been written about the taste of cold plums in the fridge (William Carlos Williams), dusting furniture and ironing (Julia Alvarez), even people sitting on a train (John Berryman). Emily Dickinson wrote dazzling poems about raindrops striking a rooftop, a bird devouring a worm, a hummingbird moving "like a rush of cochineal." The delights and mysteries of existence can be discovered in the ripple of a pond or a film of dust on a table.

Sensory details bring a moment to life because words alone can trigger the sensory experience. Sylvia Plath once wrote a poem ("Cut") about slicing open her thumb while cutting up vegetables—and we can't help but shudder when she describes the profusely bleeding "hinge of skin." When Frank McCourt, in *Angela's Ashes*, describes his flea-ridden mattress, we find ourselves scratching our arms and legs!

FOR FURTHER REFLECTION

Sensory details enable readers to identify emotionally with the people and settings of your stories, so it's important, as a writer, to heighten your sensory perceptions. Reacquaint yourself with familiar objects by concentrating on their sensory possibilities. Open a cupboard and heft a dinner plate, concentrating on the design, the texture; do the same with other items around the house. Our lives are surrounded by sensations, many of them dormant. Stimulating the senses through direct experience—and vicariously through language—heightens our awareness, makes us feel more alive.

...............................TRY THIS...................................

During the next few days compose short poems or prose paragraphs about the sights, sounds, and smells surrounding you. Challenge yourself to capture these sensory impressions in the most vivid language you can muster.

REVISION AS RE-VISION

Writing takes patience. It isn't unusual to spend months producing the draft of a novel, only to realize that it's all wrong and needs to be rewritten practically from scratch. Were those months wasted? Not at all. Writers must make their thoughts visible on paper—even if the thoughts are tentative or fragmentary—before they can work effectively with them. Writing it out allows you to see the larger design—or the lack of it—more readily. You are also likely to experience a gut feeling early on about whether a draft is working. And if your feelings tell you to start over, do it—but retain a copy of the old draft; you never know what good thoughts lie buried in it.

FOR FURTHER REFLECTION

Often we writers must not simply "revise" our stories but re-envision them whole cloth—not an easy step to take because we equate the hard work and the time spent on the first draft with its being good enough to retain. "That took me a whole month to write!" we'll complain. "It has to have *some* merit worth preserving!" But sometimes, a first draft can only serve as a starting point, one that instructs through negative example. Without the initial effort, the better performance would not be possible.

...................................TRY THIS....................................

Find the draft or partial draft of a story you gave up on, read it over, then set it aside and begin revising it whole cloth. Don't consult the original draft unless you must; the goal here is to capitalize on a freshness of perspective. Think of ways to:

- engage the reader's attention more quickly with a gripping or curiosity-arousing opening

- cut back on details that do not move the story forward

- make your characters more three-dimensional by putting them in situations that allow their personalities and eccentricities to emerge

- ensure that your protagonist is struggling to attain a worthy goal and that her opposition is formidable

DAYDREAMING WITH A PURPOSE

Daydreaming gets a lot of bad press: It's associated with laziness and nonproductiveness. No wonder writers feel guilty when they daydream. But daydreaming is one of the writer's stocks-in-trade; it is the mind's way of venturing into new realms of possibility … or impossibility, the logic centers having been mercifully turned off for a while.

Think about the fruits of daydreams: Machines that can fly, rockets that can travel to the ends of the solar system, robots that can conduct geology experiments on Mars, artificial hearts and limbs, mobile phones that are also cameras and computers not much larger than a candy bar. Not so long ago, these would have been laughable fantasies, assuming they could have been conceived at all. Daydreaming represents the mind engaged in unrestricted *play*—the kind of play that gives birth to great ideas. "Because we think of play as the opposite of seriousness," the poet-naturalist Diane Ackerman reminds us in her book *Deep Play*, "we don't notice that it governs most of society. … Much of human life unfolds as play."

FOR FURTHER REFLECTION

Reality and dream combine in storytelling. Just as a dream compresses an experience into a complex knot of symbolic images, so too does a story compress an experience (actual or potential) into a tightly woven narrative framework. When we daydream, we are engaged in a sort of instinctive storytelling. Telling stories, like daydreaming, is part of our genetic makeup.

......................................TRY THIS......................................

1. Allow yourself a half hour of daydreaming every day. Get comfortable, maybe play music that permits flights of fancy, and let your imagination break free of its worldly tethers. But keep your journal nearby so that you may record your imaginative voyage afterward—or even during, in case you bedazzle yourself with a vision you do not want to risk disappearing into oblivion.

2. Choose one of your daydream entries and fashion a poem or short story out of it.

COPING WITH LIFE'S DIFFICULTIES

What were the most difficult moments you had to face in your life? What were the most difficult tasks you performed, the toughest problems you solved, or the most challenging relationships you endured? Life is shaped by difficulties. By being able to identify and describe them in detail, whether as fiction or as fact, you are addressing a perennial public interest: How do others manage their difficulties? What can I learn from them to help me cope with my own difficulties?

As a writer, you have a knack for transforming pain into artistic gain. The first step is to use your notebook to set up a detailed and easily referenced compendium of the difficulties you have faced in your life. It won't be easy. There are moments in our lives we would prefer not to "dredge up." But despite the discomfort, doing so achieves two things: It makes the memory less painful, and it provides you with material for a story, maybe several.

FOR FURTHER REFLECTION

"I go where the pain is," Anne Rice once explained in response to how she was able to continue writing after the death of her daughter from leukemia. We inevitably benefit from the difficulties we endure. Think about how you benefited from the difficulties you wrestled with recently or during your childhood. How, exactly, did you benefit from them? As a writer, understanding the way you and other people benefit from difficulties, from failures and setbacks, will help you develop realistic characters and storylines.

......................................TRY THIS......................................

Generate a list of a dozen or more difficulties you've experienced in your life: childhood illnesses, getting involved with the wrong friends as a teenager, troublesome romantic relationships, bad career moves, and so on. Choose three, and for each, write a paragraph or two explaining how you dealt with and resolved them (or why you weren't able to resolve them).

GIVING CONSTRUCTIVE FEEDBACK

Teaching is one of the best kinds of learning there is. When you offer suggestions to a fellow writer for strengthening his draft in progress, you are deepening your own insight into the principles involved. However, you want to make sure that the feedback you give is constructive.

What constitutes constructive feedback? First, avoid making judgments about the draft. Instead of saying, "This character description is vague," say, "Try using more specific details to help readers visualize the person." The judgment has been changed into a constructive suggestion for revision. You might even go one step further and offer an example. If the writer describes a character as having "killer good looks," you might suggest, along with "Describe his good looks," the following: "His intense dark eyes—dark as onyx—seemed to radiate from some deep well of inner strength."

FOR FURTHER REFLECTION

Feedback benefits the giver as much as the receiver. As you prepare to give a fellow writer constructive feedback, you will find yourself paying keener attention to those principles of good writing you've been trying to apply to your own work. The feedback you give on story development, for example, will almost inevitably shed light on ways in which you could develop your story in progress.

........................TRY THIS....................

Maintain a record of the feedback you give during a writers' workshop session. Afterwards, apply that feedback to a draft in progress. For example, if you suggested that one of your fellow writers develop an action scene more fully, take a closer look at your own action scenes (or lack of them) and revise accordingly.

WRITING AND SOUL FOOD

Soul food or traditional African-American cooking, first popular in the South, worked its way into the American mainstream in the 1960s. But soul food can also be a metaphor for old-fashioned, ethnic, authentic home cooking based on recipes handed down over several generations—food that takes center stage, made with the freshest and choicest ingredients, prepared slowly and carefully with love. Here is a scene from Jodi Picoult's novel, *Plain Truth*, in which we get a sense of the Amish dining experience:

> Sarah made enough food to feed the whole Amish community …
> She brought bowl after bowl to the table, chicken with dump-
> lings and vegetables swimming in sauces and meat that had
> been cooked to the point where it broke apart at the touch of a
> fork. There were relishes and breads and spiced, stewed pears.
> In the center of the table was a blue pitcher of fresh milk.[*]

FOR FURTHER REFLECTION

Soul food serves to remind us of the ideals of family life, ethnic pride and tradition, and the pleasures of day-to-day living enhanced through authentic cooking. Soul food is thus a perfect metaphor for the best writing you hope to produce—writing that is never superficial hackwork, never done in haste, but writing that is enriched by devoted attention to craft.

................................TRY THIS..................................

Begin writing a series of soul-food dining moments. In one such moment, show a family for whom tradition is important dining on foods that reflect their values. In another moment, bring nontraditional family members together and draw parallels between *their* values and the food they're eating.

---

[*] Jodi Picoult, *Plain Truth*; quoted by Shaunda Kennedy Wenger and Janet Kay Jensen, *The Book Lover's Cookbook*. Ballantine Books, 2003: 38.

LOVE THROUGH THE AGES

If you're a writer of romances, or even of stories that involve romantic relationships, plan on devoting this day, Valentine's Day, to love, to learning more about the psychology, the lore, and the many manifestations of love, and, of course, to fashioning stories, poems, and essays about love. After all, love is the life-force that drives not only our individual lives but civilization itself. Virtually every writer of note has reflected on the nature of love in the context of dramatizing love relationships—painful, tempestuous, profane, sublime. Many writers have written meditations on love, most notably Stendhal (*De l'Amour*). Here are a few morsels from the English translation by Gilbert and Suzanne Sale:

- For the very young, love is like a huge river which sweeps everything before it, so that you feel that it is a restless current.

- The sight of anything extremely beautiful, in Nature or the arts, makes you think instantly of your beloved.

- In love, I have the feeling that boundless happiness beyond my wildest dreams is just round the corner, waiting only for a word or a smile.

FOR FURTHER REFLECTION

Love is the unfathomable subject; a writer can spend his entire professional life mining its mysteries. It is also the inexhaustibly popular subject, manifesting some facet of itself to some degree in just about everything we read. An enterprising writer will acknowledge the fact that every manner and form of the subject of love has found its way into literature, yet still feel confident that he can locate a relatively unusual facet of the subject worthy of exploration.

....TRY THIS....................................

Apply the "what if" question to a love topic and shape it into a story. For example, what if a pathologically shy young man somehow, through some strange circumstance, manages to befriend a pathologically shy young woman? What would their original meeting be like? What would they say to each other, if anything?

WRITING LETTERS TO ILLUSTRIOUS PEOPLE

Every aspiring writer should be an inveterate letter-writer; letters are the ideal genre for learning audience awareness. You're writing for very small audiences, typically of only one person and typically someone you know, or know of. An exception is an "open letter"—such as a letter to the editor, intended for an audience larger than its designated recipient.

Have you ever written a letter to a historical figure or a celebrity or an imaginary person? Such letters can be an effective and fun way of getting your ideas onto paper. In his posthumously published *Illustrissimi*, John Paul I, who served as Pope for only thirty-three days before his death in 1978, includes heart-warming letters to famous writers like Christopher Marlowe, Charles Dickens, and Mark Twain; spiritual leaders like Saint Bernardino and Saint Therese of Lisieux; and even legendary and imaginary figures like Odysseus's wife, Penelope, and Pinocchio. In these letters, John Paul I (whose birth name was Albino Luciani) praises the individual being addressed for his or her moral vision and inspiration.

FOR FURTHER REFLECTION

Letter writing encourages us to convey our thoughts conversationally, with candor, often with wit—some of the most important qualities we want our larger writing projects to reflect. Reading the letters of writers can teach us much about the art of honest, conversational prose.

......................................TRY THIS....................................

What would you say to some of the most famous (or notorious) persons who ever lived, if you had a chance to interview them? Make a list of such persons you would like to communicate with, and write a letter on a focused topic to one or more of them.

WORDS

Language flourishes through those who respect its power. Words affect the way we experience reality. Words can *change* reality, as when a new archaeological discovery changes our understanding of a historical event.

Exploited for ignoble purposes, language can, alas, do great harm (think of Nazi propaganda), but used to its fullest potential, it becomes great literature or enriches our most cherished beliefs. Language enables society to function smoothly. It is the basis for law and policy, for understanding how things work.

Some novice writers assume that they must acquire a large vocabulary before they can write publishable material; they spend time and money developing their "word power." But it is pointless to memorize new words out of context. The most efficient way to build vocabulary is to read a lot and reflect on an author's choice of words: why he chose those words and not others (see also the entry for April 16).

Emily Dickinson, for one, understood the power of words. She stretched the possibilities of language in exciting new ways as she sought to capture the complexities of human experience. Her poems are filled with breathtaking images such as:

> She dealt her pretty words like Blades –
> How glittering they shone –
> And every one unbared a Nerve
> Or wantoned with a Bone.

Such a poet can ignite the creative drive in any writer who reads her.

FOR FURTHER REFLECTION

What are some of your favorite words? Why do you like them? One person may love the word *enchantment*, not only for its meaning, but for its sound. Words are filled with subjective connotations that transcend their dictionary meanings. What comes to mind when you hear the words *home*, *committee*, *child*, *darkness*?

....TRY THIS....................................

Find a poem by one of your favorite poets. Why does it move you or stimulate your thinking? Is it a single word, used in a startlingly new way? A figure of speech that triggers a memory? Write a short poem in which you make commonplace words like *sing*, *fountain*, *attic*, *lamp* or *oven* take on unusual associations.

PAYING ATTENTION

The ability to pay close attention—to our task at hand, to our surroundings, to the ideas and feelings of others—is not easily achieved; it is an intellectual, temperamental, and spiritual discipline that one must patiently cultivate over the years.

The first stage of close attentiveness is intellectual maturity. We must assume that anyone's point of view is worth paying attention to, even if turns out to be a view we reject. But we cannot reject a view if we haven't listened carefully to it. If the speaker has not articulated her view fully or clearly, then that will become our first response: "Please clarify" or "Please go into more detail."

The second stage of close attentiveness is emotional maturity. Our temperament should be adjusted to be patient with even incendiary views, to respond calmly and respectfully, and not interrupt. Alas, we see abuses of this nearly every day on some network talk shows: one debater not letting the other finish a point.

The third stage of close attentiveness goes beyond intellect and reason to involve a kind of spiritual centeredness that helps ensure civility when conversing with those whose views differ from your own. If everyone possessed such civility, we would be well on our way to abolishing war.

FOR FURTHER REFLECTION

All of us can benefit from paying closer attention to our surroundings, to people, to issues. The nature essayist Barry Lopez once said during an interview that the most important skill a writer can cultivate is that of paying attention—not just to other people, but to the earth. Like any individual, the earth has important things to say to people who are able to listen with open hearts and minds.

....TRY THIS....................................

Strike up a conversation with a friend or acquaintance and be more attentive than you've ever been in the past. Do not interrupt; do not prematurely editorialize or pass judgment; listen for support points: Are they sufficient? Accurate? After the conversation, summarize the conversation and each person's contribution to it.

THINKING ABOUT THINKING

"At any waking moment the human head is filled alive with molecules of thought called notions," biologist Lewis Thomas delightfully asserts in his essay, "On Thinking About Thinking." Molecular movement as a metaphor for thinking is as ingenious as it is delightful. Like molecules, thought particles ("notions"), being "wildly variable," interact in wondrous ways, especially "when the mind is heated a little":

> New notions are flung from one elliptical path into the next, collide with unmatched surfaces and bound away, to be caught and held in place by masses at a distance. Now the motion of all the structures, large and small, becomes patterned and ceaselessly motoric, like the *Brandenburgs*. The aggregates begin to send out streamers, plumes of thought, which touch and adhere.

Dr. Thomas regarded organisms like cells or ants or even human beings as symbionts: all working interactively to produce, in effect, a super-organism greater than the sum of its parts.

FOR FURTHER REFLECTION

It makes good sense to think about thinking (what Lewis Thomas called "meta-thinking"). It is one of the crowning glories of humankind to transform an abstract idea (say the idea of a machine that can fly) into a blueprint on paper and then into a working airplane, after centuries of trial and error (from the ancient tales of Daedalus and Icarus to Leonardo da Vinci's drawings of flying machines to the Wright Brothers biplane). Thinking about thinking may just enable us to think more productively and creatively.

......................................TRY THIS......................................

1. Describe the evolution of your last story idea from inception to its completion. What specific associations came to mind following that initial flash? How did you come up with the characters for the story?

2. Outline a story in which your main character concocts a plan to do something wild yet heroic, such as bike from coast to coast in order to raise money for a noble cause. Show how his idea develops from inception to completion. What false starts or obstacles will your character encounter along the way?

ARCHIVING

Many institutions, public and private (libraries, museums, government agencies, private businesses), archive important documents—that is, they preserve them for posterity by protecting their fragility, ensuring their safety, and, of course, cataloguing them for easy reference. Writers, too, should archive their important documents by placing them in polyurethane protectors.

But what should be archived? Here is a list of possibilities:

- **Preliminary drafts.** Writers often discard their preliminary drafts, and that's a mistake; there may be flashes of genius in those original efforts—a single paragraph that could become the basis for a new work. Early drafts also are important in reminding you (and your future biographers!) of the stages in your creative process—stages that can shed light on planning new projects.

- **Preliminary character and setting sketches.** You never can tell what might come in handy later on.

- **Research notes.** Writers generally take far more notes than they can possibly use for a work in progress, but the "excess" notes should never be discarded; they could easily form the basis for a new project.

- **Photocopies of documents.** Articles, reports, interviews, surveys, and such might be relevant to future projects. Keep them in order and clearly labeled.

FOR FURTHER REFLECTION

Materials that seem like next-to-useless closet clutter today may prove to be valuable documents tomorrow. Archiving research documents and early drafts is sensible—although you may need to draw the line somewhere. Not *everything* needs to be archived; on the other hand, think twice before tossing something into the trash.

...............................TRY THIS....................................

1. Go through your research clutter and take a careful inventory of everything. Put loose papers in folders, and label them accurately with a broad-nib black marker. Duplicates, illegible pages, trivial notes can be tossed.

2. Once you have an orderly system of hard-copy files, re-create the inventory in an electronic file, and make a backup copy.

MOTIVATION AS ENERGY

Motivation is the energy burst that moves us from inspiration to accomplishment, a self-inflicted kick in the backside that allows us to overcome the inertia of languid daydreaming and start writing. A good dose of motivation bypasses the indecision that often plagues us at the onset of a writing project: How do I begin? Is my idea good enough? Such questions can shut us down before we get off the ground. Better to plunge ahead, letting your primal enthusiasm for the project be your guiding light. Sometimes, though, that primal enthusiasm gets buried by the workload, or it is weakened by disappointment. In that case, one needs to find a way to rekindle the original spark of enthusiasm. One way to do this is to revisit the moment you conceived of the project. What was the first thing that made it seem like an exciting idea?

FOR FURTHER REFLECTION

Are you a successful suppressor of your own motivation to write? Our day jobs almost require it: Tend to business first; play later—except that writing should not be regarded as play in the sense of merely having fun or relaxing. Writing is work! Even though we know this first hand, we defer to the consensus of nonwriters who regard making up stories as child's play. From now on, though, when you feel motivated to write, remind yourself that writing is honorable work, and get to it as soon as possible. Carry a pocket notebook to record thoughts and observations quickly. Hesitation douses out the flame of motivation. Promise yourself to jot down at least a few paragraphs the moment the impulse to write strikes. No more suppression!

. . . . TRY THIS . . . .

Use your pocket notebook as a writing motivator. During free but fleeting moments at work (coffee or lunch breaks), jot down story or essay ideas that you'd have fun fleshing out. When you get home, sift through those jottings, and select one idea (or a group of related ideas) and work up an outline or synopsis, or simply plunge headlong into a first draft.

FEBRUARY 21
BREATHING NEW LIFE INTO OLD STORIES

Ideas surround us: the quarrelsome couple in a restaurant, the man in a flag-draped wheelchair, the mime pretending to be a statue. Any writer worth his salt will "fill in the blanks," creating scenarios for the couple who seem to be on the verge of splitting up, the amputee who once ran marathons, the statue mime who's really a homeless person. The goal is to breathe new life into familiar stories, and that is where your unique life-experiences come into play. How might *your* marital experiences influence your way of telling the story of a couple on the threshold of divorce? What do you know of street performers and their past lives? Background research, coupled with your own experiences, will help you shape new and timely stories.

FOR FURTHER REFLECTION

Virtually every story you read is an old story imbued with new life. Put a new spin on a haunted house story by making the "house" a hotel room: You hear strange sounds inside the wall, waking you up in the dead of night. Should you investigate even though you have an early-morning meeting? Even a mundane situation, such as a neighbor walking her dog, can be spun into a gripping yarn. Imagine that her dog can sniff out buried treasure, that one of the treasures she uncovers is a cache of hundred-dollar bills from an old bank robbery. The key word is "imagine": imagination is the writer's stock-in-trade.

.................................TRY THIS....................................

Take out the first draft—or even the later draft—of a short manuscript such as a poem or short-short story and ask yourself, *Is my approach to the topic sufficiently distinctive; that is, am I adding anything new or has this already been expressed before?* Next, circle sentences or paragraphs that strike you as humdrum, boringly ordinary, hackneyed, lacking a distinctive voice. Now, revise the first page to make the opening segment more distinctive, energetic, and engaging. Spend the next few days revising another segment of the manuscript, approximately one page at a time—again, focusing on distinctiveness, originality.

CREATIVE OUTLINING

Creative *outlining*? That's an oxymoron, you protest. What can possibly be creative about outlining? Truth is, working out the framework for a story takes as much imagination as logic. Writers who rely heavily on outlining, who see outlines merely as blueprints, risk interfering with creativity and spontaneity. Obsessive microplanning can also cause the story's nuts and bolts to show through the fabric. We want our stories to seem like fluid, organic entities.

Why bother with outlines at all? Well, they're great for getting a handle on structure: Roman numerals for the main points, letters for the secondary points, lower case Roman numerals or check marks for the tertiary points—that sort of thing. Most importantly, outlining can generae ideas.

Also, outlines can be as detailed or as "scratchy" as you want them to be. You might begin with a scratch outline, then modify it until it resembles a synopsis.

FOR FURTHER REFLECTION

One can generate an outline spontaneously, intuitively—and, also like drafting, return to it for fine-tuning. Our brains are instinctive organizers, so we don't really have to push too hard to come up with a story framework.

.....................................TRY THIS....................................

1. Generate an outline as you would a discovery draft (see the entry for June 9); that is, don't worry about logical progression, just unfold the story free-associatively in outline form. Once your draft is underway, modify and expand your outline in keeping with the changes you make in the story progression. Outlines can quickly remind you of twists and turns in the plot (see the entry for September 22) that can slip out of memory.

2. Produce a discovery draft based on the outline you produced for number one. In a discovery draft you plunge ahead, using your outline as a beacon. Don't worry about plot twists and turns or character descriptions at this stage; that will come later. Draft your story, knowing full well that you're going to revise it thoroughly later on. The purpose of a discovery draft is to get as much on paper as possible before the impulse to write the story dissipates.

FEBRUARY 23
TRACKING YOUR BEST THOUGHTS

We writers are full of ideas. They're the raw materials of our profession, so it would make good sense to take an inventory of them, organize them so that they may be easily retrieved. Journals (especially when divided by subjects—story synopses, article synopses, character sketches, etc.), index-card files, and scrapbooks are all effective ways to keep track of your ideas. Try to articulate your thoughts as concisely as possible in order to save time when browsing or scanning your inventory.

When is an idea worth filing? It's hard to know when you're working with it; so when in doubt, file it. Let's say you're writing an essay about the difficulties of teaching English to immigrant children. During your research it suddenly occurs to you that reproducing words in whimsical, cartoon-like ways (say, in the manner of the late cartoonist for *The New Yorker,* Saul Steinberg) would add a dimension of fun to language learning. Whether or not you choose to include that in your current essay, the idea is worth holding onto, so should go into your idea file for safekeeping.

FOR FURTHER REFLECTION

An idea file can be a soul-satisfying way of surveying the full spectrum of your personal philosophy. Think about adding, modifying or deleting items from time to time. Also, use your file for combining one idea with another. You can enhance that potential by including cross-referencing information.

·····················TRY THIS·····················

If you haven't been keeping track of your own best thoughts—your personal philosophy, flashes of insight—it's time to start. For each of the following five questions, write a one-page response. Don't try answering them all at once—you might be tempted to settle for superficial responses.

- What do you do to combat anxiety or low self-esteem?
- What role should the arts play in American culture?
- How do you feel about the newest technological innovations?
- What is your philosophy of marriage?
- What is your philosophy of raising a family?

FEBRUARY 24
FACT-CHECKING

Publishers often include fact-checkers among their staff members for the simple reason that inaccuracies (which even the most scrupulous writer can make) can slip into your work very easily—and the longer and more complex the work, the likelier there will be mistakes.

Now, if you think that because publishers hire fact-checkers you can be nonchalant about checking the facts yourself, think again. It pays to check your facts to the extent that you are able; even a professional fact-checker can overlook something. At the same time, you don't want to obsess over factuality to the point of allowing it to interfere with your drafting. Simply make a note of it in a "fact-check" notebook, or write notes to yourself in the margins; then, when the drafting ebbs for the day, you can slip into fact-checking mode.

FOR FURTHER REFLECTION

No matter how mindful you are of factuality, it is easy to overlook things when engaged in a large project. Whether you write fiction, nonfiction, or poetry, the underlying factuality of your utterances is paramount. It is tempting to trust our memories, but even the keenest of memories may have mistaken names, places, or events.

......................................TRY THIS......................................

Drawing only from your memory, write a page or so about an event you recall from, say, a year or two ago. Name names, places, circumstances. Later, do a thorough fact-check of what you've recorded. This might not be easy (in fact, the difficulty of checking facts is probably why some writers don't bother). Begin with an Internet search. Chances are, you will have discovered errors in names, dates, locations, incidents, and so on.

CREATING ATMOSPHERE

What helps us vicariously accept the reality of a fictional world is the atmosphere the novelist builds, sometimes steadily over many pages, sometimes rapidly in a single paragraph. Notice how quickly George Orwell creates atmosphere in the opening sentences of *1984*:

> It was a bright cold day in April, and the clocks were striking thirteen. Winston Smith, his chin nuzzled into his breast in an effort to escape the vile wind, slipped quickly through the glass doors of Victory Mansions, though not quickly enough to prevent a swirl of gritty dust from entering along with him.
>
> The hallway smelt of boiled cabbage and old rag mats. At one end of it, a colored poster, too large for indoor display, had been tacked to the wall. It depicted simply an enormous face …

We quickly find ourselves in a dystopia where military time is kept, where propaganda reigns, and where springtime feels more like midwinter. How does Orwell manage it? Through choice sensory impressions, not by explicitly coming out and saying that some nightmarish totalitarian regime has taken hold of this London of the future, shattering our usual utopian visions of what a future world would be like.

FOR FURTHER REFLECTION

Open one of your favorite novels—any one by Charles Dickens will work perfectly—and pay attention to the techniques the author used to create atmosphere. Reflect on how these descriptions work on your imagination. How does each one contribute toward producing a particular mood?

................................TRY THIS....................................

Write an opening paragraph for a short story, concentrating on creating a certain kind of atmosphere—a carnival atmosphere, say, for a Mardi Gras story, or an atmosphere of foreboding for a ghost story. Over the next several days, work up a complete story outline, and then draft the story.

WRITING AS AN ACT OF LOVE

Looking back upon his distinguished career as a novelist, essayist, and playwright, James Baldwin claimed that, for him, writing was at once an act of love and an attempt to be loved. We write for many reasons, but writing out of love—for the subject, for those who have inspired us—is an especially good reason. Love not only makes the world go 'round, as the cliché goes, it inspires us to go around the world, so to speak; it makes us care enough about the world to get involved with it, to contemplate its beauty as well as its ugliness, its past glories and future possibilities.

FOR FURTHER REFLECTION

We need to recover the original meaning of the word *amateur* (from the Latin *amare*, "to love")—one who pursues activities out of love, rather than one whose skill is not up to professional standards. In addition to writing with a purpose, one should also write out of love.

....TRY THIS....................................

Describe in about 200 words a writing project in which you would like to immerse yourself purely for love rather than for financial gain or prestige. Perhaps you feel a strong urge to write about unsung heroes like paramedics who save thousands of lives every day, or aspects of American industry or agriculture that have slipped under the radar. John McPhee writes about the nature and history of oranges and the people who grow them. His book-length essay, titled simply *Oranges*, is filled with fascinating tidbits like this:

> The oranges in the Indian River packinghouse I visited had been
> gassed and were being washed in warm soapy water, brushed
> with palmetto-fiber brushes, and dried by foam-rubber squee-
> gees and jets of hot air. Brushed again with nylon bristles to
> bring out their natural shine, they were coated with Johnson's
> Wax until they glistened like cats' eyes.

And, by the way, McPhee notes how "oranges and orange blossoms have long been symbols of love."

FEBRUARY 27
BACKSTORY

Fiction writers and memoirists often open with a present predicament to arouse reader curiosity. Soon, though, the history of events leading up to the predicament must be disclosed; this can be rendered via flashbacks, which treat past events as if they were unfolding in the present, or by explaining straightforwardly what had taken place earlier. These important moments that occurred before the story's present is called the *backstory*.

The challenge in handling backstory is keeping readers from being bored or confused. Backstory material needs to be intriguing in its own right, possessing its own internal conflicts; it also needs to be presented in a way that keeps readers from confusing it with the story's present.

Backstory is also used by essayists. In his personal experience narrative "Ah, Wilderness! Humans, Hawks, and Environmental Correctness on the Muddy Rio Grande," Dinty W. Moore opens with a group of inexperienced customers and guides canoeing on the Rio Grande just east of Big Bend National Park. The present action is interrupted with backstory: "The evening before, thirteen of us meet in a motel in Odessa, Texas …" Had Moore opened with the backstory, he might have lost some readers.

FOR FURTHER REFLECTION

Readers want to become immersed in the story quickly, which is why modern-day novelists (unlike, say, their Victorian counterparts) enjoy dropping the reader into a harrowing predicament with the opening paragraph. Thrillers will sometimes open with a prologue that takes care of this. Once the reader is "hooked," the novelist can take her sweet time filling in the backstory. And, of course, backstory material can be introduced intermittently, especially if the backstory itself is leading up to some harrowing moment.

...................................TRY THIS...................................

Recall a predicament from childhood involving yourself and at least one other person. Did you and a friend ever get lost in the wilderness? Did you ever get in trouble with authorities? In one paragraph, describe the present predicament. In the next paragraph, summarize the events leading up to the predicament. Keep the reader intrigued!

THOUGHTS ON STYLE

There is some confusion over the word *style*. Your style of writing will reflect your manner of thinking and speaking. However, because you most likely do not write as copiously as you speak, your writing style will probably be more awkward than your speaking style. Just as one's handwriting is distinctive (and has matured ever since second grade), so too will one's literary style mature the more regularly it is practiced.

The most important point to make about style is that it can take care of itself. "The story invents and compels its own style," William Faulkner insisted. When you sit down to write, think about *story*, not style. Think about shaping your story just the way you feel it should be shaped, groping for just the right word, just the right sentence to convey a mood, an attitude, a touch of personality—and you will likely discover that the choices you make in telling the story will also go to shaping your style.

FOR FURTHER REFLECTION

Your writing style is a projection of your personality. Maybe you enjoy sprinkling your speech with regional expressions or tend to deliberately overstate or understate things for ironic effect. All of these things contribute to your individual voice. Of course, it takes practice to be able to transfer your voice effectively onto paper.

Another way to think of style is to regard it as an interaction of your voice with the "voice" of the story you are telling. For example, if you're writing a horror story, your natural voice will be "darkened" by the atmosphere of foreboding you may be trying to generate.

..................................TRY THIS..................................

Write a paragraph on any topic, and then read it aloud to a friend. Next, ask your friend: "Does that sound like me?" If the answer is no, try to pinpoint (with the help of your friend) the places where the writing seems stilted, unnatural. The next day, write another paragraph and read it aloud. Does it sound more like you? What did you do differently?

SYMBOLISM AND DREAMS

We are all symbolists when we dream, for symbols are what our dreams are made of. Our dreams represent experiences, fears, and uncertainties highly compressed into enigmatic images that enable our subconscious mind to process (if not resolve, at least imaginatively) the complex emotions that trigger them. Art, likewise, engages in the same kinds of condensation. The symbolism we encounter in art and in our own dreams serves to bridge the individual to the universal, the microcosm of our inner life to the macrocosm of existence.

As writers, we ought to be tuned into these marvelous mental (some would also say spiritual) pyrotechnics. Symbolism adds to the beauty and the mystery of art and life. It captures the essence of our experiences.

FOR FURTHER REFLECTION

Our subconscious minds can prove to be useful guides in weaving symbolism into our stories. By becoming more attentive to our dream lives, we can acquire a heightened sense of the symbolic undercurrents of existence that imbue life with meaning. Tune into your subconscious by recording your dreams and attempting to build stories about them. This will prove to be a more efficient way of incorporating symbolism into your writing than by "inserting" symbols arbitrarily.

...................................TRY THIS....................................

Select a dream that you've managed to record in some detail in your dream journal and turn it into a realistic short story with symbolic overtones. That is, build the story around a recognizable event, such as the struggle between a separated or divorced couple to reconcile, but describe moments, like waking dreams, in which your characters become uncertain as to what is real and what is imagined.

PARABLES AS STORY MATERIAL

A parable teaches a moral lesson by way of a story that illustrates the predicament and its outcome. Parables are effective tools of moral and spiritual instruction because we learn best by example. Parables are also short enough for us to be able to study them closely to see how they work.

One of the most famous Biblical parables is the Parable of the Sower in chapter 13 of the Gospel of Matthew. Actually, Jesus tells four parables of sowers, not just one; each offers a different perspective on the relationship between the sowing of seeds of grain and the sowing of seeds of faith. But what is especially interesting to writers about these interconnected parables is that before he has a chance to finish the first parable, one of his disciples interrupts him to ask, "Why speakest thou unto them in parables?" Jesus, in effect, explains that his parables will better convey the lesson to be learned: "Therefore speak I to them in parables, because they seeing see not, and hearing they hear not" (Matthew 13:13). In other words, the story that is conveyed by the parable illustrates the abstract moral principle which, by itself, would be more difficult to appreciate (i.e., "see").

FOR FURTHER REFLECTION

Parables remind us of the important role that stories can play in conveying abstract principles of ethical and moral behavior in concrete, dramatic terms. Human beings learn best through example. And when the examples are aesthetically as well as spiritually engaging, the lessons take root more readily.

......................................TRY THIS....................................

Write a parable based on a simple human occupation, one that can convey a moral or ethical lesson. For example, consider writing a parable of a janitor, a lifeguard, a babysitter, a factory assembly-line worker, or a schoolteacher. Try conveying, through specific actions rather than overt moralizing, how, say, a janitor's dedication to his task (a task that seems insignificant, even shameful, to some people) is honorable. Show, don't summarize, for example, how skillful custodial care ensures office productivity and efficiency.

JOHANNES GUTENBERG:
PAGE FROM THE GUTENBERG BIBLE

The printing press transformed the world with its ability to disseminate information via books and periodicals rapidly. In its earliest stages, however, it strove to continue the legacy of illuminated manuscript art. The early phase of printed books—those published before the sixteenth century—are known as *incunabula* (from a Latin word meaning "to cradle") and were very expensive. As printing technology improved and practical criteria superseded aesthetic, books became much less expensive, and more people could own them. Today, incunabula, especially the earliest printed Bibles, are museum treasures. As writers, we pay homage to these incunabula in which the great cultural legacy of the book began its long and venerable life.

FOR FURTHER REFLECTION

The invention of moveable type changed the world. Through the mechanical reproduction of books, learning became democratized. What better symbol of this milestone of civilization than that of the first book off the press, the Gutenberg Bible.

Today, the digital revolution, for all its versatility and convenience, has once again revolutionized the transmission of knowledge; but is this new revolution moving us forward the way the first revolution did? Perhaps it is too early to tell.

......................................TRY THIS....................................

After viewing the Gutenberg Bible (www.hrc.utexas.edu/exhibitions/permanent/ gutenberg), record your thoughts regarding the positive vs. the negative consequences of the Internet, of digitizing books, and of transforming libraries into "information resource centers." Do the advantages outweigh the disadvantages or vice versa?

MARCH 3
TAKING RISKS

To be a writer means to take risks, putting yourself and your ideas out on a limb, making yourself vulnerable to criticism, maybe even ridicule. Does that give you pause? If you have strong views on any subject, rest assured that there will be multitudes who will want to throw rotten tomatoes at you, no matter how carefully you present your evidence.

While it is true that no writer can please everyone—diversity of ideas and tastes is what makes the world go 'round—writers can nonetheless benefit from making an effort to persuade, either overtly, through reasoned argument, or artistically, by way of dramatically rendered scenes. Think of Atticus Finch's impassioned admonition to the jury to uphold the honor of human equality protected by the court:

> … there is one human institution that makes a pauper the equal
> of a Rockefeller, the stupid man the equal of an Einstein, and
> the ignorant man the equal of any college president. That in-
> stitution … is a court.
>
> —*To Kill a Mockingbird* (Harper Lee)

Like Atticus Finch, who rankled his fellow townspeople by daring to defy their racial prejudices, writers must guard against compromising their integrity for the sake of being accepted by the majority.

FOR FURTHER REFLECTION

Think about a topic you've considered writing on but decided against doing so because it seemed too controversial or unpleasant or risqué. Ask yourself why you wanted to write about this topic in the first place. Reconsider your decision by weighing the benefits against the hazards of pursuing the topic.

.....................................TRY THIS.....................................

Write a paragraph describing a fresh approach to a writing task you stopped working on because you felt it was too controversial or unpalatable. Focus on the importance of the topic and how you might present it in a way that would persuade those whose views on the topic oppose your own.

COMMUNICATION AND COMMUNITY

Why do we want to be writers anyway? Some writers satisfy themselves with vague or superficial answers: to be admired or to be independent. A more substantive answer takes us into the heart of the word *communicate*. We want our lives to have value—not just to ourselves and our families, but to the human community. The philosopher Rollo May pointed out that communication *leads* to community. By publishing our writing, we reach out to many members of a community, small or large; local, national, or global. Members of a community nurture one another in important ways by sharing experiences, insights, and hard-learned lessons.

Thinking about the people who make up your community—merchants, construction and maintenance workers; political leaders, lawyers, and law-enforcers, journalists and editors; homemakers, cooks, and craftspeople; entertainers and athletes, educators and those who are being educated; physicians, nurses, and other health-care professionals; religious leaders; mechanics, scientists, and engineers—what an extraordinary wealth of life-experiences for a writer to learn from and build stories around! Indeed, one could say that it is part of any writer's job to be as familiar with as many aspects of her community as possible.

FOR FURTHER REFLECTION

Good communication skills reinforce the bonds that hold a community together. Poor communication leads to misunderstandings, distortions of truth. Moreover, for communication to function properly, all channels must be open. There is no such thing as one-sided communication. Unless all views are acknowledged, respectfully and carefully considered, communication breaks down rapidly.

..................................TRY THIS....................................

Conduct "field research" on members of your community whose jobs and personal lives you would be interested in exploring. For example, if you are interested in arts and crafts, then visit an art fair or several art galleries (perhaps all specializing in a particular kind of art, like dinnerware or glass paperweights), and engage the artists or gallery operators in conversation about the kinds of artworks they produce or sell. Later, use your notes to draft an essay or story or sequence of poems about these craftspeople and the work they produce.

MARCH 5
THE JOY OF REREADING

When it comes to good books—not just "classics," but books that have stirred us profoundly or heightened our awareness of human nature—we do them and ourselves a disservice by reading them only once. Set aside time to reread the books that have made a strong impression on you. To reread an excellent book is to re-experience it, and—from a writer's perspective—to become reacquainted with important elements of the craft. Pay attention to what the author does to pull you into the story, to those verbal brushstrokes that gradually immerse you into the time and place and circumstance that acquaint you with the characters. Good writers make it seem effortless, their sentences and paragraphs unfolding like a tapestry, a magic carpet transporting you to another place. A part of us doesn't want to see the brushstrokes; but if you want to make writing your profession, you need to study such details of the craft.

FOR FURTHER REFLECTION

Reading is rereading, especially when it comes to great books; in fact, we could gauge a book's greatness by how much more we gain from it with each subsequent reading. Rereading serves as an ongoing reminder of the things we writers must learn to master: story construction, voice, dramatic rendering, historical background, setting, and so on. Something else to keep in mind: Our tastes and perceptions change over the years. When we return to a book we read a decade earlier, we will derive more from it simply because we have more experiences to relate it to.

......................................TRY THIS......................................

After rereading one of your favorite books, explain in your journal what you gained from this second reading that you hadn't gained from the first. Did you pay more attention to character personalities and motivations? Did you notice aspects of the theme or the symbolism or the plot structure that you hadn't noticed the first time? Be as detailed as you can in your response.

FINDING MATERIAL

"Anything is useful to a poet," the poet-scholar John Berryman once said. And that can be extended to writers of any stripe. To be a writer means to see the unusual in the commonplace, innovation in the routine, hidden beauty in ordinary things. Robert Frost captured the nostalgic experience of picking apples; Walt Whitman the sight of blacksmiths "with grimed hairy chests" pounding red-hot slabs of iron into horseshoes or scythes; Nathanael West the surreal sensation of movie sets momentarily being mistaken for reality.

The mysteries of existence can be discovered in the ripple of a pond or a film of dust on a table. One of the powers of literature is its ability to see significance in things that most people overlook. Keen observational skills coupled with unceasing curiosity and delight in even commonplace experiences can transform even mundane-seeming material into something extraordinary. A writer's material, in other words, is anything at all—whatever one pays close attention to and from which one is able to extract universal significance. William Blake could see the entire universe in a grain of sand.

FOR FURTHER REFLECTION

Finding material to write about is easy. Developing a poem or story out of that material is more challenging. But keep in mind that the more you try to imagine ways to turn a ho-hum object or incident into a story, the more adept you will become at it. Always have a notebook, or at least a few scraps of paper, handy for scribbling down your ideas.

....TRY THIS....................................

Compose a poem or prose paragraph about an ordinary household object like a light bulb, toothpick, potted plant, or threadbare sofa. Imagine the object (or cluster of them) in an unusual context or as having an important role to play in a story. For example, you might plot a mystery story in which a key to a safety deposit box that contains something precious is hidden underneath the soil of a potted plant. Don't try to use fancy language; rather, try to use ordinary language in unusual ways.

PEOPLE WATCHING

To be a writer is to get to know people—their bad and good habits, their distinctive temperaments, tastes, and appearances, and most of all, their deepest longings and fears. Every person you meet is a lesson in human nature. Even when simply observing people, you can learn a lot from their mannerisms, their clothing, their conversations, their jewelry, and what they carry around with them. Of course, when conjuring up characters for stories, you can make free-wheeling inferences about what you see or overhear.

Different people-watching venues will yield different results. The individuals you observe at a football game will differ considerably from those you observe at a homeless shelter, although there will likely be some overlap. It is important to take the physical environment into consideration when people watching. People will act differently in different environments.

FOR FURTHER REFLECTION

Because stories are almost always about people, we writers need to become familiar with human nature in all its variations. People watching goes a long way toward reminding us of the wide spectrum of human types. Make it a point to observe people closely (without gawking at them, of course) wherever you go. If the occasion seems appropriate enough, strike up a conversation. It's amazing how much we can learn about a person that way.

································TRY THIS································

1. Here is a fun activity that can also prove useful in working up character profiles for your future stories: The next time you're in a public place—airport terminal, restaurant, cocktail lounge, theater, shopping mall—pay close attention to someone sitting near you (do try to be inconspicuous!) and, extrapolating from that person's appearance and behavior, imagine his livelihood, hobbies, obsessions, favorite foods, and philosophy of life.

2. Using one of the character profiles you completed for number one, develop a story around that character.

OBSERVING THE DETAILS

It's amazing how much we overlook during casual observation of our surroundings. But writers, like painters and sleuths, need to pay close attention to things; that is when the *nuances* become visible: the crimson flush of joy that spreads across a mother's face as she greets her daughter at the airport; the intense but muted conversation between a man and a woman in a dark corner of the local pub—what do their gestures suggest? "You start seeing everything as material," Anne Lamott writes in *Bird by Bird*. By regarding everything as material for stories, you will enhance your powers of observation. Here are a few suggestions for enhancing your observational skills:

- **Look for the purpose or larger context.** If you see a teenager practicing skateboarding maneuvers, look for signs that she is preparing for a competition.

- **Notice the minutest details.** How does the skateboarder maintain balance? How many mishaps occur within a given time frame?

- **Form questions based on what you don't understand or would like more information about.** For example, after watching the skateboarder, interview her to learn the answers to your questions.

Yogi Berra said it best: "You can observe a lot by watching."

FOR FURTHER REFLECTION

Being a conscientious observer will enhance your powers of observation; good observational skills are developed through practice and habit, as is true of any skill. So, predispose yourself to keen observation. The best way to do that is to be an active, rather than a passive, observer. Decide ahead of time that you are going to take in every warp and woof of reality. You'll amaze yourself by what suddenly comes to your attention.

......................................TRY THIS....................................

Situate yourself in a shopping mall where you can observe shoppers inside two or three stores. Write down everything you see shoppers doing: talking with the help, inspecting the merchandise. How do shopping habits differ from individual to individual? Can you generalize about gender or age differences in shoppers' habits?

EDITING PREMATURLY

Some writers are tormented by such relatively superficial concerns as grammar, spelling, word choice, and clumsy or wordy sentences. They forget that writing is a *process* that often involves several drafts. When writing a first draft, you should be thinking only about getting ideas onto paper, to have something that can be reshaped and refined later on. The great Argentine author Jorge Luis Borges felt that one could write better by *leaving in* the mistakes, rather than stopping prematurely to edit them out.

A writing task can be thought of as existing in three stages: accumulating material, shaping an idea, refining the idea. The accumulation stage is where you ought to be writing rapidly, not stopping to edit unless you think of an alternative word or sentence immediately. The biggest danger in stopping is losing momentum and ending your writing day prematurely.

FOR FURTHER REFLECTION

The compulsion to edit at the point of utterance may stem from the false notion that writing has to be correct the first time out. Nothing could be farther from the truth. Remember your priorities when drafting: First get the ideas across; worry about structuring and fine-tuning the style to ensure readability later.

......................................TRY THIS......................................

Imagine the last time you were at the airport waiting for a flight. Try to visualize the people hurrying to and fro, getting off of planes, rushing to their gates. Write a one-page scenario of a couple or family in this setting: Where are they headed and why? What kind of lives do they lead, separately and together? What is the most urgent problem in their lives right now? As you write, do not pause to consider your word choice or sentence construction or story progression.

DREAMING ON PAPER

Are you looking for a way to capture more of your imagination on paper? One way to do it is to dream on paper—not free-associate (which is useful in itself) but actually to conjure up a dream and let in unfold in a flurry of words. To increase the likelihood that your dreams will transfer over to your fingertips, so to speak, try to engage in this activity soon after waking up in the morning (or in the middle of the night), especially after a vivid dream. Dreaming on paper is not quite drafting; it is more like hooking up with your subconscious mind, where logic breaks down but doesn't vanish—it just reassembles itself into strange patterns. Lewis Carroll's *Alice's Adventures in Wonderland* and *Through the Looking Glass* are masterful examples of dream-writing raised to the level of literary masterpieces.

When bother hooking up with your subconscious? Simply because the subconscious is a reservoir of creative possibility, and the more easily we writers can tap into it, the more creative we can become.

FOR FURTHER REFLECTION

Dreams are fanciful, symbol-laden, highly compressed stories (poems?) generated by our subconscious minds. Imagine if our dreams automatically got written down: We'd each be the authors of whole libraries of wildly imaginative books.

...................................TRY THIS....................................

Tomorrow morning when you awaken, go directly to your keyboard and begin writing in dream-sequence fashion—that is, pay no attention to transitions or logical story progression. Try to capture the juxtaposition of images and sensations typical of dreaming. Use a recent dream as a template if you wish. Refrain from holding back or editing prematurely, or else you may lose the fluid unfolding of images that often accompanies daydream-inspired writing.

EXTRACTING THE UNUSUAL
FROM EVERYDAY EXPERIENCES

We sometimes experience the unusual within or alongside the usual. A trip to the beach can quickly become an unforgettable event if porpoises suddenly leap out of the water, or if you encounter someone molding a medieval city out of sand. A ho-hum cocktail party can become memorable when you meet someone with an offbeat personality. Everyday objects acquire an unusual aura when you allow your writer's imagination to surface. Trees in winter may be commonplace, but through the eyes of a poet like Robert Frost, they acquire an almost unearthly strangeness and charm:

> ... you must have seen them
> Loaded with ice a sunny winter morning
> After a rain. They click upon themselves
> As the breeze rises, and turn many-colored
> As the stir cracks and crazes their enamel.
> —"Birches"

The world is your palette. What seems ordinary can, with the right verbal brushstrokes, become a thing of beauty or intrigue.

FOR FURTHER REFLECTION

As writers, we need to cultivate the habit of seeing the unusual within the usual. Sometimes, if we just tilt our heads a little, our ordinary surroundings can appear extraordinary. Be determined to take a fresh look at the world from a new angle of vision; it's amazing what we can discover about people and events when viewing them from a different perspective.

...................................TRY THIS...................................

Write a page in which you dramatize (not just summarize) a noteworthy experience—either from many years ago or from yesterday. Highlight what was most unusual about the experience. For example, you might write a page about the day you ran into a friend you haven't seen for ten years. What was the first thing you noticed about him other than the change (pronounced or scarcely discernable) in physical appearance? What were the first things that surfaced in your conversation?

Over the next four days, dramatize four additional experiences. At the end of this period, choose the best of these dramatizations and develop it into a short story or personal-experience essay.

MARCH 12
ADVICE

All of us can benefit from advice, provided it makes good sense in the context of what we are trying to accomplish. Sometimes, alas, that will not be the case. A fellow writer in your workshop may completely misunderstand your intentions or fail to appreciate the techniques of characterization or plotting that you're using. Advice from other writers can be intimidating, especially if those writers have been publishing their work. But that doesn't necessarily mean they can appreciate what *you* are trying to do. The advice you receive has to ring true, regardless of the reputation of the advisor. This will happen if you've already consciously or semiconsciously realized the problem on your own—or if a second reader of your draft makes a similar suggestion. (As with doctors, second opinions are often a good idea!) If the advice you receive doesn't seem appropriate, just ignore it. It was John Steinbeck who may have given the best advice ever about advice: "Beware of advice," he once warned, "even this."

FOR FURTHER REFLECTION

Giving advice can sometimes be a knee-jerk reaction—not that knee-jerk reactions are necessarily bad, but often they're not too carefully thought out. Trust your own instincts, even if you're a beginner. Get second opinions.

.....................................TRY THIS....................................

List all of the suggestions for revision you receive from members of your writers' workshop, and then apply them methodically to your draft two or three days later. Ignore the ones that don't seem relevant. For suggestions you're not sure about, ask another writer for her opinion on the matter.

CHARACTERS AND FOOD

One way to make characters distinctive is to give them distinctive culinary tastes. Think of Falstaff and his sack, James Bond and his martinis, Marcel Proust and his madeleines, Ebenezer Scrooge and his bit of undigested beef, or J.K. Rowling's Harry Potter & Co., with their chocolate frogs and pumpkin juice. Robert B. Parker's Spenser is always preparing wonderful meals for Susan, the woman in his life (although, like most detectives, he will enjoy a good donut now and then).

An excellent resource for writers who want to study how writers integrate food and fiction is *The Book Lover's Cookbook*, by Shaunda Kennedy Wenger and Janet Kay Jensen. You'll find recipes for fried green tomatoes from Fannie Flagg's *Fried Green Tomatoes at the Whistle Stop Café*; Bev's No-Fuss Crab Cakes from Patricia Cornwall's *Unnatural Exposure*; peach pie from Toni Morrison's *The Bluest Eye*; and many more.

Food and the social contexts in which foods are served add color to fiction and also to memoirs. In *Under the Tuscan Sun*, Frances Mayes describes the pleasure she experienced dining at a restaurant in Tuscany:

> Acquacotta ... is a particular local specialty, the "cooked wa-
> ter" soup of vegetables with an egg served on top; *testina di
> vitella e porcini sott'olio*, veal head and porcini mushrooms
> under olive oil ... We start with *crostini di polenta con pure di
> funghi porcini e tartufo*, polenta squares with a puree of porcini
> and truffles—rich and savory.

Mayes poetically captures the experience of encountering regional Italian food, and in so doing, reveals much about herself as well as the character of the region.

FOR FURTHER REFLECTION
We can all relate to food; it is deeply embedded in all cultures. Its immense variety can prove to be a rich palette for adding zest to character and plot—like adding spices to a recipe!

......................................TRY THIS....................................

Incorporate some of your favorite recipes into a story so that the food illuminates the personality of your viewpoint character. Include lots of sensory details—visual, olfactory, tactile—even auditory (sizzling steaks and such), as well as taste.

WRITING TO PRESERVE HISTORY

To write is to preserve the truth of the past: your past, your family's past, your nation's and the world's past, either via the direct experiences of nonfiction or the more indirect (but also truthful) renderings of fiction.

For Holocaust survivor and Nobel Peace Prize laureate Elie Wiesel, to write is to remember and bear witness. "Not to transmit an experience," he asserts, "is to betray it." From Wiesel's perspective, then, one writes out of moral obligation. History is what we shape with language. If a past event does not get written about—or if it gets written about in a superficial or distorted manner—then both the historical event and the human experience emanating from that event are betrayed.

When you prepare to write about the past, you assume a substantial burden of responsibility. You must ask yourself these questions:

- Am I aware of all aspects of the event?

- Am I aware of what has previously been written about the event? If so, what am I able to contribute to its further understanding?

- What influences does this event have on present events?

- Have I weeded out inconsistencies, falsehoods, incomplete accounts, distortions, and ambiguities from my own as well as earlier accounts?

FOR FURTHER REFLECTION

Writing is essential to preserving history. Not only that, the quality of the writing—its precision, its depth of coverage—determines the quality of the historical record. If you plan to write about a historical event, you must be faithful to the historical record and correct inaccuracies in the existing record.

......................................TRY THIS....................................

Write the first page of an essay about a historical event with which you feel some emotional bond. For example, choose a battle fought in Vietnam because a relative or friend had participated in it. After the draft is complete, check for accuracy by consulting appropriate documents.

As an alternative, choose a pivotal moment in history, such as Alexander Graham Bell's testing out his first telephone. Plunge into a draft, but take time out to do some in-depth reading about the event.

ESTABLISHING THE JOURNAL-WRITING HABIT

Writing in your journal regularly is important. If you are not already in the habit of writing regularly in your journal, make an effort to do so every day for three weeks—enough time for the habit to take hold. Once that happens, you will have taken a major step toward making writing an integral part of your life.

To get yourself to write in your journal every day, you need to come up with stimulating things to write about. Don't bore yourself by recording what you ate for breakfast or what chores you're resolved to tackle. Here are some journal writing possibilities that could some day spark a story or essay:

- gut responses to articles in this morning's newspaper
- experiences during your last trip out of town
- one-sentence story ideas (later to be expanded into paragraphs)
- on-site descriptions of people you observe in public places
- pet peeves
- superstitions, rituals
- embarrassing moments
- mystical or frightening moments
- immediate reactions to movies just watched, books just finished
- records of ongoing progress—toward learning a new skill, toward breaking a bad habit, toward solving a difficult problem

FOR FURTHER REFLECTION

Journal writing primes the mind for big projects as well as serves as a reservoir for new ideas. The habit of writing regularly in your journal predisposes you to observe more keenly, to be more receptive to ideas for essays, stories, poems. Keep in mind that the act of writing is itself an effective means of generating ideas—or to put it another way, writing is a mode of thinking.

...................................TRY THIS.....................................

Write a journal entry of at least half a page every day for two weeks. Choose from the above list of suggestions. Vary the type of entry (description, list, reflection, analysis, free-association, poem, reading notes, etc.) each day. During the second week, elaborate on each of the previous week's entries.

LE MOT JUSTE

The French expression means "the most precise word for the occasion." It's a lovely three-syllable whisper in the ear reminding us of the value of precise communication. Language, of course, being merely a symbolic system, can never totally capture the reality it strives for—nor do we need for it to do so. But if you're writing a poem or critical essay, you will be after the most precise words possible. In some cases, you will need to provide what is sometimes called a stipulative definition, one that is more precise than the standard dictionary definition ("When I use this term I intend for it to mean such and such").

Words may have "established" dictionary definitions, but most have subtle shades of meaning that are context-dependent. In a very real sense, there is no such thing as interchangeable synonyms. Synonyms may be similar in meaning but not exact. Think, for example, of the words *photograph* and *snapshot*: Yes, you can use one in place of the other and get your basic meaning across, but the word *photograph* implies formality and at least a minimal amount of skill on the part of the photographer. A *snapshot*, on the other hand, can be taken much more quickly, without artistic design, by anyone.

FOR FURTHER REFLECTION

On the vast palette of language, words are the individual pigments. Think of synonyms as shades of a major color. Take some of the words that are synonymous with *big*: *large*, *huge*, *enormous*, *oversized*, *immense*, *grand* (or *grande*, if you're ordering a latte from Starbucks), *colossal*. Substituting *blue* for *big*, our palette would consist of *azure*, *aquamarine*, *turquoise*, *cerulean*, *powder blue*, *ultramarine*, and so on.

.....................................TRY THIS.....................................

Using a thesaurus as a prompt-book, write a brief poem or descriptive passage using several synonyms of a given word separately. Let's say you choose the word *home*: First write a paragraph using that word; next, write a second paragraph using the word *abode*; and then write a third paragraph using the word *cottage*, and so on. Capitalize on the different connotations that each synonym generates.

ACTIVE LISTENING

Along with training the eye to see what is before us, writers need to train the ear to listen actively, to "put your ear close to your soul," as the poet Anne Sexton eloquently put it, "and listen hard." This kind of listening has more to do with acute and sensitive mental alertness than with literally hearing anything. Active listening can also be thought of as intentional thinking, or rapt attentiveness—a way of opening oneself up to the easily overlooked nuances of human behavior. It is the kind of listening that doesn't just happen: It has to be actively practiced.

Shakespeare, through Falstaff (*Henry IV*, Pt. 2), concerned about becoming lethargic, speaks of "the disease of not listening" that has begun to plague him. Not listening is a disease because it can cause misunderstanding, undermine precious family bonds, interfere with job efficiency, and lead to social ills on a grand scale.

FOR FURTHER REFLECTION

What do you suppose Anne Sexton means when she advises writers to put their ear close to the soul and listen hard? What does she expect writers to be listening for? What can the soul disclose that is important to writers? Listening well recruits the soul as well as the mind and the heart.

...................................TRY THIS....................................

1. Put your ear to your soul and listen hard. What do you hear? Write a paragraph describing what you are listening to when you put your ear to your soul.

2. Keep an ongoing list of problems you or others in your family have experienced as a result of not listening; then write an essay about the consequences of problems arising from not listening.

THE ART OF QUESTIONING

Here is a rock-solid bit of writerly advice: Question everything. Resist passively accepting received truths without thinking them through. This is not a symptom of paranoia, but of healthy, critical skepticism—the kind of skepticism that gives birth to scholarly inquiry. If someone says, in response to your desire, at age fifty, to learn to play the violin, "You can't teach an old dog new tricks," turn the claim into a question: "*Is* it true that you can't teach an old dog new tricks?"—or deconstruct the metaphor, "Is it true that older people can't learn new skills like learning to play a musical instrument?" When you feel curiosity about a natural phenomenon like mountains, ask yourself, "What geological forces caused mountains to form?" or "How long does it take mountains to form—or to wear away?" (the Appalachians once resembled the Rockies). Resist the temptation to pass it off as, say, "God's creation." That may well be the cause, but it begs the question, "How did God use the forces of nature to create the mountain?" Making a habit out of questioning is making a habit out of in-depth thinking, a prerequisite for writing.

FOR FURTHER REFLECTION

Reflect for a moment on some of your own assumptions—perhaps those regarding male-female differences (physical, behavioral, psychological) or the proper way to raise children or how to stay healthy. Now pose questions about these assumptions and then question your responses to those assumptions.

...................................TRY THIS....................................

Write down an assertion—something less certain than a hard fact, but which you nonetheless feel fairly confident is true. Perhaps an assertion like, "The American Civil War put an end to slavery," or "If intelligent life existed beyond the earth, we would have heard from them by now." Now turn that statement into a question: "*Did* the American Civil War truly put an end to slavery?" "Are there any reasons that could explain why we haven't heard from intelligent aliens, assuming they exist?" You now have a topic to research!

TRAINING THE MEMORY

Writers are memory artists; that is, they take what has been and recast it as a work of art—a story or poem or (if the emphasis is going to be on what actually happened) work of nonfiction (and by the way, any work of nonfiction is "artistic" insofar as it is being reshaped in carefully orchestrated language). Memory, as Mark Van Doren eloquently wrote in *Liberal Education*, "holds together past and present, gives continuity and dignity to human life." It stands to reason, then, that writers should train their memories—not just to memorize superficial facts and figures but to acquire deep understanding of the roles those facts and figures have played in the larger scheme of things.

Memory training is an ancient art (see the entry for May 18). These days, with our many systems of information storage and the Internet, memorization is no longer the crucial tool that it used to be. But the memory can still be trained in ways that are useful to writers. Regularly engaging in the following tasks should strengthen the memory:

- reread important books and articles
- take notes
- write detailed responses in your journal
- share your responses with family and friends

FOR FURTHER REFLECTION

Memory training is important not just for more efficient retention of facts but for assimilating them more readily into our worldview. Memory training also helps us to see linkages between past and present experiences. After all, memory (short-term and long-term) is what enables us to know ourselves and our place in the world.

...................................TRY THIS....................................

Compose a synopsis for a story, stage play, or film script in which memory plays an important role. You might want to read or view such classics as *Citizen Kane*, *Spellbound*, or *Death of a Salesman*.

MOTIVATED BY IDEAS

"It is a love of ideas that motivates the deep writer," asserts Eric Maisel, a psychotherapist and creativity consultant. "Deep writing" is Maisel's term for passionate, caring writing. Writers who are passionate about ideas, who care about sharing their intellectual passions with others, are motivated by their passion and their caring to get the writing done.

Think about the ways in which ideas can motivate us to write:

- They stimulate our imaginations. The idea that millions of earth-like worlds may exist in our galaxy alone has inspired many a writer of science fiction.

- They deepen our understanding of the past and of historical trends or scientific progress. Ideas have their own histories. Take any idea from biology or medicine, for example—infectious disease, blood circulation, brain function—and you will discover that it has a long history.

- They inspire us to contribute to their legacy. Once we acquire deep knowledge about a subject, it is natural to want to share it with others. Some wish to share their knowledge directly, face-to-face: They become classroom teachers. Others would prefer to share their knowledge indirectly, through writing or painting: They become authors or painters.

FOR FURTHER REFLECTION

Good ideas are their own best motivation to write, so it will pay to spend time doing a lot of idea brainstorming. It's likely that a lot of duds will pour out—idea gems, like jewels, are rare and precious—but be patient. Think of panning for gold: An idea is a nugget of potential story-ness that you can develop into an entertaining work of fiction.

......................................TRY THIS....................................

Set up an idea file, alphabetically arranged using index cards, or just maintain an e-file. The nice thing about index cards, though, is that you can shuffle them around and connect them in interesting ways. At least once a week, select one of your ideas from the file and begin drafting a story, essay, or poem around it.

MARCH 21
TRADITION VS. INNOVATION

Any literary work is both old and new: It belongs to a tradition—of genre (e.g., romance, mystery, science fiction) or subgenre (e.g., Gothic romance, police procedural mystery, cyberpunk science fiction), of character development ("flat" caricatures or "round" nuanced individuals, to adopt E.M. Forster's terms in *Aspects of the Novel* [see the entry for November 7]), and extends that tradition in an innovative way. Highly innovative works, if crafted with sufficient artistry, often become literary classics. James Joyce's *Ulysses*, for example, with its consummate stream-of-consciousness narration and brilliant language play, revolutionized the novel for the modern age. At the same time, it follows the most ancient of literary structures: the hero's journey—the odyssey, named after its most famous and greatest example, Homer's *Odyssey*, a work that dates back to the seventh century B.C.E. As a writer you need to be aware of the tradition in which you are working, no matter how innovative you hope to be—which is why it's so important to read widely within your preferred genre as well as outside of it.

FOR FURTHER REFLECTION

Tradition and innovation are both vital to culture. In art, though, the scales are tilted toward innovation because part of what makes art pleasurable is its novelty. An artist, whether a painter, filmmaker, or poet, knows that the aesthetic experiences thrive not only on new twists to old motifs or plots, but on entirely new paradigms for paintings, films, or poems.

...................................TRY THIS....................................

Write a page of conventional narration—a dramatization of a personal experience, such as a close encounter with a rattlesnake or the day you and a friend got lost in the woods. Give it a conventional beginning, middle, and end. Wait a day or so, and then rework the episode, using innovative techniques. For example, include three viewpoint characters instead of one (maybe even including the snake's), and shift unexpectedly from one viewpoint to the next. Or employ a stream-of-consciousness narrative voice.

MARCH 22
CRAZY QUILTING

Conventional narratives progress chronologically, sometimes spatially. But there's no reason to be chained to convention. Maybe the story you want to tell would be most effectively rendered as a mosaic, or (less tidily) as a crazy-quilt. That is, the story might shift from narration to description to explanation to report, and then back to description—following no pattern whatsoever. There are many precedents for this: Melville's *Moby-Dick* is something of a crazy-quilt novel, disrupting, as it does, its narrative thread to expound on the science of cetology (whale biology) or go into technical detail about whale hunting or whale lore. A very different kind of crazy-quilt novel is John Dos Passos's *U.S.A.*—a trilogy, actually (*The 42nd Parallel*, *1919*, and *The Big Money*). These novels, with their newsreels, newspaper headlines, camera-eye exposés, and character profiles, create a Whitmanesque collage of a frenetic America during the first three decades of the twentieth century. Reginald Marsh's copious illustrations add to the crazy-quilting effect.

FOR FURTHER REFLECTION
Crazy-quilt (or collage) novels attempt to paint a full picture of an age, a culture, a complete human experience (like whaling or warfare). The scope is necessarily epic-like, the text coming as close to visual art as prose can possibly get; in fact, Dos Passos makes liberal use of visual images via his newsreels and camera eye segments.

...................................TRY THIS...................................

Study the organizational schemes of Melville's *Moby-Dick* and Dos Passos's *U.S.A.* trilogy, and then work up a preliminary design/outline for a crazy-quilt novel of your own. Think in terms of collage, multimedia presentation—a kaleidoscopic array of scenes that, taken together, can create a feeling of energy and excitement to your novel. Think more in terms of *scenes* than of temporal progression.

MIND STRETCHING

The most important thing we can learn from a formal education is how to continue educating ourselves on our own—learning how to learn, appreciating the power and potential of new ideas. "A mind that is stretched around an idea," Oliver Wendell Holmes, Jr., once said, "never returns to its original dimension."

Mind stretching should be a daily exercise for writers—hence the purpose of this book. But also think about mind-stretching opportunities in contexts other than writing or preparation for writing. Let every facet of your life involve mind stretching. When you're out planting flowers or vegetables, for example, find out all you can about the flowers and vegetables you're planting: their physical and nutritional properties, the history of their cultivation, their cultural contexts. Start with the Internet but don't stop there. Find books on the subject in your local library or favorite bookstore. Nothing stretches the mind like a book you can hold in your hands, page back and forth in, retrieve on an instant's notice.

FOR FURTHER REFLECTION
The hunger to know is one of our basic appetites. Take care that it isn't satisfied with mental junk food—i.e., with quick encyclopedia-type blurbs. "A little learning is a dangerous thing," Alexander Pope famously wrote in his philosophical poem, "An Essay on Criticism," "Drink deep or touch not the Pierian spring."

...................................TRY THIS...................................

Stretch your mind by launching an in-depth reading campaign into your favorite subject. No matter how familiar you think you are with a subject area—be it ancient Chinese history, Baroque music, scholastic philosophy, radio astronomy, French impressionist painting, or bridge building—there is a lifetime's worth of additional learning left to absorb. To keep from being overwhelmed by possibilities, though, decide on a specific course of mind stretching for a given month. Devote this month to learning more about the Spanish Civil War; devote next month to learning more about existentialist philosophy. For months with important holidays, learn more about that holiday; for example, how images of Santa Claus have evolved since the nineteenth century; or the pagan origins of Halloween; or the history of Mardi Gras.

SHOWING RATHER THAN TELLING

Depicting an action scene in fiction is typically more complicated than describing one in nonfiction. The fiction writer needs to capture an invented character's emotional responses and present them with all the authenticity of nonfiction. (By the way, writers of what has come to be called "creative nonfiction" also employ such fiction-writing techniques to describe real-life characters and events.) Dramatization is not an easy skill to master. As Ernest Hemingway pointed out, you must include "what the actual things were which produced the emotion that you experienced" and give them dramatic immediacy through the eyes of your viewpoint character. Such rendering enables your readers to experience the resulting emotions vicariously—which is more effective than merely telling your readers what the emotions were like.

FOR FURTHER REFLECTION

Let the events in your narrative speak for themselves. Dramatize a scene rather than summarize it ("Ralph slammed the door so hard the house shook" rather than "John would typically slam the door so hard the house would shake"). Being overly explicit about how cruel a deed was (as opposed to simply depicting the deed and letting the reader decide for himself how cruel it was) leads to melodrama. Of course, telling (in the form of background explanation and description) has its place in fiction and can enrich a story immeasurably. But the story itself should predominate.

...............................TRY THIS...................................

Take one of the following explicit statements and render it dramatically so that the reader will experience the desired emotional response on his own:

- Barney reacted with extreme anger when he saw the thug push the old woman to the ground and take her purse.

- The children were dressed in such scary costumes that Arthur experienced a sudden awful memory from the war.

- As she approached the finish line, Janice could barely hold back her emotions.

- Eric could no longer control the car as it slid across the ice-slick road toward the edge of the cliff.

MARCH 25
INTERIORS

When you think of "setting," you might automatically think about external settings: rugged landscapes, rolling plains, dense forests. But "setting" includes interiors as well—the interiors of homes, offices, hospitals, schools, cathedrals, factories, laboratories. If you're writing a novel or memoir, you will find yourself describing not one interior but several. To do this effectively, visualize each interior as a kind of stage set; everything you describe should contribute to the overall atmosphere of the story that you're telling. Highly specific details go a long way, as Edgar Allan Poe, that master of interiors, everywhere demonstrates in his tales. Consider "The Pit and the Pendulum," in which the frantic narrator lay bound inside his dark cell:

> For many hours the immediate vicinity of the low framework
> upon which I lay had been literally swarming with rats. They
> were wild, bold, ravenous—their red eyes glaring upon me as
> if they waited but for motionlessness on my part to make me
> their prey. ... In their voracity, the vermin frequently fastened
> their sharp fangs on my fingers.

FOR FURTHER REFLECTION

Interior settings can generate atmosphere just like exterior ones. If you enjoy writing about old-world high society, read the novels of Edith Wharton for the way she captures the elegance of Gilded Age salons, opera houses, and the like; and if you're a writer of supernatural or Gothic fiction, you'll want to study such masters as Poe, H.P. Lovecraft, and their modern-day disciples Stephen King, Dean Koontz, and Peter Straub. If you're a playwright, then interior settings will become a major consideration when mapping out the play's storyline.

...................................TRY THIS...................................

1. Compose a dark, Poe-esque interior scene in which the narrator is at the brink of losing her mind out of fear. Use details that generate a sense of foreboding. Think of the inexorably descending pendulum or the rats' glowing eyes in Poe's "The Pit and the Pendulum."

2. Describe the interior setting of that play you've been planning to write. Is it a living room, as in a Noël Coward domestic drama? Is it an office, as in David Mamet's *Glengarry Glenn Ross*? Read the setting descriptions of several plays before writing your own.

MARCH 26
PASSION

If we are too cerebral, too logical or rule-bound in our writing, our writing might turn out "flat"—proper but anemic. Just as readers love to have their emotions stirred by a good story, so too, must writers permit their passions to carry them forward. This isn't as mystical as it sounds. To re-create, with words, a suspense-filled or heart-rending scenario takes a lot of emotional energy.

Where does it come from, this emotional energy? We all possess it; although with some writers, it takes a little prodding to bring it to the surface. Rationality, circumspection, and decorum are powerful regulators: They help get us through our workday without losing our sanity. To be good artists, however, we must let down our guard—must tranquilize our superegos—and allow a little emotional turbulence into our writing. It makes us vulnerable, but it also taps us into the soul of humanity.

FOR FURTHER REFLECTION
The word *passion* is derived from a Latin word meaning "suffering"—specifically, Christ's suffering on the cross; it also can refer to profound or divine submission. We can see how these meanings relate to passion in the more romantic sense. When one feels passionate about an individual or a cause, we can sense a fusion of love with self-sacrifice and a willingness to endure whatever pain is necessary to become one with the beloved ... or with God. Books that detail the sufferings of saints, by the way, are known as passionals—a sort of counterpart to devotionals.

...................................TRY THIS...................................

What topics fire up your passions? Finding new ways to fight bigotry? Giving recognition to the marginalized? Improving public education? Make a list of them, and then choose one as the subject for a poem, short story, or essay.

CONFLICT

Stories require conflict—one or more powerful obstacles that all but prevent the protagonist from reaching his urgent goal—until the climactic moment of reckoning when the protagonist brilliantly overcomes the conflict. The danger of losing the battle is not only sustained until the showdown, it intensifies. Conflict too easily resolved does not make a satisfying story.

Opposition need not be between the "good guys" and the "bad guys." It may come from those whom the protagonist loves or least suspects—spouse, children, parents, close friends, colleagues). Our complex needs lead us into conflict with those whose needs differ.

In order for the conflict to be satisfyingly resolved, there must be confrontation. "Without contraries," wrote the visionary poet William Blake, "is no progression." Things are better off in the end as a result of enduring the conflict.

FOR FURTHER REFLECTION

Conflict is as elemental to real life as it is to story. Story implies conflict; it's what the story builds around. Hero learns of bomb threat; hero finds bomb, quickly defuses it; everyone is safe without ever knowing their lives were threatened: not a story. But: Hero learns of bomb threat, uncovers one false lead after another; meanwhile, time is running out; in one desperate gamble, hero learns that there are two bombs planted, one in an area where lover is close by, the other in a heavily populated area; hero must choose. *That's* a story. By the way, it's part of the plot of Richard Donner's 1978 blockbuster film *Superman*.

......................................TRY THIS....................................

Neil Simon once explained that he begins a play by placing two persons with seemingly irreconcilable differences in the same room (think of Felix and Oscar in *The Odd Couple*). Follow Simon's strategy. Begin a play or story set inside a hotel room where two people are having it out. Who are they? Why are they there together? What are they arguing about? What is at stake?

TRANSPARENT STYLE

Novice writers sometimes assume that in order to make a strong impression on their readers they must sound impressive, that they must use big words and complex, ornate sentences and paragraphs to be taken seriously.

Nothing could be further from the truth. Readers want clarity above all: clarity in depicting a scene, a predicament; clarity in explaining a complicated problem or concept. In short, readers want an author's style to serve as a window into the story or essay, not as a slab of polished chrome that only calls attention to itself. Yes, graceful prose is desirable but only insofar as it contributes to clarity, not distracts from it. Graceful prose should never be verbose, using more words than are necessary to convey the intended meaning.

Words look "big" when they're not familiar—a problem aspiring writers experience when they do not read as widely or as often as they should. Also, language, unfortunately, is sometimes used to obscure meaning or deceive—a phenomenon sometimes called *doublespeak*. If an employer tells her staff that she will be "compressing the department in order to achieve optimal efficiency in light of recent market trends," she may well be saying, "You're being laid off."

FOR FURTHER REFLECTION

A transparent style of writing—in other words, writing that is devoted to transmitting story or information the way a window transmits sunlight into a room with minimal attention to itself—should be every writer's goal.

...................................TRY THIS....................................

Comb through recently completed drafts of stories and essays looking for paragraphs that are difficult to process—are more opaque than transparent—and revise them so that the story or the information is conveyed as clearly as possible. Look for words and phrases that obscure rather than clarify and for sentences that call too much attention to themselves and make reading a chore.

WORKING WITH SYMBOLS

The best way to give your writing symbolic richness is to let it come naturally, to let the story itself suggest its symbolic possibilities to you. Are you writing about courage during wartime? Think about Stephen Crane's "red badge"—the bloody head bandage he wore to represent his ironic courage in the context of his deserting the front. Do you want to convey the magic of the rebirth that accompanies spring? Think of T.S. Eliot's images of fertility and sterility in "The Waste Land" ("dull roots mixed with spring rain ... Earth in forgetful snow, feeding / a little life with dried tubers"). Do you want to write about the way ugliness can usurp beauty, or evil usurp good? Consider one of William Blake's *Songs of Innocence and Experience*, such as "London," in which the speaker encounters "Marks of weakness, marks of woe" in every face he meets, and senses "How the Chimney-sweeper's cry / Every blackning Church appalls, / And the hapless Soldier's sigh, / Runs in blood down Palace walls."

Symbolism enables us to capture profound experiences and phenomena with specific concrete images—a kind of metaphysical shorthand that synthesizes beauty with profundity.

FOR FURTHER REFLECTION

Reading poetry is an excellent way to get a keen sense of the way symbolism operates in literature. The Romantic poets—especially Blake, Coleridge, and Keats—are ideal sources. Let the symbols—the albatross in Coleridge's "Rime of the Ancient Mariner," the painted figures on Keats's Grecian urn or the nightingale in his respective great odes—work their alchemy on your imagination.

......................................TRY THIS.....................................

After reading the poems in Blake's *Songs of Innocence and Experience*, try your hand at writing a poem about one of Blake's subjects (a rose, a lamb, a fly, a tiger, an angel) and give it a modern spin. Don't worry about poetic form; focus exclusively on exploring the symbolic potential of the subject.

WRITING YOUR WAY OUT OF WRITER'S BLOCK

This is not as oxymoronic as you think. Writers who get blocked the most are perfectionists: Either they must try working out what they want to say in their heads first, or they balk at the prospect of having to squeeze the words out. Someone once said that writing is like opening a vein or pulling teeth. If that sounds like you, try "gushing" on paper, assuming that it's just warm-up stuff that you'll throw away. Just pick up your pen and start scribbling. Start with the difficulty you're having and try figuring out—on paper—why it's giving you so much trouble. Before you realize it, coherent thoughts and bright ideas will emerge out of the chaos—it's the nature of the human mind to move away from chaos and into coherence. The trick is to be patient and tolerant of the gibberish that might pour out. And don't be too hasty in discarding that gibberish either—a single word or phrase could contain the spark of an original idea.

FOR FURTHER REFLECTION

Our brains consist of hundreds of billions of neural interconnections. Is it any wonder that our thinking processes get a little scrambled or seize up now and then? Writing is a great way to unscramble. The very attempt to place unformed thoughts on paper helps to make the thoughts cohere.

......................................TRY THIS....................................

If you're blocked, write out a question to yourself, such as, "What might be keeping me from finishing this project?" and proceed to write down possibilities. If you run out of possibilities, write out another question, such as, "What other parts of this project (new scene, new subtopic, new character to introduce) can I turn to instead?"

MARCH 31
MANAGING TIME

We all seem to be slaves of time, especially when the clock says we must report for work at such and such a time and pay our bills by the deadlines. For Native American peoples of the past, time was not regimented externally by clocks, but generated internally by the rhythms of nature—the rising and setting sun, the phases of the moon, the cycles of the seasons, the rhythms and growth stages of one's body.

Engaging in artistic work, like writing, gives us a chance to escape clock time. The universe of the imagination cannot be regimented. Creative activity takes us out of external, regimented time and puts us back in touch with internal, natural time. Some writers will "allot" themselves x number of hours for their writing, but this smacks too much of the regimented time of the workplace. Try, instead, slipping gradually into a pensive state of mind, one that allows the doors of imagination to open—for it is from that same door that words will begin to flow. This kind of mental receptivity must not be equated with indolence or daydreaming, however. With it, the creative artist allows "natural" time to take over, so that instead of clock hands describing temporal progression, we now have the beating of our hearts, the intake of our breath, the flow of our thoughts.

FOR FURTHER REFLECTION

Finding writing time is tricky if you have a full-time day job or are attending school full-time. Tricky but doable; you can carve out odd periods during even a busy work day if you are so motivated (and you should be). Even fifteen minutes of uninterrupted writing before bedtime every night can yield dramatic results after a month.

......................................TRY THIS......................................

Write a page in which you describe the influence of conventional time in your life. Do not pay attention to the time as you work on this page. Instead, pay attention to your thinking process. Do not work as if you're under a deadline. Pay attention to the way you shape your sentences, how one thought follows another.

APRIL 1

THE VALUE OF ARCHETYPES

Archetypes are foundation stories; they give rise to innumerable variations over time and across cultures and are closely associated with what Carl Jung called the universal or collective unconscious. No matter what our cultural upbringing, we all relate to and interact with these foundational stories.

Jung singled out four archetypes as especially important:

- **The mother archetype:** mother as the fertility principle, the nurturer (as in "mother nature"); but also the mother as devourer, presiding over the underworld—the terrible, inescapable, all-devouring mother

- **The rebirth archetype:** reincarnation, resurrection; the transmigration of souls

- **The spirit archetype:** transcending the physical body; but also the psyche or mind (as distinct from brain) and (according to Jung) the manifestation of spirit in dreams and in fairy tales

- **The trickster archetype:** the joker, the prankster, the sly fox, the poltergeist, the urchin, and most especially, the devil (we might call this the villain archetype)—the negative energy in a story

FOR FURTHER REFLECTION

Think of archetypes as reservoirs for stories that play out one of innumerable variations on a fundamental (archetypal) theme. Consider the trickster archetype: You could fill an entire notebook on variations of that one—some harmless, like the practical joker; some malicious, like the identity thief or the hacker intent on sabotaging bank computers (see the entry for September 10).

..................................TRY THIS....................................

Create detailed character profiles for your novel in progress. Pattern each character after one of the Jungian archetypes—mother, rebirth, spirit, or trickster. Try not to let the archetypal patterning be too obvious, however. Include whatever variations to the archetype you consider necessary to make the character seem realistic and contemporary.

EDWARD HOPPER: "NIGHTHAWKS"

Many of Edward Hopper's paintings make ideal objects of contemplation for writers because they depict some sort of internal conflict. His most famous painting, "Nighthawks," you can probably visualize in your mind's eye: a late-night diner brightly lit, a couple and a lone man seated, a counterman saying something to the couple. Outside, all is oppressively dark and deserted. There are so many thoughts that this powerful scene is able to generate! Here is one: It is the darkest year of World War II—1942 (the year Hopper painted "Nighthawks"); the world is splitting apart at the seams, and in the painting, the man and woman seated next to each other in the diner are as detached as the man sitting alone. The counterman is speaking to them, but they are too wrapped up in their separate thoughts to pay attention, as much as they might like to. Nothing coheres, and yet the painting is itself a masterpiece of coherence. "Nighthawks" may be viewed by going to www.artchive.com/artchive/H/hopper.html.

Likewise, in "Office at Night," the man and the woman clearly have a workplace-related connection, but they are nonetheless profoundly disconnected despite the fact that they are keenly—almost painfully—aware of each other's presence.

FOR FURTHER REFLECTION
Edward Hopper's paintings are like parables. The scenes they depict reflect the modern predicament: people finding themselves disconnected and struggling to find ways to re-establish connection in a cold urban environment—scenes where people normally go to relax (hotels, restaurants, theatres, etc.), but are unable to relax there because of their loneliness or inner turmoil.

..................................TRY THIS..................................

Locate a collection of Edward Hopper's paintings in your public library or view them on the Internet. Which aspects of American life do Hopper's paintings capture? Which ones speak to you most poignantly, and why? Select a painting that seems to suggest a story to you, and then write the story.

APRIL 3

CANDOR

Are you able to call a spade a spade? Do you dare to see the world without rose-colored glasses? Do you avoid the temptation of sugaring up the unsavory and the unseemly aspects of reality? Fiction as well as nonfiction thrives on candor—on seeing the world and human nature as they really are (insofar as we are capable of seeing things as they really are).

In other words, don't overlook the blemishes, the distasteful quirks of your characters' personalities and actions. Learn not to flinch when you dramatize scenes in which one of your villains beats someone to a bloody pulp or speaks in an offensive manner. By taking care to represent what you consider to be unsavory behaviors or viewpoints candidly, you heighten the authenticity of your story.

FOR FURTHER REFLECTION

Unless you go into the gory details, your characters will seem made of cardboard, unconvincing. On the other hand, don't be sensationalistic—that is, refrain from including graphic detail just to shock your readers. Whether you write fiction or nonfiction, you need to treat your subjects in an uncompromisingly honest way, without glossing over the unseemly details. Readers are very good at sensing when things have been left out, whatever the reason.

...................................TRY THIS...................................

1. Check over one of your short stories for its candor. Have you left things out because it makes you uncomfortable to think about them, much less write about them? Revise the story by including the unsavory details—if necessary. Be careful not to exploit graphic descriptions or acts of violence just for shock.

2. Write a poem containing blunt observations. Recall Allen Ginsberg's opening to "Howl": "I saw the best minds of my generation destroyed by madness, starving hysterical naked …"

APRIL 4

A WRITER'S SOCIETY

Writers and artists are sometimes regarded as solitary individuals who have cut themselves off from society in order to work. This may be true of some writers and artists, but certainly not all. Besides, working in solitude should not be perceived as a cutting-off experience. For any painting, musical composition, poem, or novel to succeed, it must speak to the hearts and minds of the community.

The great Swiss psychologist Carl Jung taught that all of us are linked together by our common needs and desires. "The secret of artistic creation and of the effectiveness of art," he wrote, "is to be found in a return to the site of the participation mystique." As different as each of us may seem to be from one another, in terms of temperament and tastes, we all share fundamental human needs, and the deeper we tap into that subterranean human stream, the better artists we'll become.

Instead of feeling that we must shut out the world when we write, we should think instead of shutting out the *distractions* that keep us from tapping into the common stream of humanity, of which our own lives are tributaries.

FOR FURTHER REFLECTION

We writers need society, including the most reclusive among us. It's a bit paradoxical, though: We need to interact with society in order to write about human situations of any kind, but we also need solitude to get the writing done. Writers with families sometimes find it difficult to strike the right balance. It requires understanding and a little compassion from all parties involved.

......................................TRY THIS....................................

Work out a writing regimen around your social obligations—job, family, and friends. Go over it with your spouse. Put it to the test by following it for at least two weeks, and then make whatever adjustments you deem necessary.

LITERATURE AND LEARNING

A good book teaches as it entertains; a great book—one that we are willing to admit to the pantheon of Literature—also makes us wiser, not just more knowledgeable, and may even enlarge us spiritually.

Think of all the virtues that human beings need to learn—compassion, self-discipline, patience, hard work, honesty, loyalty, integrity—and now think of books that dramatize the value of these virtues.

Literary critics often battle over which works of literature should be considered part of "the canon"—a term borrowed from Biblical scholarship. As cultures change, so do the criteria for what constitutes indispensable reading—reading that can teach us what we most need to know about the human condition.

A fine resource for determining which of the "great books" to read, at least in the literatures of Europe and the Americas, is Harold Bloom's *The Western Canon*. Bloom's principal criterion is aesthetic rather than sociocultural or political—art over ideology. At the center of Bloom's canon are the works of Shakespeare, Dante, Chaucer, Cervantes, Milton, and Goethe. (Homer, strangely enough, is scarcely discussed.) Central to Bloom's American canon are Whitman and Dickinson.

FOR FURTHER REFLECTION

We learn something about life from any book we read, including potboiler mysteries, adventure sagas, and fantasies. Such novels primarily entertain us, but we also learn a thing or two about investigating a crime, how to maneuver a raft through white-water rapids, how to ride a horse into battle, or how to uncover a scheme to overthrow a warlord.

However, if we want to steep ourselves in the most brilliant and memorable—and, yes, most challenging—works that illuminate the human condition, then we must turn to the great books.

......................................TRY THIS......................................

Write a review of a literary classic you've recently read. If it has been awhile, reread it first. In your review, explain why you think the book deserves to be part of the canon of great literature or not. Refer to its themes, its scope, the way it sheds light on a historical period or a culture.

APRIL 6
GETTING IDEAS

"Where do you get your ideas?" the nonwriter asks the writer. Goethe, the great eighteenth-century poet, playwright, and novelist, would have reminded the asker that writers get their ideas from the same places as nonwriters—from their life experiences. "All my poems are occasional poems," he once explained, "suggested by real life." But what the nonwriter is really asking is not "where" but "how": *How* do you take an idea or experience and make it work as a poem or story?

The key word in Goethe's explanation is *suggested*. The nonwriter may live a richly eventful life, but cares little about reflecting on the significance of those events, or on their retelling for the entertainment and edification of others, except perhaps for an anecdote here and there. The aspiring writer, on the other hand, will take notes, will strive to capture, through sensuous details that fix the experience indelibly in memory, and perhaps, more importantly, will fit the experience into the bigger picture—the writer's life as a whole.

FOR FURTHER REFLECTION

If you take writing seriously, start thinking of yourself as a writer rather than as someone who writes. The distinction is important. Writers perceive the world as material; they see language as their tools, reading as finished writing. And writers are sponges for ideas, even when they're asleep. James Thurber was such a writer. Once, while at a party, his wife caught him sitting and gazing into space. "Dammit, Thurber," she snapped, "Stop writing!" Needless to say, he did not.

...................................TRY THIS...................................

Get into the habit of weaving seemingly insignificant events into your stories. Are you frying hamburgers? Write a story about a chef at a world-class restaurant who has just been told he will be preparing a meal for the president of the United States. Are you lying inert on the beach? Write a story about an adolescent who is magically transported to a Greek isle—let's say the home of the Cyclops. Never be reluctant to let your imagination fly free.

APRIL 7
DEVELOPING CHARACTERS

Fiction writers ought to take seriously W. Somerset Maugham's claim that one can never know enough about one's characters. If you wish to create realistic, complex characters—if you want your characters to seem like people, not just types, then you need to think deeply about them; indeed, you need to research them in depth.

How should character research proceed? A good way is to prepare detailed descriptions of each of them. Such descriptions will include more information than you might ever explicitly use in your novel, but their purpose is not merely to serve as data sheets; they are to help you develop characters that seem alive in your own mind—complex enough to seem like real persons. Also, when writing a novel, you can easily lose track of your different characters' attributes. Having their profiles in front of you will prevent mix-ups. For specific character-development criteria, see the entry for January 7.

FOR FURTHER REFLECTION

Creating engaging characters takes homework. By developing detailed profiles of each character, you'll be better able to present them three-dimensionally as well as consistently. (If you don't have profiles to refer to, behavioral inconsistencies can creep into your story which may prove time-consuming to undo.) It is also possible to get a stronger handle on your story line when describing characters in detail.

......................................TRY THIS....................................

Prepare a one- to two-page description of the principal characters in your novel or memoir. Be as detailed as you can. Allow yourself several days to complete these profiles. Keep adding or modifying them as you work on the book.

ENHANCING YOUR POWERS OF OBSERVATION

Observing keenly is a fundamental skill for writers to learn. One of the best ways to improve your powers of observation is to paint, in words, many of the things or events you observe in the course of a day. Once you've cultivated this skill, you will be more apt to scrutinize your surroundings better. Mountains will become more than towering, cloud-shrouded peaks; you will see them in much richer detail, perhaps as John Muir does in his writings on the Sierras:

> The highest peaks burned like islands in a sea of liquid shade. Then the lower peaks and spires caught the glow, and long lances of light, streaming through many a notch and pass, fell thick on the frozen meadows.
>
> —"A Near View of the High Sierra," from
> *The Mountains of California*

Of course, creating memorable descriptions takes a lot of practice. The biggest obstacle will probably be to avoid overused expressions, to describe something in a way that not only captures its nature but does so in a delightfully original way, as Muir does by describing mountain peaks silhouetted by sunlight as "islands in a sea of liquid shade" or beams of light as "long lances."

FOR FURTHER REFLECTION

Writing is a wonderful way of celebrating the beauties of the natural world and the accomplishments of our techno-industrial civilization. It is also a way of discovering (or rediscovering) the little things, the inconspicuous things, that would otherwise slip by our radar. Think of how much less distorted a view of reality people would have if they only opened their eyes and observed like writers.

......................................TRY THIS.....................................

Go through old drafts of stories, essays, poems, and journal entries and look closely at the way you describe things. Pluck out one or more of those descriptions and improve upon it. Make note of what you added or modified to strengthen the description.

DRAFTING

John Milton, blind when he began working on *Paradise Lost*, dictated large portions of his epic masterpiece to his daughters, composing in his head as he went along. Since most of us lack Milton's prodigious intellectual gifts, we need to put our words down on paper. Only then can we see what we need to do to strengthen the draft. You've probably heard novelist E.M. Forster's famous saying regarding this basic step: "How do I know what I think 'till I see what I say?" If a novelist like Forster needs to revise, we shouldn't balk at our own need to revise.

Accepting the inevitability of revision is actually liberating. You can plunge into a draft without worrying about whether you're "getting it right." This frees you to concentrate on what is most important—and difficult (if you ask me): generating content, developing the story, bringing your characters to life.

Some writers think of their very first drafting efforts as "rough drafts" or "discovery drafts." Only after revising *that* draft do they come up with a "first draft," which they define as a draft that is ready for someone else's eyes—not the public's, but someone objective enough to give useful feedback.

FOR FURTHER REFLECTION

The drafting stage should proceed swiftly: You're writing at the speed of thought. You need to keep your focus steadily in view, but you do not want to fret over stylistic matters. If something doesn't sound right, it would be better simply to make a note to yourself in the margin.

..................................TRY THIS....................................

Take out a draft of a story or essay, finished or unfinished. Reread it, then immediately begin revising it. Do not take time to worry about where it's going or how polished your sentences are. Keep working on the draft in thirty-minute intervals. Once it's "finished," reread it with an eye to showing it to someone whose critical judgment you trust, and revise it accordingly. At that point, you will have produced a first draft.

NIGHTMARES AS A RESOURCE

It is often said that writing is a lot like therapy; by writing, we find a way to face our inner demons. That can scare the bejeebees out of anyone, but writers are a special breed: Everything is reinforced—from their thick skin to endure harsh criticism to their reinforced stomach lining to confront the unsavory underbelly of life.

If some of your nightmares cause you to awaken in a cold sweat, consider getting them under control by writing about them. Because nightmares tend to linger in the mind longer than regular dreams, you have a better chance of capturing them on paper before they fade away.

Disturbing dreams and nightmares reveal much about a person's obsessions, hence, they can add an aura of mystery to your characters as well as make them realistic.

FOR FURTHER REFLECTION

Nightmares can be put to good use. Their intensity, their atmosphere of foreboding or outright terror, the hideous distortions of persons and circumstances, the sense of imminent doom—all of these feelings can be re-channeled into psychological thriller fiction.

......................................TRY THIS......................................

1. Soon after scribbling down the gist of a nightmare, go to your keyboard and expand the notation into a detailed scenario of one or two pages. Try to maintain the original sensation of terror or foreboding or weirdness. The next day, start working on the story itself. Begin with a rough outline / opening situation—increasing suspense leading to a climactic moment / climax and denouement. Next, write a discovery draft of the story.

2. Outline a sequence of disturbing dreams or nightmares for one or more of your characters, and use these dreams as the premise of a story about someone who is being tormented by his dreams, while at the same time those dreams offer clues to some deeply hidden trauma. Alfred Hitchcock's thriller *Spellbound* is a classic example of this scenario.

APRIL 11
THE SCHOOL OF HARD KNOCKS

We all know this school, don't we? For all the benefits we derive from a formal education, nothing in academe can quite match up to the classroom of the streets or the workplace. These "real world" experiences bring you in contact with a wider range of people and worldly situations than you are likely to encounter in school—more grist for the story mill. The trick is to be able to take good artistic advantage of that raw material. For example, a writer who tends bar part time will want to pay close attention to what his customers divulge to him (or to other customers) after belting down a few. If you're a health-care worker, patients' woes can become the basis for intimate stories about sickness and recovery—"illness narratives," as they're sometimes called. And health-care professionals have harrowing stories of their own to tell. Two fine books that will enrich your understanding of the world of work are *Working* by Studs Terkel (dozens of interviews with blue-collar workers), and *Intensive Care: The Story of a Nurse* by Echo Heron.

FOR FURTHER REFLECTION
The laborers of the world, from dishwashers to brain surgeons, have important stories to tell, and writers can learn much from them. The experiences that members of your family alone have gained from their respective jobs—professional, blue collar, white collar, military, theatrical—can serve as springboards for many stories.

...................................TRY THIS...................................

1. Interview a family member or friend about his job experiences, then use that information in a short story centered on a specific conflict situation. For example, if your grandfather worked as a bus driver, write a story in which your grandfather-counterpart character has to avoid a major accident during rush hour.

2. Keep a detailed record of a friend's recuperation from an accident or illness. Include objective facts about the affliction as well as the patient's ongoing reactions to aspects of the recovery.

COURSES AND WORKSHOP GROUPS

Creative writing courses are usually taught as workshops: Each student writer's draft is shared with the class, which in turn offers feedback. If there's general agreement on the problems with the manuscript, the author would be wise to heed the group's suggestions. Sometimes, however, there is widespread disagreement. In such cases, the author should trust her own judgment.

If you're acquainted with other writers in your community, you might organize your own monthly workshop group. Here are a few pointers for you to consider or adapt:

- Ground rules should be distributed beforehand: e.g., the writer(s) whose work is to be discussed must distribute (say, by e-mail) copies of the draft sufficiently ahead of time (say, one week for each draft to be discussed).

- Each reader must participate orally and submit a written critique.

- The author of the work being critiqued is to listen and ask questions only to clarify what has been said, not argue a suggestion.

FOR FURTHER REFLECTION

Creative writing courses or community workshops are not every would-be writer's cup of tea. If you've never taken a course in creative writing, it is well worth the experience. If nothing else, the external pressure to get work completed will make you more productive.

...................................TRY THIS...................................

Sign up for an evening course through one of the colleges (two-year or four-year) in your community. Before you enroll, though, talk to the instructor to find out about how the class will be organized, what will be expected of you, and the assigned readings, if any. Do this with at least two candidate classes so that you'll have a basis of comparison.

As an alternative to taking a course, join a community writers' workshop on a trial basis to see if you find it helpful. Use this checklist to help select a workshop that would suit you best:

- Would it welcome the genre(s) I work in?
- Is it neither too large nor too small (seven to ten members is ideal)?
- Is the leader a published author?
- Does it meet regularly?

APRIL 13

FOOD AND LOVE

Many love stories involve food. That's because food and love go so beautifully together. The Mexican novelist Laura Esquivel built her famous novel, *Like Water for Chocolate*, around food; its subtitle is *A Novel in Monthly Installments With Recipes, Romances, and Home Remedies*. The novel even opens with a recipe for Christmas rolls (sardines, chorizo sausage, onion, oregano, chiles serranos, and hard rolls), together with instructions for preparation from the narrator:

> Take care to chop the onion fine. To keep from crying when
> you chop it (which is so annoying!), I suggest you place a little
> bit on your head.

Food and cooking always seem to work harmoniously in love stories. Different foods, and different venues for eating them, can symbolize a love relationship in its various stages. Tita, in Esquivel's novel, experiences her love for Pedro in terms of cooking:

> She was really excited as she started to prepare the mole. ...
> Pedro, hearing her from the living room, experienced a sen-
> sation that was new to him. The sound of the pans bumping
> against each other, the smell of the almonds browning in the
> griddle, the sound of Tita's melodious voice, singing as she
> cooked, had kindled his sexual feelings.

FOR FURTHER REFLECTION

Think about your own associations for food with romance. Perhaps a certain kind of food recalls a special moment with a special someone? As a writer, you will want to exploit the connection between food and love the next time you write a story with romantic content.

......................................TRY THIS...................................

1. Compose a romantic scene in which food or drink is integrated with the expression of love between the two persons. The associations can be serious or humorous.

2. In a journal entry, free-write on whatever comes to mind when you think of different foods. Resist overdone associations (apples with forbidden desire; garlic with vampires, for example). What associations come to mind when you think of the following: cauliflower, marshmallows, watermelon, mushrooms?

FAMILY HISTORIES

Every family is a treasure trove for researchers. Along with diaries, scrapbooks, and photographs, records from school, church, weddings, and correspondence, are the memories of the elders, which can prove to be even more valuable than the documents. But gathering "oral histories," as they're called, takes time and patience. Don't expect to obtain all the information you need in one or even two sessions. Memories need to be tweaked and supplemented. Before interviewing a family member, formulate well-focused questions, and supplement them with any documents, photographs, or maps you can bring along. Or you might ask the family member to provide such documents herself. You'll be amazed by how effectively a single letter or photograph can trigger a chain of dormant memories.

FOR FURTHER REFLECTION

We tend to think of history on a global, national, state, or municipal level, but families have histories too; in fact, family histories often shed important light on the larger historical contexts. First, there is the history of the nuclear family: parents and siblings; then there's the extended family of grandparents, aunts, uncles and cousins; and then there's the more historical family: the ancestors that can be traced back for dozens of generations, assuming records have been kept. Alas, many family records get lost or destroyed in fires or floods. That is why oral histories are so important.

.....................................TRY THIS....................................

1. Interview the oldest member of your family on a very specific topic, one you feel confident she could address in detail. If one of your parents or grandparents served in World War II, for example, direct the questions toward her specific activities during the war.

2. Find out all you can about one of your earliest known ancestors, and write either a biographical sketch about her, or write a short story centered around one of her more interesting deeds.

ON PRACTICE

If there is any one secret to literary success, it has got to be practice—in both senses of the word: to work at your craft in a professional context and to work at your craft in a never-ending effort to improve it. The twentieth-century American poet Conrad Aiken, who, like many other poets and prose writers, maintained a notebook, compelled himself to complete an exercise in verse every day of the year. Aiken knew that in order to become masterful at poetry, he had to become familiar with many different techniques, not merely record ideas for poems. Science-fiction writer Ray Bradbury taught himself to write short stories by disciplining himself to writing a story a week every week without fail, year after year.

Do these examples seem extreme? They shouldn't if you have devoted yourself to becoming a successful author. Unless you are a literary genius, the apprenticeship will be long—but it will be more pleasurable than painful provided you practice regularly with iron-willed determination and not be fazed by negative criticism or rejection slips. Practice may not make perfect, but it will certainly make a writer out of you.

FOR FURTHER REFLECTION

Think about allotting extra time for practice sessions to strengthen specific skills such as structuring a story or writing in sonnet form or bringing scenes from early childhood to life. Don't regard such practice as a "necessary evil." Instead, think of it as spiritual exercises of a sort—as a devotion to your craft and to getting language to convey your most cherished ideas and experiences as accurately and as movingly as possible.

...................................TRY THIS...................................

If you haven't yet begun keeping a notebook devoted exclusively to practice, do so now. Before you begin practicing, indicate in a heading what specifically you intend to practice—be it a particular poetic form or conflict scene between two or more characters, or a description of a natural phenomenon.

APRIL 16
VOCABULARY BUILDING

There are effective ways and ineffective, even counter-productive, ways of building vocabulary. Let's start with the latter. Memorizing long, increase-your-word-power lists of words accompanied by perfunctory definitions has little benefit because you're trying to learn words out of context. By trying to learn words this way, you risk misusing them, causing yourself considerable embarrassment. Part of the problem is that vocabulary lists present only one definition, when in fact several definitions may exist—and each of those definitions may require an extended definition (sometimes covering several pages) in order to be fully understood. Take a term like *platonic*: A vocabulary list might define it merely as "nonsexual, as in a platonic relationship between friends of the opposite sex"—completely overlooking its larger philosophical context—its allusion to Plato's Socratic idealism whereby Truth (including moral truth) transcends particular circumstances.

A much better way to develop your vocabulary is to read more, and take the time to look up words—ideally in an unabridged dictionary—whose meanings you cannot glean from their context.

FOR FURTHER REFLECTION

People sometimes assume that one needs a "large vocabulary" to be a writer. Yes and no. Yes in the sense that language is a writer's stock-in-trade, and the more you know about the language, the better—not just different words but the different levels of usage and the different ways in which sentences and paragraphs may be constructed. No in the sense that a large vocabulary for its own sake can actually interfere with good writing, if one assumes that "big" words are more impressive than familiar ones. Your aim should be to communicate clearly, not to impress.

..................................TRY THIS....................................

As an alternative to vocabulary building lists, spend a few hours with your dictionary. Open it at random and study the unfamiliar words you encounter, paying attention to its etymology (origin). Next, use each of these words in a sentence or short paragraph of your own devising. (See also the entry for November 16.)

SPIRITUAL ATTENTIVENESS

There is always a difference between surface truth and underlying truth. What is mirrored on the surfaces of things is not only frequently opaque but deceptive. We writers need to be attentive to those deeper truths underlying our subjects. A happy face, an air of contentment can easily disguise a soul in torment. Think of Richard Cory from Edward Arlington Robinson's famous poem.

> ... And he was rich—yes, richer than a king—
> And admirably schooled in every grace:
> In fine, we thought that he was everything
> To make us wish that we were in his place.
>
> So on we worked, and waited for the light,
> And went without the meat, and cursed the bread;
> And Richard Cory, one calm summer night,
> Went home and put a bullet through his head.

Writers usually are the first to realize how deceiving appearances can be. But what does it take to be able to see through the mask? The surface may reflect a false image, but if you are a compassionate as well as meticulous observer, you may notice darker stirrings underneath.

FOR FURTHER REFLECTION

Detecting underlying truth requires what might be called contemplative observation—observing with our third, inner eye that can penetrate like metaphysical X-rays to the underlying truths. But what does that mean, exactly? When we observe the physical world, we observe only mirror surfaces. To see beneath surfaces, we must see with insight. Call it creative insight, call it spiritual—our language does a poor job of capturing the essence of contemplative observation. Suffice it to say that the whole of reality is comprised of far more than the sum of its physical parts.

...................................TRY THIS...................................

Write a profile of someone you know well, whose outer behavior seems inconsistent with his inner nature. Dramatize a scene in which that repressed inner nature suddenly becomes manifest.

CREATIVE THINKING

In a way, "creative thinking" is redundant. Isn't thinking, by definition, creative? Yes, in the sense that, through the miracle of millions of brain synapses interacting, a thought is brought into being. Even if we say that most of the thinking we do is practical, rooted to the here-and-now, there is nothing necessarily uncreative about practicality.

Be that as it may, when most people apply the word *creative* to thinking, they mean innovative and unusual ideas. Writers of every stripe, from investigative reporters to poets, need to be good creative thinkers in this sense of the word—that is, to imagine not only effective story scenarios (if they're fiction writers or playwrights), but effective methods of literary "texturing," of making those scenarios come to life: weaving in backstory, explanation, character description, interior monologue, mood-setting description, and so on. Such modes of thought are said to be creative because they draw from many different facets of experience and weave them into a unified whole.

FOR FURTHER REFLECTION

A thin line exists between so-called ordinary thinking and creative thinking, and both are necessary. We want to think practically when we work out household budgets and be mindful of our health; however, we can be creative about the kinds of nutritious meals we prepare, since there are so many possible foods and styles of preparation. When we write, too, we combine practicality with imagination. We invent dramatic situations involving imaginary persons; yet these situations need to be conveyed in well-written, grammatically correct prose.

....................................TRY THIS....................................

1. Begin writing a fantasy story as if you were writing a factual news story. That is, approach the fantasy elements as if you were reporting on the results of the latest city council meeting; emphasize facts, keep descriptions as objective as possible.

2. Compose a story about a magician who suffers from memory loss and winds up as a homeless person in skid row. Describe the circumstances leading to his affliction and the stages that lead to his living on the streets.

APRIL 19
SNAPSHOT GROUPING

We not only gather our family photographs in albums, we organize them—usually by event—and organize the events chronologically. There are other ways to organize photographs, though. Take any family member—grandparent, nephew, your pet Golden Retriever—and arrange the snapshots of them in chronological order: You now have a photographic history of that individual or pet. Once in sequence, they may suggest a narrative; in fact, you may want to build the narrative explicitly around the photographs, even to the point of describing how you searched all over the house (and your relatives' houses?) to gather them together. Also, snapshot groupings need not be chronologically arranged; you might arrange them spatially (Mexican Riviera; Volcano National Park; Versailles) or thematically (nature hikes; zoo visits; pilgrimages).

FOR FURTHER REFLECTION

Photographs by themselves can easily suggest stories. Grouped into sequences or similar themes, they not only suggest stories but virtually outline them for you. Taking a fresh look at your photo collection can yield more ideas and story lines than you had earlier realized.

....TRY THIS....................................

1. Spend the next several days gathering snapshots of a single family member (if the snapshots are not yours, you may want to make photocopies or simply ask the owners to e-mail you copies if the photos are digitized). Once they're gathered together and properly sequenced, begin work on a profile of the individual, with each photograph, perhaps, introducing a different phase of that person's life.

2. Create a photo sequence for a short story. Let each photograph represent an aspect of your protagonist's life—for example, you might include her birthplace, first home after marrying, favorite recreational sites, city of ancestry, and so on. For each photo, write a page of narration or exposition that embodies the significance of the stage of that character's life.

APRIL 20

DISCONTENT AS INSPIRATION

There's a wonderful cartoon by Alex Gregory in *The New Yorker*, in which a college student is perched in a window seat writing to her parents: "Dear Mom and Dad: Thanks for the happy childhood. You've destroyed any chance I had of becoming a writer." Of course, many successful writers have had happy childhoods; they simply find other things to write about! The point of the cartoon is that negative experiences imply conflict, the struggle to rise above debilitating circumstances, and such conflict is the essence of story. So, if your life has been replete with negative experiences, then you can draw from your own life when searching for marketable stories. As the cliché goes, "When you're dealt lemons, make lemonade." If your life has not been so afflicted, then you may want to spend time delving into the lives of those less fortunate in order to gain insight into the way people grapple with conflict at different stages of their lives.

FOR FURTHER REFLECTION

Discontent, anger, painful awareness of injustice—all of these intense negative emotions can be rechanneled into productive writing; there's nothing quite like being outraged to get the fingers racing across the keyboard. Novelist and essayist William H. Gass cites getting even as one of his great motivators to put words on paper. You just need to be careful that the anger doesn't cloud your judgment. It's a delicate balance: Wait too long and you'll "cool off" to the point of losing the motivation; don't wait long enough and the red you see will transfer onto the page.

....TRY THIS..

Tune into a news show whose political views are opposite of your own so that the likelihood of your getting angry is good. Have pen and paper ready for taking notes. Start writing as soon as you feel the urge (writing at once will defuse the anger just a bit so that you'll be able to think more rationally later on). Wait a half hour, but not much more than that; then whip out the draft of a well organized rebuttal.

SURPRISE

"The road to banality," the psychologist Jerome Bruner writes in *On Knowing: Essays for the Left Hand*, "is paved with creative intentions." What is tougher to pinpoint than being merely "creative" (a word that gets attached to just about anything these days, from creative advertising to creative financing) is generating what Bruner calls "effective surprise"—creative thinking that grows out of the artist's (or scientist's) ability to see a connection between dissimilar ideas and combining them in a way that "takes one beyond common ways of experiencing the world." The result astonishes us at the same time that it makes us exclaim, "Of course!" That must have been Isaac Newton's reaction when, as the famous story goes, he saw an apple falling from a tree and in a flash of recognition realized that the same force that caused the apple to fall was keeping the moon in orbit around the earth—an "orbit" meaning nothing more than continuously falling toward a center of gravity, but moving too swiftly around that center of gravity to actually fall inward. If the apple had been moving horizontally as fast as the moon, it too would orbit.

FOR FURTHER REFLECTION

Metaphors, puns, jokes, cartoons—these are all examples of effective surprise that delight us and, in the case of jokes and cartoons, make us laugh out loud. If only we could be that creative, we sometimes sigh with envy. But there's no reason why we can't be: we just have to work at it, to put ourselves in the habit of seeking underlying similarities in dissimilar things.

......................................TRY THIS...................................

1. Find a cartoon, say from *The New Yorker* or from a newspaper's editorial page, and transform it into a narrative, making the surprise element—the basis for the cartoon's humor—the dramatic focus.

2. Write a story about a woman who decides to host a surprise birthday party for her abusive husband. What kind of surprise do you suppose she has in mind?

APRIL 22

SHIFTING VIEWPOINTS

Novelists frequently make use of two or more narrators: a hero and a villain, let's say, with the viewpoint shifting from chapter to chapter. This shifting of viewpoints allows the story to be told from radically different perspectives—useful in developing suspense. The narrator knows things the opponent does not, and vice versa. The bad guy may be getting ready to ambush the hero, for example, and the reader wants to leap into the novel to warn him of the imminent danger.

Shifting viewpoints also help readers gain a deeper understanding of complicated situations. If one character is a scientist conducting an experiment in quantum physics, his thinking processes might overtax some readers (assuming the writer is being at least marginally accurate about the way physicists think); but shifting to a nonscientist's viewpoint—say a nonscientifically trained government official—could make the experiment more understandable.

The challenge to the novelist, of course, is to be able to capture the personality, the obsessions, as well as the scheming of each viewpoint character without disrupting story continuity.

FOR FURTHER REFLECTION

Short stories are usually told from a single viewpoint; there isn't enough time to develop multiple viewpoints. But novels are different: Readers enjoy moving from the consciousness of one character to another. "No more than one viewpoint character in a short story" is a *convention*, remember; short stories have been written with multiple viewpoints. Always remember: if you feel a need to depart from convention, then do so. If your experiment doesn't work out, you'll know it soon enough. Ends tend to justify means, in creative writing, as in real life.

..................................TRY THIS....................................

Write a chapter-by-chapter synopsis of a novel (or at least Part I of a novel), with each chapter showing a shift in viewpoint—say, from hero to villain, or from three or more eyewitnesses to an incident, each eyewitness interpreting the incident in a different manner.

THINKING ABOUT MEANING

Even stories written chiefly to entertain convey a deeper meaning. What will your readers learn from the crew competition your hero lost despite months of arduous training? What is the larger meaning behind the pleasure your heroine derives from training horses? What survival lessons are learned from catastrophes like droughts and earthquakes? Of course, the quest for deeper meanings can be satirized. "Can we actually 'know' the universe?" Woody Allen quips. "My God, it's hard enough finding your way around Chinatown."

Be that as it may, we are creatures who continuously wonder about the deeper meanings of life. Writers are in the business of exploring deeper meanings—maybe not directly, maybe not at all, but at least grappling with it in a story, hinting at possible answers, then deferring to the reader to carry the ball.

FOR FURTHER REFLECTION

Invoking the M-word (what is the underlying *meaning*?) as you're working on a draft will help you stay mindful of the larger purpose: What will your readers gain from reading the piece? But it's just as important to keep the draft centered on the story instead of on the underlying meaning; otherwise, the story will seem preachy and contrived.

.....................................TRY THIS...................................

1. Reread the last piece of writing you've completed, and ask but one question of it: "What is the deeper meaning?" That is, what value will reading your piece have for your readers? Revise the piece to produce a more fulfilling answer to the question.

2. Outline a new story, keeping the "so-what" question firmly in mind. How does it influence the plot structure, especially the ending? The way you conceive your characters?

PSYCHOLOGICAL REALISM

There are two kinds of reality: objective reality—the reality of the external world—and subjective reality—the reality of our internal lives, our pleasures, fears, meditations, anxieties. We have come a long way over the centuries in our ability to distinguish one reality from the other—but even in our high-tech age, the two realities tend to blur. When a character perceives certain kinds of behavior as an affront to her religious beliefs, for example, the external behavior she is observing "objectively" is inevitably colored by her system of values. The two realities intertwine. The writer must be true to both, while simultaneously distinguishing between them. In John Updike's novel, *Terrorist*, a young Muslim man, Ahmed, considers succumbing to extramarital temptations a sacrilege. But from the viewpoint of Ahmed's girlfriend, Joryleen, the notion of sex as sacrilege is ludicrous. These are both subjective realities; the objective reality thus made manifest is that human beings have conflicting views about sex outside of marriage.

FOR FURTHER REFLECTION
Psychological realism can be traced back to Sophoclean tragedy—to the horror and anguish Oedipus experiences when he discovers that he has unwittingly married his mother. But psychological realism blossomed in the late nineteenth century with the Russian novelists, especially Dostoevsky. In *Crime and Punishment*, we enter the mind of the murderer-intellectual Raskolnikov and vicariously experience his struggle existentially to place himself above the trappings of human morality. And in the early twentieth century, following the Freudian revolution, novels and plays such as Arthur Miller's *Death of a Salesman* and *A View From the Bridge*; Edward Albee's *Who's Afraid of Virginia Woolf?*, and Tennessee Williams's *Suddenly Last Summer* are memorable examples of the way modern dramatists have shed light on the darkest recesses of the psyche.

......................................TRY THIS.....................................

Write a minidrama in which you capture a psychological phenomenon such as paranoia or sexual repression or jealousy. You may want to reflect first on the dynamics of repression. How does one rechannel a feeling of contempt over the behavior of a family member or friend?

APRIL 25
SETTINGS AND SITUATIONS

In fiction and poetry, settings often reflect the situations unfolding in them, and vice versa. Regardless of the genre you're writing in, the setting you choose should connect somehow to the drama that will unfold upon it. Think of the dark, mysterious forest in Hawthorne's tale, "Young Goodman Brown," where the townspeople secretly meet to partake in their satanic rituals; think of the correspondence between the mock-fertility image of the ash heap or the enormous but sightless eyes of the oculist T.J. Eckleberg's billboard, and the sterile, morally blind characters that they foreshadow, in Fitzgerald's *The Great Gatsby*:

> This is a valley of ashes—a fantastic farm where ashes grow
> like wheat into ridges and hills and grotesque gardens ... But
> above the gray land and the spasms of bleak dust which drift
> endlessly over it, you perceive, after a moment, the eyes of
> Doctor T.J. Eckleburg. The eyes of Doctor T.J. Eckleburg are
> blue and gigantic ... They look out of no face ...

FOR FURTHER REFLECTION

The harmonious correspondences between humanity and the natural world is a romantic concept that is often treated ironically in modern literature: We have cut ourselves off from nature so that the beauty and harmony of the wilderness belies the degradation and disharmony of urban blight. An optimist, though, may write about urban blight but call attention to, say, a lovely, peaceful park in the city's heart, one that can come to symbolize future promise.

....TRY THIS...................................

1. Begin a short story or personal-experience narrative with a description of the story's setting. Describe the setting in a way that can serve as a foreshadowing of what is to come.

2. Practice your skills at describing interior settings. In a paragraph or two describe one or more of the following:

   - your bedroom from early childhood
   - your grandparents' kitchen
   - the basement or attic of an old Victorian house
   - a sculptor's workshop

APRIL 26
DEVOTION

We dedicate ourselves to causes we feel a strong ethical or aesthetic commitment toward; but we *devote* ourselves to causes that speak to our spiritual selves. This book has been conceived with the assumption that serious writing requires not just dedication to a particular task at hand but devotion to the very enterprise of writing, of sharing your innermost thoughts with your fellow human beings. John Updike tells us, in his essay "Religion and Literature" (found in *More Matter: Essays and Criticism*), that "the literary artist, to achieve full effectiveness, must assume a religious state of mind—a state that looks beyond worldly standards of success and failure. A mood of exaltation should possess his language." This may sound overly idealistic to some writers, but without feeling exalted by the power of language, its capacity to educate and to inspire, it would be a lot more difficult to sustain the enthusiasm and energy required for completing literary works.

FOR FURTHER REFLECTION
It is good to pause now and then in order to meditate on what it means to be a writer. It is a moral and spiritual undertaking as well as an intellectual and artistic one. Writers have the capacity to bring joy, insight, and hope to the multitude. The craft of writing, then, truly is worthy of devotion.

..................................TRY THIS....................................

1. Over the next few days, use your journal to reflect on your commitment and devotion to writing, what you hope to bring to humanity through your writing, how you see writing as a means of enriching your own life.

2. Work the entries you've written for number one into a substantive essay on writing as a moral force or as a means of promoting higher consciousness and civility in the world.

DRAMATIC INCIDENTS

There are two ways to think of incidents in the context of your novel or memoir. One way is to think of them as the conflict situations experienced by your characters. How do they struggle to resolve the conflict? The second way is to think of incidents as a pattern of events (random or otherwise) that leads to something significant. A conversation with a stranger on a plane, for example, leads to an interview with a major corporation, which in turn leads to a money-making opportunity that enables your protagonist to finance a lifelong dream.

FOR FURTHER REFLECTION

Our lives are filled with incidents that comprise who we are. If you are going to write your life story or a novel based on events in your own life, pay attention to the way your life has been shaped by the things that have happened to you. Even slight incidents might have provided the spark to change the course of your life: words of praise from your piano teacher just when you felt ready to give up the instrument, rekindling your desire to master a difficult Rachmaninoff piece, which in turn results in your winning a major competition.

......................................TRY THIS....................................

Make a list of things that have happened to you within the past year. Next, choose one of the incidents and write a paragraph about how it has affected your life. Finally, expand the paragraph into a full-fledged short story in which the dramatic incident is pivotal. For example, if you wrote out a dramatic incident in which your viewpoint character is a teacher trying to restrain a student who is beating up on another student, build a story around the teacher's experiences with troubled youth in an inner city school.

APRIL 28
CRAFTING EFFECTIVE SENTENCES

Sentences are crafted and orchestrated, not just written. They're like a painter's brushstrokes or palette-knife texturing of the pigment. Sentences govern the rhythm of a piece, and rhythm is as important to prose as it is to poetry. William Faulkner's intricate sentences, often reflecting interior monologue, will be very different, say, from Ernest Hemingway's or Raymond Carver's go-for-the-jugular minimalist sentences, or John Updike's highly nuanced, artistic, almost musical sentences. Some writers' sentences, like those of Tom Wolfe, are almost manic in their vitality. Here's an example from *The Right Stuff*: Notice how his sentences capture Chuck Yeager's state of mind after having broken some ribs falling off a horse:

> Yeager gets up before daybreak on Tuesday morning—which is supposed to be the day he tries to break the sound barrier—and his ribs still hurt like a sonofabitch. He gets his wife to drive him over to the field, and he has to keep his right arm pinned down to his side to keep his ribs from hurting so much.

FOR FURTHER REFLECTION
Study the way your favorite writers shape individual sentences as well as orchestrate sentence flow within a paragraph. Pay attention to the rhythmic pattern their sentences generate: how two short sentences may follow a much longer sentence; how transitions like *however* and *on the other hand* and *in the meantime* add to the coherence, the flow.

......................................TRY THIS....................................

Your manner of sentence construction inevitably affects the reality of the world you're building out of language. Take a "root" sentence like "Joe tackled the thief," your basic subject-verb-object construction, and experiment with variations. Add subject modifiers ("Old Joe, feeling a surge of strength and daring that belied his sixty-two years, tackled the thief") or verbal modifiers ("Joe tackled the thief, twisting his neck in a headlock and then jerking him backwards hard enough to produce a distinctly audible CRACK from his lower vertebrae").

Next, add two or three more sentences to complete the scene, paying attention to sentence variety and length. Aim for a richly rhythmical texture that enhances the readability of the paragraph.

APRIL 29
CONTEMPLATING RELIGIOUS SYMBOLISM

The beauty and sublimity of religious experience are captured in its symbols—not just the symbols that embody the religions themselves (the lotus blossom for Buddhism; the crucifix for Christianity; the crescent for Islam; the Star of David for Judaism; the Yin Yang circle for Taoism, and so on), but the symbols that embody the spiritual experiences within a given faith. Think of the Buddha sitting in his lotus position; of Kali's ambivalent dance of destruction and creation in Hinduism; of the "straight path" from the first sura of the Qur'an that Muslims utter during *salat*, the five daily prayers; or of the *Ninety-Five Theses* that Martin Luther nailed to the door of Wittenberg Cathedral in 1517.

The symbolism generated by the world's religions are of universal importance, not just of importance to the followers of a given religion—a good reason for writers to be aware of religious symbolism when developing characters and story ideas.

FOR FURTHER REFLECTION

Religious symbols—icons— enable the faithful to wrap their minds (and hearts) around the reality underlying the icon. A gold cross worn around the neck embodies the true cross on Golgotha two thousand years ago; and that cross in turn embodies Christianity itself. If you wish to integrate symbolism into your writing, think first of the way symbols are experienced in spiritual contexts.

...................................TRY THIS...................................

1. Write about your experience with symbolism in a spiritual context. Explain how a religious symbol (icon) helps you become more spiritually centered, how it helps with meditation or prayer.

2. Write a poem in which you capture the ecstasy of a religious vision—a famous one such as Ezekiel's vision of the celestial throne or Bernadette Subaru's vision of the Virgin Mary or a religious vision of your own.

APRIL 30
LOCATING THE ROOTS OF WRITER'S BLOCK

Psychoanalysts remind us that we need to confront our demons in order to vanquish them. If one of your demons happens to be writer's block, then you ought to put into writing the cause of the block. According to the poet Howard Nemerov, "Being unable to write, you must examine in writing this being unable." You might simply make a list of possible reasons, such as:

- I can't organize my thoughts.
- I can't create a conflict situation, or one that is strong or complex or original enough.
- I don't know enough about my subject.
- I'm too lazy to write.
- I can't make my characters seem like real people.

When you hit upon the right thing, a light will probably flash in your brain. When that happens, the next step will be to probe the obstacle intensively. Let's say the light flashes when you write "can't make my characters seem like real people"; your next step will be to prod that statement with a barrage of questions: *Why* can't I make them seem like real people? What *kinds* of "real people" do I want to write about? What do I *mean* by "real"? And so on.

FOR FURTHER REFLECTION
Sometimes knowing the root of a problem is the most important step toward solving the problem. It takes a good deal of mental courage to confront what is really at stake behind your anxieties or procrastinations.

.....................................TRY THIS.....................................

A good way to get to the root of writer's block is to engage in a bit of self-therapy. Divide yourself into two persons: Writer and therapist. Allow the therapist persona to ask probing questions ("Do you really want to be a writer?" "Have you found the right angle for this topic?" "Are you uncertain about how to create a conflict situation?"). Then let your writer's persona answer the questions—in writing!—as candidly as possible.

ON FAIRY TALES

There are at least three reasons why writers should read and reread fairy tales. They embody the essence of story (deeply desired goal, struggle against daunting opposition, satisfying final outcome). They return us to our child selves. And, perhaps most importantly, like ancient myths, they can be retold in modern contexts, the way Donald Barthelme retells the story of Snow White in his novel by that name. It begins, "She is a dark beauty containing a great many beauty spots: one above the breast, one above the knee …"

Fairy tales can serve as springboards or templates for modern stories. Take Cinderella, for example: Instead of her being a char-maid abused by her jealous stepsisters, you can transform her into an entry-level employee manipulated by senior managers with ignoble motives.

FOR FURTHER REFLECTION

Fairy tales, like ancient myths and folktales, dramatize archetypal struggles between good and evil, the consequences of foolish actions (think of Pinocchio and his lies), and the exploitation of the innocent (think of Hansel and Gretel and the witch). Fairy tales remind us writers of the essence of storytelling. (See also the entry for September 27.)

......................................TRY THIS....................................

Read Anne Sexton's poetic retelling of fairy tales in her *Transformations*, then write a fairy-tale transformation of your own. If poetry isn't your cup of tea, then do a prose transformation of your favorite fairy tale.

MAY 2
M.C. ESCHER:
"ASCENDING AND DESCENDING"

One of the most peculiar attributes of the modern era has been the fascination with and almost obsessive exploration of the paradoxical, the surreal, and the mystical that resides deep within the heart of the mundane. M.C. Escher is a kind of philosopher among graphic artists; his images question our assumptions about everyday reality. Stairways move constantly upward yet somehow meet up with the bottommost step. Interiors magically become exteriors; birds magically morph into humans. He is especially fond of the Möbius strip: It has only one side. How can that be, you wonder? Take a long strip of paper, and just before you tape the two ends together, twist it once. Now take a pencil and draw a line along the center ... you'll meet the beginning of the line without turning the strip over—and you couldn't turn it over if you wanted to, since it has only one side. Magic exists in the real world!

FOR FURTHER REFLECTION

As writers, we delight in ways to extend notions of reality out of its complacent definitions. If we look hard enough we will find the magic in the mundane, ir-rationality lurking in the very core of rationality.

......................................TRY THIS......................................

1. Work up a fantasy story about Escher's "Ascending and Descending," the image of which may be accessed at www.mcescher.com. Tell the story from the viewpoint of one of the figures on the stairs.

2. Compose a poem about the bizarre world that Escher's image embodies.

FACING YOUR FEARS

In *The Courage to Write*, Ralph Keyes describes how E.B. White, the essayist and author of children's books (*Stuart Little*; *Charlotte's Web*), wrote about the very things he feared. "White personified courage," Keyes writes, "by being so willing to sail boldly into the squall of his own fears, commenting on the trip as he went."

It takes a lot of courage to put your feelings on paper. Once you face your inner demons and start writing about them, you've taken a major step toward making it as a writer. "Learning technique does far less to improve our writing," Keyes asserts, "than finding the will, the nerve, the *guts* to put on paper what we really want to say"—emphasis Keyes's; and perhaps emphasis should also be added to *really*. It is easy to fudge on what we *really* want to say when what we *really* want to say is painful, embarrassing, or frightening even to ourselves.

FOR FURTHER REFLECTION

Some of the issues we feel compelled to write about may contain experiences we're not prepared to deal with emotionally. Be patient. If possible, work around these obstacles, but don't ignore them. You might find it useful to write about these emotional hurdles in your journal first. Writing, remember, is a good form of therapy. By externalizing our demons, we're well on our way to exorcising them.

...............................TRY THIS...................................

1. Write a page in your journal that begins like this: "One of the fears I have a difficult time thinking or writing about is ..." See if writing about this fear in your journal will make it easier to incorporate it into your novel or memoir.

2. Write an essay that probes the origin of one of your deepest fears. For example, do you have a fear of water because you had a near-drowning experience as a child? Describe that early traumatic experience in as much detail as you can.

"I WRITE FOR MYSELF"

There are times when writers would rather not concern themselves with readers. There may be issues they want to get off their chests without having to worry over whether readers (including editors) will approve or disapprove of the topic or approach, or whether readers will understand their intentions. On the other hand, writing implies being read, whether by an audience of one or a billion. This also implies that certain basics of communication need to be fulfilled: Sentences need to be grammatical, and words need to conform to standard definitions. It also means that the discourse needs to progress in a coherent, logical manner.

FOR FURTHER REFLECTION

When writers say they wish to write only for themselves, perhaps what they're really saying is that they want to express their ideas their own way without having to conform to expectations. Well, writers can do that within the framework of basic standards like accurate word choice, clearly written sentences, and coherent presentation of ideas. Of course, there are also moments when writers want to record private thoughts in a journal. Even here, though, it could be argued that they are writing for an audience: themselves or a part of themselves they need to get in touch with—their rational side trying to communicate with their emotional side, for example.

.....................................TRY THIS....................................

Just for fun, prepare a list of about a dozen words. Now, write a paragraph in which you give new, arbitrary meanings to some or all of those words. A week later, see if you can decode what you've written. As an alternative, create a list of nonarbitrary neologisms—words you have coined that make good sense. Use these words in a poem or story, making sure that the meaning becomes clear in context.

INDISPENSABLE BOOKS FOR WRITERS: FICTION

A must-read list should include works that are most closely related to the kind of works you want to write and works you should read simply because they are good books. This first list will focus on works of fiction. Other entries (see June 5, July 5, and August 5) will focus on other genres. Here is a list of important novels and their themes:

- *Don Quixote* by Miguel de Cervantes: Imagination can triumph over adversity.

- *Gulliver's Travels* by Jonathan Swift: Vanity, avarice, and injustice are examples of human folly.

- *Candide* by Voltaire: Folly exists in blind optimism.

- *Frankenstein* by Mary Shelley: There are consequences to be had when a creator neglects the created.

- *Jane Eyre* by Charlotte Brontë: A young woman with ingenuity can overcome oppression, even in a patriarchal society.

- *David Copperfield* by Charles Dickens: A child can endure hardship and lack of parental guidance and still become honorable.

- *The Scarlet Letter* by Nathaniel Hawthorne: Love can overcome prejudice and injustice.

- *Moby-Dick* by Herman Melville: The more one seeks to uncover the mysteries of existence, the greater the mysteries become.

- *Anna Karenina* by Leo Tolstoy: Profound psychological forces underlie love.

- *The Adventures of Huckleberry Finn* by Mark Twain: A boy undertakes a river journey from innocence to experience.

- *The Great Gatsby* by F. Scott Fitzgerald: Romantic love can endure even in an age that threatens to stifle love.

FOR FURTHER REFLECTION

The shelves of libraries and bookstores are teeming with wonderful novels; and while reading lists are useful, you mustn't feel chained to them. Follow their suggestions, but supplement them with discoveries you make on your own.

......................................TRY THIS....................................

Prepare your own list of novels (in addition to the novels listed above). In a paragraph or so, explain what writers can learn from them.

MAY 6

ON SERENDIPITY

Because writing is such a demanding craft, writers must work persistently for years in order to perfect their skills. Important as skill is, however, a certain amount of good luck also is needed—or rather a very special kind of good luck called serendipity.

The *Random House Webster's Dictionary* defines *serendipity* as having the aptitude for making discoveries by accident. To put it another way, it means knowing, from past experiences, when a lucky find might occur. A researcher may "just happen" to pick a book off of a library shelf that contains exactly the bit of information she was looking for: a lucky find—but she had increased the odds of making that find by knowing (or at least making an educated guess) where in the library that happy find might occur.

Serendipitous moments can be downright uncanny. The great photographer Ansel Adams thought of them as moments of divine intervention: "Sometimes I get to places just when God is ready to click the shutter," he once said.

FOR FURTHER REFLECTION

Serendipitous moments may seem almost like supernatural intervention, but it's more like heightening your receptors—your keen observation together with your intuition to increase the chances of discovery that might otherwise have slipped by. Writers will often experience moments of serendipity when, immersed in their subject matter, will stumble upon ideas seemingly out of the blue, from unexpected sources (a bit of overheard conversation or a scene from a sitcom), seemingly irrelevant to their projects, but somehow providing a flash of insight.

......................................TRY THIS....................................

Grab a book off the shelf—any book! Don't bother searching for anything in particular. Open it at random and begin reading. Write down every idea you get from reading what is on that single page. Now turn to another page and do the same thing. Later, stroll down the aisle, pick another book whose title arouses your curiosity; once again open the book at random, and record any ideas that come to mind.

MONOLOGUES AND DIALOGUES

Dialogue is an effective way to capture a character's temperament. Writing effective dialogue, though, is not as easy it looks: You need to develop an ear for individual manners of speaking—which includes favorite words and expressions, ways of putting sentences together, habits of repetition, regionalisms, and ethnic dialect. Even poets need to be attentive to manners of speech should they wish to write dramatic monologues, like the notorious Duke in Robert Browning's "My Last Duchess":

> ... She had
> A heart—how shall I say?—too soon made glad,
> Too easily impressed; she liked whate'er
> She looked on, and her looks went everywhere.

As the award-winning short-story writer Alyce Miller points out, "When your characters are allowed to talk, you begin to learn who they are."

FOR FURTHER REFLECTION

Dialogue is conversation between two or more persons; monologue is one person speaking—it could be to another person, but we never hear the other person speaking (compare this with interior monologue; see the entry for June 28). Dialogue is a basic tool of both character development and story development.

...............................TRY THIS...................................

Write a two-page confrontation between two characters. Use both dialogue and narration, but place more weight on dialogue for carrying the conflict progression. Here are three confrontation possibilities:

- A batter confronts the umpire over whether the pitcher had delivered a strike ball.

- A pro-life activist argues with a pro-choice activist over whether a blastocyst deserves the status of a living human being.

- Two professors argue whether college students should take an introductory literature course as a prerequisite for graduation.

OBSERVING BEHAVIOR

To help bring your characters to life, you need to describe them in detail—not only their physical details but their behavioral details, so that your readers can see them in action. It is tempting simply to say that a character has "lost his temper" or "became frightened"—those are merely summative descriptions that fail to bring the individual into sharp focus. In *Pride and Prejudice*, instead of merely telling the reader that Mr. Darcy finally told Elizabeth that he loved her, Jane Austen conveys the moment poignantly through skillful characterization:

> [Mr. Darcy] sat down for a few moments, and then getting up walked about the room. Elizabeth was surprised, but said not a word. After a silence of several minutes he came towards her in an agitated manner, and thus began,
>
> "In vain have I struggled. It will not do. My feelings will not be repressed. You must allow me to tell you how ardently I admire and love you."
>
> Elizabeth's astonishment was beyond expression. She stared, coloured, doubted, and was silent. This he considered sufficient encouragement, and the avowal of all that he felt and had long felt for her, immediately followed.

Instead of summarizing what your characters are doing, let your readers observe your characters in action.

FOR FURTHER REFLECTION

Writers don't so much "tell" a story as dramatize a story; they delineate their characters and the action in a way that enables readers to observe the drama in their mind's eye. This requires writers to show what the characters are doing, show what is going through their minds (either through overt actions and speech or by bringing the reader inside their heads).

......................................TRY THIS...................................

Turn each of the following summative statements into detailed scenarios that readers can observe in their minds' eye:

- Clarence was too scared to jump off the high dive.
- Louise's mother scolded her for staying out so late.
- The children were playing happily in the park until the drunk scared them away.

CONCISION

"Make this paragraph more concise," writing teachers remind their students with great frequency. "Try to say the same thing in fewer words!" Of course, students need to distinguish between writing in which the language is richly textured and evocative, and writing that is merely verbose. Concision in itself is not a virtue. Hamlet's "to be or not to be" soliloquy, for example, could be condensed into a single sentence (say, "One often wages an inner struggle between the torments of being and the eternal nothingness of nonbeing")—but who would want to? The principle to follow here is that of common sense: If, by cutting or condensing, the passage can still mean the same and have the same or greater impact, and convey its meaning just as efficiently, then do so.

When reviewing a draft for concision, check for redundancies (such as saying that the sky was gray on a rainy day) and wordiness (e.g., "Carl had an urge to walk in the woods"; the wordy noun phrase "had an urge" can be tightened up with a strong verb, *longed*).

FOR FURTHER REFLECTION

When it comes to good writing, less is often more. Expressing the same idea with fewer words enhances readability and strengthens the prose. Avoiding unnecessary explanations and redundant expressions will facilitate comprehension and better enable readers to enter your story world.

....TRY THIS....................................

Do a sentence-by-sentence edit of a recent draft, looking for ways to transform verbose sentences into concise ones. Keep an eye out for wordy phrases like "at the present moment in time" instead of simply "now," or, "In my opinion I think that writers should be paid more" instead of "Writers should be paid more," since it's clear that what you're saying is your opinion. At the same time, make sure you don't throw out the emotional-impact baby with the stylistic bathwater.

PROPHETIC DREAMING

In ancient times, dreams were associated with prophecy. A ruler would consult a dream interpreter about his dreams in order to find out what they augured. Even today, we hear of people who dream about an event before it actually takes place—but they need not be regarded as possessing supernatural powers. Like good weather forecasters, they may simply possess an exceptional ability to extrapolate from present circumstances. Even so, learning that something you dreamt occurred the next day can be a little eerie. Sometimes, the human mind seems to have inexplicable links to the supernatural. In any case, it's a provocative scenario, especially if you're interested in writing horror stories à la Stephen King, Dean Koontz, Clive Barker, Peter Straub, or Ramsey Campbell.

FOR FURTHER REFLECTION

Where does the natural world end and the supernatural world begin? Artists throughout history have been obsessed with this boundary (or lack of it). In today's world, dominated by science and technology, people search for transcendent meaning—through religion, through magic, through art. Perhaps prophetic dreams are symptoms of a genuine human capacity to tap into the supernatural.

....................................TRY THIS....................................

Write a journal entry in which you reflect on the possibilities of prophetic dreaming. Describe prophetic dreams you or someone you know may have had. Think about making prophetic dreams the basis for a short story.

TURNING EXPERIENCES INTO STORY MATERIAL

You probably have a lot more experiences capable of triggering stories and essays than you realize. Some of these experiences you've forgotten; others you've overlooked on the assumption that they couldn't possibly yield story material, forgetting that such experiences merely need to be enhanced with a little imagination. Still other experiences are "too close to the bone"—just thinking about them distresses you.

A single day is filled with experiences—some of them trivial, like weaving your way through traffic to get to work. But even a drab experience like this can serve as a catalyst for a story. What if, on the way to work, you decide to take a detour to avoid a traffic jam but get lost and wind up on an old mountain road leading to a shack inhabited by an ex-convict? Or what if a love letter you wrote to a co-worker got intercepted by your boss, who was secretly in love with the same person? Unexpected developments like this add spice to life, and especially to stories.

FOR FURTHER REFLECTION

Mundane reality can easily be tweaked to form story scenarios; you just need to exercise your imagination on a regular basis. Just as importantly, write down your experiences as soon as possible after they occur so that you can better capture their urgency. If you're writing fiction, you may want to enhance things a bit by adding or modifying characters and enhancing the conflict situation.

...................................TRY THIS....................................

Set up a "Personal Experiences" section in your journal; organize it chronologically (e.g., "Childhood Experiences," "Adolescent Experiences," "Most Recent Experiences") or thematically (e.g., "Experiences in Nature," "Religious Experiences," "Holiday Experiences"). There are dozens of other possible experience categories, depending on the kinds of experiences that have made up your life. Perhaps you were born and bred on a farm or ranch, or in a congested urban area, or in a mountain wilderness. Add those categories to your journal, and fill those pages on a regular basis.

MAY 12
THREE-STAGE CRITIQUING

Giving and receiving feedback on a manuscript is enormously helpful if done properly. For many beginning writers, sharing one's work with strangers can be intimidating. Keep in mind that giving feedback should be more like coaching from the sidelines than instructing. Another useful metaphor is *catalyst*: initiating a desired chemical reaction without actually being part of the reaction or the result.

It is also a good idea to approach manuscript feedback in three stages, as follows:

1. **Content-critiquing stage:** Are the characters, setting, opposing forces delineated in sufficient detail? Is the plot sufficiently "textured" with enough unexpected twists and turns?

2. **Structure-critiquing stage:** Is the opening strong enough to engage the reader's attention immediately? Does it arouse curiosity or a sense of anticipation for what will follow? Do the story events unfold in a coherent manner? Is there a rising curve of tension or conflict leading toward a climactic moment or epiphany?

3. **Style/mechanics-critiquing stage:** Are the sentences sufficiently varied, emphatic, concise? Is the word-choice accurate, the level of usage appropriate to the characters and circumstances? Is the dialogue formatted properly?

If you're organizing the workshop, you may want to distribute prompt sheets to each member ahead of time.

FOR FURTHER REFLECTION

Critiquing drafts is a learning experience for all involved. By giving feedback, we reinforce important facets of storytelling in our own minds; by receiving feedback, we are reminded that writing is a product for public consumption, and that writing for publication is, in effect, negotiated between author and reader (represented by members of a writer's group and later by editors).

.........................TRY THIS.........................

1. Prepare a detailed prompt sheet for yourself or for your writer's group. Organize it by content, structure, and style.

2. Use this same prompt sheet to critique your own work in progress.

MAY 13
FOOD AND SPIRIT

There's something about food and dining that speaks to our spiritual nature. Saying grace at the table is one manifestation of this association; but there is also an affinity between growing food, preparing food, and eating food that heightens our spirituality. We feel a need to express our gratitude, to acknowledge our awareness that food is always a gift of plentitude and that it could be cut off from us for any number of reasons.

One cannot fully understand human nature until one understands the role that food plays in daily life as well as for special occasions.

Because food is associated with (and sometimes even the occasion for) gatherings of friends and family, a spiritual bonding seems to take place. Think of family gatherings, especially at dinnertime when everyone is more relaxed and more communicative or weekend get-togethers, especially during the summer—either at home or at the beach or a favorite park—when food and fun and the outdoors generate a keen sense of *joie de vivre* and a willingness to be with others. Food brings out the best in people; for that reason alone, it is worthy of a writer's close attention

FOR FURTHER REFLECTION

What food-related events in your life have heightened your *joie de vivre*, your spiritual well-being? Can you remember the particular foods involved? Perhaps that mushroom sautéed tenderloin steak dinner or that delectable chocolate fondue dessert somehow enlivened everyone's spirit during a special get-together. Perhaps a special dish served for Easter or Christmas, Hanukkah, Ramadan or Kwanza, or during Lent helped to enhance the religious experience.

......................................TRY THIS....................................

1. Write a story in which eating a certain meal contributes to your character's spiritual awakening.

2. Write an autobiographical essay in which you describe a dining experience of your own.

BRINGING A HISTORICAL PERIOD TO LIFE

We love reading historical fiction because it transforms abstract, generalized facts—essentially *summaries*—into suspenseful human *dramas*. Whether your novel in progress takes place during a well-known or historical period or an obscure one, you want that period to come to life in the reader's mind. But what do we mean by that? It means focusing on minute details, not just on the big picture. It may mean giving less emphasis on the recorded "facts" in order to foreground the human drama. Thus, if you're writing about Galileo's recantation or the D-Day invasion or a slave rebellion in ancient Rome, you need to give readers the sensation that they are eyewitnesses. That means using sensory imagery—sounds, smells, and sights. It means using psychological coloring—fears, uncertainties. What were the Grand Inquisitor and the other members of the clergy wearing? What was the weather like at Omaha Beach that fateful dawn morning of June 6, 1944? What was it like to be fired upon as you rushed for cover, knowing you could be shot and killed any moment? Good writing strips away the veil of time to make history visceral, intimate, and immediate.

FOR FURTHER REFLECTION

The history of an event is deepened by the experiences of those who participated in that event. In his essay, "History," Emerson reminds us of the intimate connection between history and human life:

> There is a relation between the hours of our life and the centuries of time. ... Every revolution was first a thought in one man's mind, and when the same thought occurs to another man, it is that key to that era.

......................................TRY THIS....................................

Randomly select, from a world history survey, one specific incident. Study it thoroughly—in the book at hand and elsewhere. Then, bring the incident to life through an invented or historical character, adding sensory descriptions to create dramatic immediacy. Don't just explain that a battle was fought; describe in detail the preparations being made; show the soldiers interacting with each other. Use dialogue. Build suspense.

MAKING LISTS

Lists are a delightful way to conduct a mental inventory of things you know but don't know you know. The very effort to create a list rekindles the memory; we are bound to surprise ourselves with what we come up with on the spur of the moment. Listing things is also an ideal way to initiate a train of associations from any one of the items you write down.

You can create lists for anything—and one list can trigger ideas for another. Let's say that you're listing favorite parks you've visited. Any one of them could suggest a secondary list: your favorite landmarks or most memorable camping moments in Yosemite.

FOR FURTHER REFLECTION

Lists are easy to produce and they're also fun because we rediscover things we forgot we knew. For that reason, listing things can be an excellent way to generate ideas for stories, essays, or poems. By developing a habit of making lists whenever we feel at a loss for ideas or content, we can maintain a healthy level of productivity.

......................................TRY THIS.....................................

Make a list based on any or all of the following prompts:

1. I like to write because …

2. Some of the most embarrassing moments of my life include …

3. Magical or spiritual moments I've experienced …

4. People in history I'd like to learn more about; or: people in history I wish I could invite over for dinner …*

5. Stories I loved most when I was a child / teenager / young adult …

6. Things about myself I want to improve (e.g., memory, eating habits) …

7. Friends and family members who have influenced me most …

8. The scariest experiences I've ever had …

---

* Plato, through the mouth of Socrates, refers to it explicitly as "a parable of education and ignorance" (W.H.D. Rouse's translation, *Great Dialogues of Plato*; NAL, 1956).

WORDS WITH MULTIPLE MEANINGS

When D.C. Denison, editor of *The American Heritage Dictionary*, was asked which words had the most meanings, he mentioned *set*, *take*, and *go* as among them. Not only do these words each have dozens of different meanings, they also function as different parts of speech—namely nouns, verbs, and adjectives. Writers, especially poets, can also make words acquire more than one meaning. Consider Yeats's "The Lake Isle of Innisfree":

> I will arise and go now, and go to Innisfree,
> And a small cabin build there, of clay and wattles made:
> Nine bean-rows will I have there, a hive for the honeybee,
> And live alone in the bee-loud glade.
>
> And I shall have some peace there, for peace comes dropping
>   slow,
> Dropping from the veils of the morning to where the cricket
>   sings;
> There midnight's all a glimmer, and noon a purple glow,
> And evening's full of the linnet's wings.
>
> I will arise and go now, for always night and day
> I hear lake water lapping with low sounds by the shore;
> While I stand on the roadway, or on the pavements grey,
> I hear it in the deep heart's core.

The meanings of the words at first seem straightforward enough, but with subsequent readings, they begin to suggest different meanings. *Arise*, for example, seems to suggest the soul rising from the body, and *Innisfree* suddenly takes on the additional meaning of heaven: where the soul shall be eternally "free" from the body.

FOR FURTHER REFLECTION

Words have the power to resonate, to take on different meanings depending on the context. Poets look for opportunities to make words mean several things at once. By using words with multiple meanings—or by making words yield multiple meanings, we writers enhance the aesthetic experience of reading.

························ TRY THIS ·······························

Write a poem in which at least one of the words takes on more than one meaning. Recall the repeated closing lines of Robert Frost's "Stopping by Woods on a Snowy Evening"–"And Miles to go before I sleep"–notice how the repetition of the word "sleep" generates a double meaning.

HEEDING YOUR HUNCHES

Writing is largely a rational act. We have a story to tell or a topic to probe, and we go about telling the story or probing the topic in a more-or-less logical manner. But rationality alone does not a writer make. Sometimes the writing process must proceed intuitively, rather than adhere to rules. And the writing itself can be intuitive as well, in the sense of following a nonlinear progression, such as intertwining narration with explanation, or unfolding the story spatially instead of chronologically.

We want our writing to appear fluid, organic—a living entity. For that to happen, we need to let go of stubborn assumptions that may have been drilled into us years ago. Conditioning is a powerful force, so you need to be patient with yourself and to be encouraged by writers whose works have an organic feel to them—Eudora Welty, Italo Calvino, Raymond Carver, Annie Dillard, Lewis Thomas.

FOR FURTHER REFLECTION

Trust thy intuition! The subconscious mind is a cauldron of powerful ideas and associations. Bring it to a boil, and let it drive your fingers across the keyboard, at least during the discovery draft stage. You can always switch to your logical brain and work on coherence later on. The first step is to sensitize your inner ear to the stirrings of your intuition. Intuition speaks to us when conventional rational thought is not enough. Our perception of reality is complex, and we pick up more than we realize. A hunch can be a subtle insight not yet shaped by language.

. . . . TRY THIS . . . .

Conjure up an idea for a piece of flash fiction (two to three pages), and write the story in one sitting. The idea is to put your intuition in the driver's seat. It may be a bit risky, and you might wind up with gibberish (your intuition probably doesn't have much driving experience), but then again, you might strike a vein of crude that, with later reshaping, might yield a treasure.

WRITING TO IMPROVE THINKING

Writing extends the capacity of the human brain. Once we record a thought, we are also laying the groundwork for analogous thoughts. Before long, we have, before our eyes, a repertoire of interconnected thoughts that can serve as springboards for any number of writing projects.

In ancient times, before writing became the predominant means of communicating, orators used elaborate forms of memorization to retain large quantities of information. Rhetoricians like Cicero and Quintilian wrote treatises on utilizing the memory for oratory. Frances Yates, in her scholarly study of the art of memory from ancient times through the Renaissance, demonstrates how memory training was fundamental to training in rhetoric, which in turn was one of the cornerstones of formal education. Even though the art of memory is no longer practiced (or valued) the way it was back then, it continues to play an important role in writing. We could not attach one sentence to another, let alone unfold a narrative or develop a thesis if it weren't for our memories.

FOR FURTHER REFLECTION
Many people fail to realize what a vast storehouse of memories get accumulated over the years or how important it is to keep our memories active. Writers benefit tremendously from exercising their memories, say, by writing detailed responses to books after they've been read or writing full-fledged reviews of books, plays, concerts, and art shows. The ancient rhetoricians discouraged orators from writing down their speeches because they felt that it interfered with memorization (this is amusingly presented in Plato's dialogue *Phaedrus*)— and they were probably right. It's a little like the way pocket calculators have discouraged mathematical computation in one's head. On the other hand, our memory skills have deteriorated so radically since the Middle Ages that writing can now be used to strengthen them.

......................................TRY THIS.....................................

Embark upon a memory safari with your pen. That is, think of a distant memory that has grown blurry with time and begin writing about it. You may be surprised by what you begin to recall after a few sentences of probing.

MEMORY PUZZLES

Memory itself can become central to your story. There are at least three approaches. The first, although it has been over-used, can still utterly fascinate readers if handled skillfully: The protagonist suffering from amnesia. Who is this person? He has no idea, but gradually clues begin to pop up or fragments of the memory begin to return, but in an incoherent manner (see also the entry for August 19). The second approach is to give your protagonist a memory that has been disguised and distorted by trauma, and with the help of a therapist, he is able to remove the protective mask or distorting lens. Think of the Gregory Peck character in Alfred Hitchcock's *Spellbound*, or Tom Wingo, the narrator in Pat Conroy's novel, *The Prince of Tides*. The third approach is simply to mete out the backstory one piece at a time, thereby creating, in effect, two story lines. All three of these approaches have been influenced by Freudian psychology and the culture of psychotherapy that has played such an important role in modern Western culture for the past hundred years.

FOR FURTHER REFLECTION

Memory puzzles, traumatically shattered then gradually pieced back together to reveal a shocking secret, make for exciting reading. Understanding the complex workings of the human mind is a big undertaking, but fascinating. Psychologists, for example, have discovered that the way one recalls and event is often influenced by deeply rooted beliefs. Thus, five eyewitnesses might give five different versions of the same event.

......................................TRY THIS....................................

After reviewing some of the basics of psychoanalysis and reading some choice psychoanalytic fiction (such as *The Prince of Tides*) and viewing psychological thrillers (such as *Spellbound*), outline a psychological thriller of your own in which memory loss or memory distortion plays a significant role.

EXTERNAL MOTIVATION

Self-discipline is a wonderful attribute, but sometimes it's not enough to get through a time-consuming writing project. In college, one needs the external motivation of required courses and assignments with their accompanying due dates to get through. In the workplace, one needs the external pressure of quotas to ensure that merit evaluations are high. To put it bluntly, we usually need someone to crack the whip over us before we can feel motivated to get the work done. It's only human nature.

For writers, the supreme external motivators are editors and publishing contracts. Beginning writers, however, need to have more preparatory kinds of external motivation. An extreme example is to have your significant other lock your study door and not let you out until you've completed your quota. A less radical option is to have your significant other not prepare dinner until you show her finished pages. Other options: no dessert, no television, no games, no …

FOR FURTHER REFLECTION
Setting up an external source of discipline for completing writing tasks takes some ingenuity, but it pays off in the end. It may seem rather gimmicky, but the ends will most likely justify the means. Ground rules need to be established and adhered to; whether it's "No glass of wine until you show me five pages," or, "You owe me twenty dollars for every day past the deadline," you have to stick with it.

······································TRY THIS···································

Commit yourself to finishing a writing project in *x* number of days. Be realistic! Translate that into number of pages per day. Now, recruit your significant other to enforce the law: no dinner, no dessert, no whatever, until the pages are completed. Keep a record of the progress you actually make each day. Don't worry if your quota is irregular (e.g., three pages one day, one page the next, four pages the next). The most important thing is to keep working day after day, ideally within a predetermined period of time.

DISCOVERY

Writers, like scientists, are in the discovery business. That is, they are always seeking to discover new ways of bringing a character to life or new twists and turns to thicken their plot or new insights into old issues. Like surprise (see the entry for April 21), discovery "favors the well-prepared mind," as the educational psychologist Jerome Bruner asserts.

Discovery is itself a powerful story thread. There are many kinds of discovery stories: the search to unravel secrets or buried treasure, the steadily growing education and intellectual/artistic maturity of the protagonist—James Joyce's *A Portrait of the Artist as a Young Man*, for example. Some discovery stories open with a mysterious or catastrophic set of circumstances, and as the story unfolds, the full nature of the disaster is slowly pieced together. Margaret Atwood's *Oryx and Crake*, about a global environmental catastrophe resulting from genetic engineering run amuck, is a fine example of this kind of story.

There is also the story of self-discovery: a narrator's search for the roots of his ethnic heritage, like that of Kunta Kinte in Alex Haley's celebrated novel, *Roots*.

FOR FURTHER REFLECTION

Art, like science, engages in discovery—a basic human impulse. All learning is driven by the desire for discovery—of the nature of things, of who we are, of the complete pictures that fragments lure us into discovering. Paradoxically, the more we discover, the more we realize how much is left to discover. "Writing, like life itself," writes Henry Miller, "is a voyage of discovery."

......................................TRY THIS....................................

Imagine a scenario in which the protagonist must discover certain clues to be able to solve a mystery. Let's say, for example, that someone has planted a bomb in the center of a large city, and it is up to you, an antiterrorism expert, to hunt for clues leading to the device. To keep your story filled with suspense, consider making some of those clues false ones—red herrings the terrorists had planted to throw you off scent.

TYPES OF PLOTS

If you're setting out to write a novel, first consider the different types of plots. Now, in a very basic sense, all plots are similar in that a problem or crisis is introduced that the protagonist must solve or else. The "or else" refers to the obstacles, typically in the form of formidable opponents, who will do all they can to keep your protagonist from reaching his or her goal—and that goal must be important enough and urgent enough to justify the battles being fought, the risks undertaken, to achieve it. What is more, the suspense increases as the plot progresses toward a showdown: The hero is running out of time, or the villain is becoming ever more resourceful

As for categorizing plots, much overlap exists. There are love-triangle plots and solve-the-mystery plots and voyages-of-discovery plots and escape plots. If the scope of your novel is broad enough, it might include a little bit of everything. For more information about plot variations, see Ronald B. Tobias's *20 Master Plots*.

FOR FURTHER REFLECTION
Understanding basic plot devices and different kinds of plots can be enormously helpful when plotting a novel for the first time. The most important ingredient is a vitally important goal, which an enterprising hero sets out to achieve despite almost overwhelming opposition.

...............................TRY THIS...................................

Lay out a bare-bones plot for your novel, one that answers these questions:

1. What is the predicament? What is at stake? Why should anyone care?

2. Who is your hero? What are his qualifications and motives for resolving the predicament?

3. Who is the opponent and what are his qualifications and motives for preventing the hero from achieving success?

4. What obstacles must the hero overcome, and how?

5. How are things going to turn out?

FICTION AS APPLIED PHILOSOPHY

Just as a parable illustrates an abstract moral principle with a story, so do modern literary works illustrate their authors' philosophies. Albert Camus, who was a philosopher as well as a novelist and playwright, bluntly asserted that "a novel is never anything but a philosophy put into images." However, it would be a mistake to think of novels as illustrated philosophical works. Story must come first, otherwise the basic purpose of reading fiction, to experience vicariously an imagined world, is forsaken. Strive to connect story particulars to the philosophical abstractions they represent without being too formulaic about those connections.

FOR FURTHER REFLECTION

A story is indeed a philosophy translated into images, as Camus noted, but the images must take center stage. There's a quantum difference between a philosophical novel and a story-rich philosophy (think of the difference between a Platonic dialogue and a play by Sophocles or Shakespeare). The play is devoted to stirring the emotions through a story that also happens to embody a profound idea; the philosophical dialogue is devoted to anatomizing the nature of the profound idea, using story elements to illustrate key concepts.

............................TRY THIS....................................

1. Take one of your short stories or your novel in progress, reread it carefully, and then write a paragraph in which you distill the philosophical basis for the work. If you are unable to do this, consider reworking the manuscript so that it more readily embodies a philosophical premise.

2. This reverses the task requested in number one: Select a philosophical premise that you consider to be urgently in need of sharing with readers—let's say a strong belief that children must learn about other cultures at a much younger age then they usually do in school. Now, build a story around that conviction. Perhaps your viewpoint character is a teacher who finds herself forced to confront less enlightened parents or school administrators.

CENSORSHIP

Censorship, in the context of banning or blocking from publication or purchase works of literature for unwarranted reasons (a character uttering a racial slur, for example, but which happens to be consistent with the character's nature), is a bad practice. Many would agree it is a violation not only of freedom of speech as protected by the First Amendment, but a corruption of a work of art. As Walt Whitman proclaimed, "the dirtiest book of all is the expurgated book."

However, there is such a thing as "good" censorship: blocking works that advocate harming people or undermining national security, for example. If you were to write a book unambiguously advocating a terrorist activity, not only would the book be censored, you could be arrested. Other examples of justifiable censorship include uttering words (the proverbial yelling "Fire!" in a crowded theater) that could induce panic and even cause loss of life.

FOR FURTHER REFLECTION

Freedom of speech has its limits. While it is true that books and media represent cornerstones of political and intellectual liberty, it is possible for books and media to be used for nefarious purposes. Wisdom comes with knowing where to draw the line. That said, writers should feel free to write their stories the way they want to without worrying about censorship, or else their stories would become sanitized to the point of sterility.

......................................TRY THIS....................................

Write a journal response to a current censorship case, such as the effort to ban the Harry Potter novels on grounds that it teaches the "devil's work" (i.e., magic); or to *Huckleberry Finn*, on grounds that the characters use racially offensive language; or to *The American Heritage Dictionary*, on grounds that it includes obscene words. Give fair consideration to both sides of the argument before presenting your own case for or against such censorship.

MOOD

Mood, like atmosphere, needs to be sustained before readers begin to feel it in their bones. Whereas atmosphere is generated by physical surroundings, mood is generated by the interaction of character with surroundings. In Primo Levi's memoir, *The Periodic Table*, the predominant mood is one of imminent doom (mood spelled backward!) as Levi conducts chemical research for the Fascists—his only means of survival:

> There were no escape routes, or not for me. Better to remain
> on the Earth, ... purify benzene and prepare for an unknown
> but imminent and certainly tragic future.

Ironically, Levi's experiences are filled with fanciful moments as he thinks about his life in chemical metaphors. His relatives are aloof life the noble gases, for example. His work with nickel (meaning literally "little demon") reminds him of one of his lab assistants, "a rather raw-boned girl of eighteen, with fiery red hair and green, slanting, mischievous, alert eyes."

FOR FURTHER REFLECTION

The mood of a story emanates from the viewpoint character's reactions to his surroundings. A good way to study mood is to read ghost stories. Note how the feeling of dread, of gloom, of fear arising from the viewpoint character's reactions to being inside a haunted house adds to the aesthetic pleasure of the story.

..................................TRY THIS....................................

1. Write a story that sustains a dark, somber mood—or a bright, optimistic mood from beginning to end. Look for opportunities to match the viewpoint character's emotions to the interior setting.

2. Write a story in which the mood keeps shifting—say, from eerie and murky to bright and cheerful and back again.

"LETTING IT ALL HANG OUT"

Freud taught us that the suppressive super-ego serves an important function in civilization, for it is the wellspring of our moral sensibility. If we didn't hold back on our savage desires, there wouldn't be much left of civilization. Sometimes we may wonder, looking at what has happened to Western society over the past half century, whether we haven't been suppressing enough.

But writing—all art—is another matter. Too much suppression and the writing will feel disingenuous and self-serving; it will not "ring true." Readers have an uncanny ability to sense when the author is holding back. At the other end of the spectrum, however, an unfiltered disclosure dump can make readers uncomfortable. Bottom line: Exercise integrity when sharing intimate or unsavory experiences.

FOR FURTHER REFLECTION

Candor is a virtue. So is unity and centrality of purpose. Resist omitting material that can serve to illuminate an important facet of human nature. What may seem on the surface to be a violation of morality could prove to be a heightening of moral awareness. If we wish to raise consciousness of the evils of prostitution, for example, we may need to write graphically about the lives of prostitutes. Stephen Crane, at the end of the nineteenth century, was well aware of this when he wrote *Maggie: A Girl of the Streets*.

..................................TRY THIS.....................................

Write a page or two describing a personal incident you would normally feel uncomfortable writing about; only this time, "let it all hang out"—be completely candid about what happened. If you just can't bring yourself to get the words out, try writing the incident in the third person.

MAY 27
THE PLEASURES OF STORY

"What happens next?" we wonder as we reach the end of a chapter. Stories are life-dramas in miniature, delicious concentrations of real life that enable us to see the whole picture as it were. Maybe that is why we love stories so much: They capture the essence of real life in taut, absorbing narratives that help us better understand real life, which is not nearly so orderly or comprehensible.

A good story has the power to draw us into its world from the opening lines. Fairy tales open with the archetypal "hook": "Once upon a time … " Reading a story is like taking a flying-carpet ride into a world of enchantment, someplace "long ago and far away"—even in another galaxy.

And a good story involves us in the moral or philosophical issues it generates in the character's efforts to reach a goal—whether that goal is to find a purpose in life, to win someone's love, to escape from oppression.

FOR FURTHER REFLECTION

Stories are pleasurable because they take us outside of ourselves. They enable us to think about human problems we might not otherwise be aware of. In this sense, storytelling is a profoundly humanistic activity. The more insight we gain into the human condition, the better place our world will become. That stories can achieve this pleasurably is a small miracle.

...................................TRY THIS...................................

1. Write a journal entry describing your favorite stories and the pleasures you experience reading them. That of escaping to a faraway land? Of gaining insight into complex problems through fascinating characters?

2. Using the journal descriptions of the favorite kinds of stories you prepared for number one, outline a story of your own based on one of them. Make sure that you incorporate those story elements—characters with mystifying, complex personalities; plots with unexpected twists and turns, enchanting settings—that you find pleasurable when reading stories.

DIFFERENT CHARACTERS, DIFFERENT VOICES

Many novelists create two, three, sometimes four or more viewpoint characters, shifting from one to the other in different chapters. Each viewpoint has to project the voice of the character whose viewpoint is being presented. This can be tricky, which is why it's always a good idea for novelists to get to know their characters ahead of time. One common way to do this is to prepare a character notebook and fill it with detailed profiles of each character in the novel: their behavioral characteristics along with the physical ones; their speech, mannerisms, favorite words, and phrases (see the entry for April 7).

Mark Twain was a master at capturing different personalities through different voices. Consider this scene from *Roughing It*, his account of his adventures in Nevada during the silver rush, in which a member of the clergy tries to communicate with Scotty, a frontiersman:

> "I am the shepherd in charge of the flock whose fold is next door."
>
> "The which?"
>
> "The spiritual adviser of the little company of believers whose sanctuary adjoins these premises."
>
> Scotty scratched his head, reflected a moment, and then said:
>
> "You ruther hold over me, pard. I reckon I can't call that hand. Ante and pass the buck."

FOR FURTHER REFLECTION

Writers need to be ventriloquists, able to project different voices into different personalities, particularly through dialogue, but also through their patterns of thought. As a character speaks and thinks, so is her character projected to the world. When putting words into your characters' mouths, think of ways to make their respective habits of speech distinctive.

......................................TRY THIS....................................

Write a dialogue scene between two very different individuals. Try capturing their personalities through their manner of speech. Also contrast them dramatically through their behavioral eccentricities, and physical characteristics.

MEDITATING ON SYMBOLS

Just about any object can be given symbolic weight. A bowling trophy can embody a special time in a character's life before he met up with the wrong crowd; a ringlet of hair can embody a long-ago tempestuous love affair; a discarded key can embody a family secret. For Walt Whitman, a locomotive symbolizes a kind of mythic beast embodying a new technology and a new destiny for America:

> Thy black cylindric body, golden brass and silvery steel
> … Thy metrical, now swelling pant and roar, now tapering in
>   the distance,
> Thy great protruding head-light fix'd in front
> … Fierce-throated beauty!
> Roll through my chant with all thy lawless music, thy swinging
>   lamps at night,
> Thy madly-whistled laughter, echoing, rumbling like an
>   earthquake, rousing all …

Symbols concentrate the essences of people's lives in a way that can generate sensations beyond what meets the eye.

Meditating on symbols will help us to manage them more effectively in our writing. We want to experience the symbolism for ourselves to ensure that it will work in the context of the story scenarios we develop.

FOR FURTHER REFLECTION

A good way to meditate on symbols is to read about the nature of symbolism, how symbols function in different cultures, in religion, in art. Carl Jung's writings on dreams, for example, include studies of dream symbolism. J.E. Cirlot's *A Dictionary of Symbols* describes a great many mythic and religious symbols that have characterized our collective consciousness throughout history. Animals, mythological creatures like dragons, fruits, houses, and castles—these are just a few of the many symbols that inhabit our mental lives. A symbol, writes Cirlot in his introduction, is a "dynamic … reality, imbued with emotive and conceptual values; in other words, with true life."

..................................TRY THIS...................................

Write a story or poem in which you include a creature with the capacity for symbolic resonance–a horse, a butterfly, a deer, a rat, a snake. You might even consider making the creature the narrator (ideal for a fantasy tale).

MAY 30
STARTING UP THE WRITING

Quite often, a writer is blocked simply for lack of an initial little spark to light the fire. But sometimes, writers mistake the spark for the fire—that is, they think they must have a full-blown plot or a fully articulated thesis in mind before daring to put the first words on paper. No: Instead of a plot, think of a room in which the plot will unfold, and then think of someone inside that room about to do something, anything:

> Mary Jo had been lying on the sofa wide-eyed and unmoving
> for nearly an hour before she decided to call the police.

It doesn't matter whether Mary Jo calls the police; it doesn't matter whether, ultimately, Mary Jo is really going to be lying on her sofa or inside a tent in Uganda when the story opens. Or even that you'll be opening with Mary Jo instead of Mary Jo's ex-husband. What matters is that you're starting up the writing.

FOR FURTHER REFLECTION

It is easier to remain inert than to muster up enough energy to get moving. Have you ever watched the Space Shuttle lift off from Cape Canaveral? For several seconds it seems to rise ever so slightly despite those massive plumes of fire. There's a striking, if slightly exaggerated, analogy for getting the writing going: Overcoming inertia seems almost superhuman at times.

..................................TRY THIS....................................

Keep a log of your start-up moments. Write down everything you do up until the moment you begin or resume working on the draft of your essay or story. Include rereading, brainstorming, or engaging in any of these activities.

MANAGING YOUR WRITING PROJECT

Have you ever felt, while working on a novel, or book-length work of nonfiction, that the different parts of the project become tougher and tougher to manage, even if you use an outline? Before you know it, you run into contradictions in the plot, or character traits that are forgotten or contradicted. Well, if it's any consolation, even the most experienced writers face this obstacle on occasion. "A work in progress quickly becomes feral," is the way Annie Dillard expressed it in *The Writing Life*. One way to avoid such problems is to keep a running log of facts about settings, plot twists and turns, and character traits in a notebook, using those very headings. For example, if you're planting clues in a mystery, you might open your notebook to Plot Twists and Turns—or even a special section or subsection titled Clues.

Managing the details of your book this way has another advantage, that of keeping you concentrating on the details that make a book worth reading. If you feel that your project does not need such management, perhaps you need to take another look at it to make sure it's as substantive as it should be.

FOR FURTHER REFLECTION

If you like to work spontaneously without first working up a plan for completing a project, then do so; but sooner or later you will need to bite the project-management bullet. It might not be so annoying, though, once you've generated momentum on the writing.

................................TRY THIS................................

Notebooks are as good as their ease of reference. Divide a three-ring binder into discrete sections such as Character Traits, Plot Details, Settings, using subject dividers with plastic tabs. Next, begin inventorying every trait you can think of for each character. Take similar inventories for Plot Details and Settings.

RECURRING THEMES IN ANCIENT MYTHS

The ancient myths have been serving writers with innumerable themes, and they always will. Consider the tragic love story of Jason and Medea. After Medea helped him find the Golden Fleece, he abandoned her; in revenge she murdered their two children. John O'Hara, for one, in his short story "Natica Jackson," places the ancient tale in a Hollywood context. After the Jason counterpart, a young chemist, has an affair with a lonely film actress, his wife quietly takes their children out to the middle of a lake, tells them to dive in, and then leaves them there to drown. Retelling these ancient stories in a modern context adds richness to the human drama across the ages. The consequences of infidelity, betrayal of trust, arrogance, and revenge transcend time and place.

FOR FURTHER REFLECTION

The beauty of ancient myths lies in their wonderful relevance to the modern world. That's because their themes truly are timeless and universal. Whether it's Jason betraying the woman who devoted her life to him, or Prometheus re-appropriating divine power and knowledge to benefit humanity, or young Phaeton daring to drive his father Apollo's chariot carrying the sun across the heavens, there are modern counterparts just waiting to be told by enterprising writers.

...................................TRY THIS....................................

Take a favorite myth or folktale and use it as a springboard for two different modern-day adaptations. For example, take the myth of Persephone (Roman name, Proserpine) and her underworld abductor Hades (Pluto) and adapt it first as a story about a poverty-stricken woman forced to receive money in exchange for secret information; then adapt the same myth into a fantasy story about an angel who is kidnapped by a demon and held for ransom.

JOHN TENNIEL: ILLUSTRATIONS FROM *ALICE'S ADVENTURES IN WONDERLAND*

The word *imagination* comes from image, and some of the most imagination stimulating images ever created for children are those which John Tenniel created for Lewis Carroll's *Alice's Adventures in Wonderland* and *Through the Looking Glass*. Tenniel's illustrations are, strangely, both whimsical and darkly realistic; they conjure up an Alice more in keeping with Lewis Carroll's intentions than, say, the Walt Disney rendering of Alice. You may view these illustrations online by going to www.johntenniel.com.

Writers who wish to include illustrations in their books will want to work closely with illustrators to ensure that the images reflect the nature of the story world and the characters as they intended.

FOR FURTHER REFLECTION

Humans are visually oriented creatures; even when books are not accompanied by illustrations, we readily supply them with our imagination. That said, all of us, but especially children, delight in illustrated stories. They somehow enhance our willing suspension of disbelief. Writers will sometimes illustrate scenes from their novels in progress so that they'll feel three-dimensional.

......................................TRY THIS...................................

Write a visually intense children's story of about five hundred words, then illustrate it, either with pencil (any colors), watercolors, or pastels. It doesn't matter whether you have "drawing talent." The experience of creating visual counterparts to your scenes will help you develop your description skills.

PERSISTENCE

Sometimes you just have to be stubborn. No matter how difficult the writing task, how slowly the words come, how altogether discouraging the act of writing seems to be, your stubborn streak keeps you going. Persistence is an art: You find ways of challenging yourself to continue. That Chinese proverb of the longest journey beginning with a single step is a nice bit of wisdom, but it's not enough to keep up your will to complete a long and difficult project.

There are all sorts of ways to keep up the momentum when you seem to have run out of stamina:

- **Take a break.** Sometimes a few minutes away from the keyboard will give your brain a chance to recalibrate.

- **Shift tasks.** The notion that you should only work on one thing at a time is nonsense. Shifting from one writing task to another is a common and useful practice.

- **Establish external deadlines.** Promise your spouse that you'll complete the writing task or else … If you have enough self-discipline, establish a hard deadline for yourself. It will be good practice for when you negotiate a contract and have to come up with some hard deadlines.

- **Go into further-research mode.** Maybe what's interfering with your persistence is your subconscious realization that you need to learn more about certain aspects of your topic.

FOR FURTHER REFLECTION

Persistence is an effective antidote to writer's block (see the entries for the 30th of each month), but persistence itself can falter: You can run out of steam, you can become mentally fatigued or lose confidence. Fortunately, there are ways to rekindle your persistence, but it may take some mental gymnastics to pull them off. No one ever said that a writer's life is easy.

.....................................TRY THIS.....................................

Keep a record of the strategies you use to sustain or rekindle persistence. Refer to this list whenever your will to continue starts to ebb.

IMAGINING YOUR IDEAL READER

Audience-targeting can be tricky. After all, even an audience of mystery fans can have such diverse tastes that it's difficult to isolate a common denominator of expectations. For that reason, instead of dreaming about reaching an audience of millions, it would be more helpful to envision one ideal reader.

Envisioning such a reader might go something like this: Let's say you want to write a fantasy novel in which two powerful rulers fight against each other in an effort to control the entire world. How will you tell the story to keep your ideal reader enthralled? Does your ideal reader love scenes with dungeons? Evil wizards casting horrific spells on people? Would she enjoy a medieval setting? A modern one? A setting on a different world altogether?

Your ideal reader, if you haven't guessed by now, is you. You want to write the kind of novel that you, as a reader, would most enjoy. But don't think of the ideal reader as you; think of her as another person, maybe someone whose tastes are almost like yours, but just a bit more discerning.

FOR FURTHER REFLECTION

Like actors or singers, writers need to feel assured that they are delivering the goods to their audiences. Being conscientious of that will ensure a following. Without being audience-aware (at least of your ideal reader), you may fall short of the high standards of storytelling that such readers will expect.

............................TRY THIS...................................

1. Write a profile of your ideal reader, similar to a profile you would create for a character in your novel. Describe her in as much detail as possible, paying special attention to level and type of education, artistic tastes, and favorite books.

2. Using the profile of the ideal reader you prepared in number one, write a short story in which this person plays an important role. For example, confront her with an ethical dilemma, such as competing in a grueling race for personal profit or to raise money for the homeless.

INDISPENSABLE BOOKS FOR WRITERS: NONFICTION

Great works of nonfiction such as the following convey wisdom and have the power to enrich one's life.

1. The Holy Bible. Perhaps history's single most influential book (actually, many books, but seldom published separately). It should be supplemented by other sacred books, such as the Qur'an, the Bhagavad Gita, and the Upanishads.

2. *Bulfinch's Mythology* by Thomas Bulfinch. A retelling of the legends of the gods and heroes from ancient Greece, Rome, and Scandinavia.

3. *Walden; or, Life in the Woods* by Henry David Thoreau. A meditation on self-reliance and how a rediscovery of essential values can overcome the "quiet desperation" that dislocation from nature can cause.

4. *The Diary of a Young Girl* by Anne Frank. This masterpiece of private writing presents a microcosm of social interaction and coming of age within a confined space while embodying the macrocosmic tragedy of the Holocaust.

5. *Bury My Heart at Wounded Knee* by Dee Brown. American westward expansion from the perspective of the displaced and subdued Native peoples. A richly documented revisionist history.

6. *The Right Stuff* by Tom Wolfe. Wolfe's energetic prose style bedazzles us as it informs us of the experiences endured by the original seven Mercury astronauts and the man with the most "right stuff" who wanted no part of the program—Chuck Yeager.

7. *Cosmos* by Carl Sagan. One of the most widely read science books of all time, an awe-inspiring, visually rich introduction to astronomy and the history of science; the basis for an award-winning PBS series hosted by Sagan.

FOR FURTHER REFLECTION

Unlike fiction, nonfiction can become dated, depending on the subject. But even outdated nonfiction can be valuable reading if it is superbly written. Much has been discovered archaeologically about the history of ancient Rome since Gibbon wrote *The Decline and Fall of the Roman Empire*; on the other hand, no other history work can match its eloquence and depth. The same holds true for works of science, such as Darwin's *The Origin of Species*.

......................................TRY THIS....................................

Write a short essay in which you discuss a topic you know well, but in a manner that stirs emotions as well as educates.

GENERATING IDEAS QUICKLY THROUGH FREE-WRITING

Once you begin thinking and observing like a writer, ideas will begin to rain down, sometimes in torrents. If you're too lazy to get those ideas down on paper, or (even worse) if you're too worried that what you do write down won't be good enough, you'll be inviting writer's block. The very act of writing can help you figure out what it is you're trying to convey. So whether you have only the merest figment of an idea, or are not even sure if you have an idea at all, let the words out, *quickly.* "In quickness is truth," Ray Bradbury reminds us in *Zen in the Art of Writing.*

At first, writing spontaneously—what writing teachers call *free-writing*—may not be as easy as it sounds. We've become so conditioned to worry about grammar, word choice, and punctuation that we deny ourselves the luxury of unimpeded thought. Grammar, word choice, and punctuation are important—do not misunderstand; but the time to be concerned about such matters is during the final-draft stage, not the idea-generating stage. To get your story off the ground, think content; don't worry about sentence construction or semicolons.

FOR FURTHER REFLECTION

It sometimes pays to let our spontaneous minds do the writing, to turn off the editor (who insists we start correcting right away, like the schoolteachers who made us error-paranoid with their red pens) and just follow our thoughts wherever they may take us.

...................................TRY THIS...................................

Get ready to open the floodgates of your subconscious. Write *nonstop* for ten minutes about a single incident from a work in progress. Do not pause if you're unsure about a word or sentence (simply circle it instead). Talk to yourself on paper if nothing comes to mind. For example, write, "What personality strengths and flaws does this character possess? What is her biggest obstacle or fear?"

JUNE 7
VILLAINY

Almost by definition, stories are about struggling against villainy. In popular fiction, the distinction between hero and villain (or the forces of good and the forces of evil) are fairly clear-cut (as in Harry Potter vs. Voldemort). But villainy comes in a wide variety of guises; it's not just the white-hat good cowboys valiantly fighting against the black-hat bad cowboys. A "good guy" can be a "bad guy" in disguise, and vice versa; sometimes it isn't easy to distinguish between good guys and bad guys. Tom Jones, in Henry Fielding's novel by that name, evolves from an undisciplined rogue to a man of conscience and caring. Julien Sorel in Stendhal's *The Red and the Black* is a womanizing, power-hungry schemer who nevertheless strives to give meaning and purpose to his life in a society characterized by pettiness and bigotry. And how do we categorize Bigger Thomas in Richard Wright's *Native Son*, or Humbert Humbert and Lolita in Vladimir Nabokov's masterpiece?

FOR FURTHER REFLECTION

Without villainy in one of its many manifestations, there can be no story. One of the appeals of popular fiction is its sharp distinction between good and evil, hero and villain. In "literary" fiction, however, where emphasis is placed on the complexity of modern society and the psychological dynamics of human motives, the differences *become* ambiguous. Villains can seem like heroes and vice versa; villains can also become heroes, and vice versa.

......................................TRY THIS......................................

Create two profiles of a single character. In the first profile, imagine the character as the protagonist in a popular novel. Focus on his unambiguously heroic qualities. In the second profile, imagine this same character in a novel of psychological realism, in which he is torn by conflicting desires.

JUNE 8
COMPARING, CONTRASTING

We live in a relativistic universe: Nothing is "strange" or "ugly" or "heroic" except in comparison (explicit or implicit) to things less strange or ugly or heroic. Writers sometimes compare (emphasize similarities) or contrast (emphasize differences) one character or setting with another: "Sylvia, unlike her sister Margot, could not keep a secret if it meant her life"; "Like Notre Dame, the late medieval cathedral of Chartres is supported by flying buttresses." Or consider Bruce Catton's contrasting descriptions of Civil War generals Ulysses S. Grant and Robert E. Lee in his essay "Grant and Lee: A Study in Contrasts":

> The Virginia aristocrat ... saw himself in relation to his own region. [Lee] lived in a static society which could endure almost anything except change. ... He would fight to the limit of endurance to defend it. ... The Westerner, on the other hand, would fight with an equal tenacity for the broader concept of society ... tied to growth, expansion, and a constantly widening horizon.

By comparing one general to the other, Catton emphasizes the complexity, the three-dimensionality of each man, thus allowing us to appreciate their greatness as heroes all the more.

FOR FURTHER REFLECTION

By comparing persons and places, writers add depth of understanding to human nature, to moments in history. Such comparisons can be explicit, as in Bruce Catton's comparison of Grant and Lee, or implicit (more often the case in fiction) by dramatizing, say, the good queen's actions in one chapter with the evil queen's actions in the next.

...................................TRY THIS...................................

Here are comparison/contrast exercises for you to practice in your journal:

- your personality with the personality of one of your siblings
- Ray Charles's style of blues singing with Billie Holiday's
- Darth Vader and Voldemort as villains
- yourself at age fourteen compared to yourself at age eighteen, at twenty-three ...

WRITING A DISCOVERY DRAFT

A discovery draft (or zero draft) is what some writers like to call a rough draft. Roughness isn't the issue (even eighth drafts can still be "rough"), but finding out what you're trying to say is. Writing generates more writing—even when you're outlining or writing a synopsis; but a discovery draft opens all the stops. You might think of it as focused free-writing, oxymoronic as that sounds. Our brains, after all, are wired to think in logical sequences. Any sentence you write generates prompts for the next sentence and the next.

Writing a discovery draft is a little like free-writing (see the entry for June 6), except that with the former, you keep your sights focused on the story you're trying to write. That said, you will have more freedom than you might initially think staying within the story framework.

FOR FURTHER REFLECTION

Working on a discovery draft stimulates a writer's ability to make rapid connections between story elements, which can serve as a shortcut to plotting. You'll be amazed by the elaborate plot details you can come up with spontaneously by producing a discovery draft.

....TRY THIS....................................

As soon as you work out a bare-bones framework for a short story, plunge into a discovery draft. Think about story progression, character, and setting; let twists and turns in the plot, dialogue, and atmosphere fall where they may. Don't spend time fretting over what to write next. The goal here is to discover things as you go along.

DREAMS AND THE SURREAL

The significance accorded to dreams by psychoanalysis early in the twentieth century gave rise to an art movement known as surrealism. André Breton published the *Surrealist Manifesto* in 1924 in which he protested against the sterile efforts of artists to represent the so-called real world. For Breton and his painter and writer followers (Duchamp, Ernst, Magritte, Tanguy, Dali, etc.), dreams were windows that opened to a superior reality (the root definition of *surrealism*); that is, the reality of mind and of dreams. Dream content became the material for this new wave of modern art. Surrealism, in Breton's words, was "psychic automatism ... by which one proposes to express ... the actual functioning of thought."

Armed with this ideology of the superiority of dream visions and the forces of the unconscious mind as disclosed by Freud, the Surrealists explored new possibilities of artistic expression in all genres: the visual arts, painting, poetry, the novel, and theater. "The Marvelous," wrote Antonin Artaud, who wrote his own surrealist manifesto for the theater, "is at the root of the spirit."

FOR FURTHER REFLECTION

The Surrealist revolt against logic and reason, coming as it did in the wake of World War I, and the birth of psychoanalysis, created a revolution in art. No longer would art be enslaved to the logic-based reality that produced war and suffering. The Surrealists taught artists to make valuable use of their dreams and subconscious impulses.

................................TRY THIS..................................

Study the paintings of Giorgio de Chirico, René Magritte, Salvador Dali, or Dorothea Tanning and write a poem on one of them—in the Surrealist spirit of letting your subconscious mind or your dreams guide the writing. Bring in objects and ideas that you would not expect to be linked together in a conventional setting. Magritte, for example painted a huge rock suspended over the ocean, tree leaves shaped like birds, a locomotive emerging from a fireplace. Such surrealist imaginings can help pull your imagination out of the groove of conventionality.

TAPPING INTO THE EXPERIENCES OF OTHERS

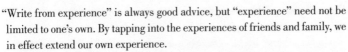

"Write from experience" is always good advice, but "experience" need not be limited to one's own. By tapping into the experiences of friends and family, we in effect extend our own experience.

The best way to tap into others' experiences is to study them on their home turf. Robin Williams—in preparing for his role in the film *Awakenings* as Dr. Malcolm Sayer, the slightly fictional counterpart of the neurologist Oliver Sacks, the author of the book on which the film is based—shadowed Sacks, accompanying him on rounds to study his temperment, his personality quirks, and his diagnostic techniques. Williams's resulting performance is masterful.

Like dedicated actors striving to create Oscar-winning performances, we writers need to immerse ourselves in the lives of others in order to gain "gut" knowledge of those experiences, which in turn will enable us to write about them forcefully and convincingly.

FOR FURTHER REFLECTION
Interviewing people about their experiences can yield a lot of useful information—but to get the fullest sense of what it's like to work in a certain occupation, a writer needs to get as close to the first-hand experience as possible.

......................................TRY THIS....................................

Write a story about a worker's experiences at his job. Try to capture the sensation of the workplace—the atmosphere, the specific tasks, the hazards and frustrations, the way one interacts with co-workers. In order to capture this ambiance, pay a visit to the workplace. Ask if you can volunteer to assist with some of the work.

JUNE 12
MARGINALIA

The notes you scribble in the margins of books or on manuscripts you're work-ing on are known as marginalia. Why would something so trivial be accorded such a fancy term? Because marginalia are not trivial: They serve as useful glosses when rereading a complex work, as a means of "talking back" to the writer, establishing a dialogue in the margins, so to speak. Many writers, such as Samuel Johnson, Samuel Taylor Coleridge, Joshua Reynolds, Charles Darwin, and Carl Jung, wrote great marginalia. Edgar Allan Poe's marginalia have been published as such (in the Library of America edition of Poe's literary criticism). The Canadian literary scholar H.J. Jackson has published a study of marginalia (*Marginalia: Readers Writing in Books*). In her chapter on Mo-tives for Marginalia, Jackson observes that annotators, being "self-conscious readers," often experience an "irresistible impulse" to annotate.

FOR FURTHER REFLECTION

Reading can be just as creative as writing in the sense that as you assimilate the ideas of another, you feel a strong impulse to engage the author in conver-sation. An author's assertion can elicit excited agreement or disagreement, or trigger additional ideas in a similar vein. The reader, in a sense, becomes a latter-day disciple (or detractor) of the author.

..................................TRY THIS...................................

Copiously annotate a work of nonfiction (make sure the book is your own, not the public library's). Include the following types of marginalia:

- additional thoughts triggered by the passage
- reasons for agreeing or disagreeing
- comparisons/contrasts with other passages or other authors' views on the topic
- cross-references

Write a review of the book, using your marginalia as prompts.

JUNE 13
DRINK

No one needs to be reminded of the role that alcoholic beverages play in story-telling. Who can think of a Noël Coward play without thinking of martinis? One of the standard moments in film is the hero or villain preparing a drink—usually whiskey on the rocks or something involving seltzer.

Beverages, alcoholic or otherwise, are also standard fare in mysteries, especially if someone is going to be drugged or poisoned. Think of that bizarre concoction Rosemary is urged to drink regularly in Ira Levin's *Rosemary's Baby*; and of course there's the beverage of choice for vampires …

> The Lords took up a stance on either side of the first kettle,
> and each, extending a right hand, slashed his right wrist with
> a knife which he held in his left hand, and let the blood flow
> copiously into the brew.

That appetizing moment, not surprisingly, is from the pen of Anne Rice (*Vittorio the Vampire*).

The abuses of alcoholic beverages—in drama and comedy alike—have long been a staple of novels, theater, and film, particularly in the plays of Eugene O'Neill. In the films *Days of Wine and Roses* and *Leaving Las Vegas*, we witness the horrific ways in which alcohol leads to the destruction of personhood. A comedic reversal of this is *Cat Ballou*, in which Lee Marvin plays the part of a famous gunslinger gone to seed because of drink, but finds himself in a situation where he must sober up in order to face an enemy gunslinger who has set out to kill him.

FOR FURTHER REFLECTION

Like food, beverages—tea, coffee, wine, beer, hard liquor, nectars, and mysterious concoctions—add flavor and even important story content to a novel. A character's choice of beverage can be a reflection of personality, culture, historical period.

..................................TRY THIS....................................

Write a scene for a play or short story in which an important conversation unfolds over the consumption of particular beverages. The type of beverage should directly or indirectly add to the mood of the story and maybe even relate to what is being discussed.

JUNE 14
HIDDEN HISTORIES

Much of history is hidden. Even major historical events like World War II, for all the books devoted to them, include "blind spots" that historians or novelists have not yet tapped into—like the story of the Russian women volunteers who dug anti-tank trenches—many of whom were gunned down from the air; or the many medical histories of the war, such as the efforts to protect the troops against lockjaw and malaria. Explore any period in history in depth and you will discover stories yet untold, or needing to be retold. The ancient world is an especially fertile area for discovering story material. Very little attention, for example, has been given to Çatal Hüyük, the earliest known city (in Mestpotamia); or to Mistra, the lost Byzantine capital and fortress situated in southern Greece. While mystery-steeped places like Troy have been endlessly written about, other places just as mysterious—like the Hittite capital, Boghazkoy, or the hidden city of Petra in the middle of Jordan's desert—are untapped.

Writers looking to create historical fiction based on little known sites and events would find an excellent resource in *The Encyclopedia of Mysterious Places*, by Robert Ingpen and Philip Wilkinson.

FOR FURTHER REFLECTION

Stories set in obscure but mysterious places never fail to enchant readers. A combination of intrepid research combined with creative imagination can bring a lost moment in history to life. Every city and country on earth has many unexplored or overlooked facets of its history that can yield fascinating stories.

......................................TRY THIS....................................

Choose a moment of "hidden history"—ancient or modern—and research it in depth and use it as the setting for a story. Create imaginary characters and situations but be faithful to the historical record, or what there is of it.

IMAGE JOURNALING

Images and words complement each other, which is why many historical and biographical works, and even novels and collections of poetry, contain photographs and other illustrations. Think of Blake's watercolors that accompanied his poems, or the illustrated novels of Lewis Carroll, Charles Dickens, Mark Twain, or John Dos Passos. Contemporary novelists like Kurt Vonnegut (in *Breakfast of Champions*) incorporate illustrations into their fiction. Umberto Eco's *The Mysterious Flame of Queen Loana* is an especially fascinating example. We live in a visual age, and while images can never replace texts, they can certainly supplement them.

Journal writing, too, can be supplemented with photographs, drawings, or collages. Likewise, photo albums and scrapbooks can be supplemented with descriptive passages. Illustrating your journal entries is not only fun, it can heighten your descriptive and analytical skills and suggest narrative angles you might not otherwise have considered.

FOR FURTHER REFLECTION

Images and language involve different "reality-processing" centers of our brains, so it makes sense that, when we interconnect the two modes of recording our impressions of the world around us, we are giving ourselves—and potentially our readers—a greater range of possibilities for representing reality.

........................TRY THIS....................

Create a "collage" journal entry consisting of text, drawings, or cutouts from magazines or newspapers. Give it a thematic focus—e.g., "The Horrors of War"; "Architectural Marvels"; "Memories of My Trip to Hong Kong"; "Stages of My Kitchen Remodeling Project"; don't just create a collage haphazardly.

JUNE 16
WORKING WITH JARGON

There is good jargon and bad jargon. Every profession or recreational activity (e.g., mountain climbing or skiing) has its own jargon or specialized language, which enables members of a given profession to communicate more quickly and efficiently. Take a word like *feverish*: It can mean an abnormally high body temperature; but it can also mean (more metaphorically) a heightened, excited state of activity. Health-care professionals, however, prefer the word *febrile* because it has only one meaning, that of abnormally high body temperature. If you were to use *febrile* to mean feverish in a nonmedical sense, it would seem forced—a mere display of "highfalutin'" vocabulary.

Writers should become familiar with the jargon of professions in which their characters are involved. If you're writing a novel about espionage, then you'll need to learn the jargon of military intelligence. Working on a mystery novel? You need to understand not only police procedures and forensics, but the jargon of these professions as well. Be careful, though: You have to use this language so your lay readers can understand it—by providing a clear enough context or by unobtrusively defining the expressions.

FOR FURTHER REFLECTION

Jargon, used judiciously, can add authenticity to a story, especially when you want to convey a character's expertise in a particular field. You yourself need not become an expert in that field, but you will have to become sufficiently knowledgeable to make your character seem like an expert. It's not unlike an actor preparing to play the part of an expert. Think of Tom Hanks as astronaut Jim Lovell in the Ron Howard film, *Apollo 13*: Hanks had not only read Lovell's book (*Lost Moon*) on which the film was based, but also visited with Lovell and his family for a week.

....................................TRY THIS....................................

Write a "shop talk" dialogue scene between two individuals from similar but distinct professions, each with its own colorful jargon–a professional golfer, say, in conversation with a professional bowler or basketball player. You can make the conversation humorous, as one athlete struggles to understand the jargon of the other.

LISTENING TO NATURE

To be a good naturalist, listen to nature. This is not as mystical as it sounds. In *Silent Spring*—the book that helped bring about the modern environmental movement—Rachel Carson describes how she woke up one morning and could not hear birdsong. Carson, a birder, discovered that huge bird populations had diminished due to widespread DDT spraying.

Nature is filled with marvelous sounds. Thoreau devotes an entire chapter to it in *Walden*. Here he rejoices in birdsong:

> The whippoorwills chanted their vespers for half-an-hour, sitting on a stump by my door; ... [he was also] serenaded by a hooting owl. ... [Y]ou could fancy it the most melancholy sound in Nature, as if she meant by this to stereotype and make permanent in her choir the dying moans of a human being.

But the sound that obsesses him most is as unnatural as could be: that of the locomotive. This symbol of technology, Thoreau depicts as something that both terrified and fascinated him (he was, after all, a land surveyor and pencil maker):

> The whistle of the locomotive penetrates my woods summer and winter, sounding like the screams of a hawk sailing over some farmer's yard ...

FOR FURTHER REFLECTION

Nature speaks to us with many different sounds, or voices: the voices of the wind and rain, the grumbling of thunder, the rustle of leaves, the symphonies of crickets and birds, even (in early spring) the cracking of melting ice shifting on the lake. These natural sounds speak to us because we are a part of nature, and these voices have been stirring us ever since we were painting bison on cave walls.

.....................................TRY THIS.....................................

Go on a nature walk and be sure to bring along a pocket notebook (and perhaps small guidebooks to trees, wildflowers, and birds). Describe what you observe and hear in as much detail as you can. In addition to sketching tree leaves, flower blossoms, and such, try to capture as many nature sounds—the rustling of the canopy, the gurgling of a mountain stream, the rumble of distant thunder ...

"WHAT IF ... ?"

This is the operative question for science-fiction writers, of course: What would happen if androids used as slaves began murdering their slavemasters? (the premise of Philip K. Dick's *Do Androids Dream of Electric Sheep?* and the excellent film based on it, *Blade Runner*). But it is also a key question for any writer of fiction. "What if ... ?" sets the brain's plotting wheels in motion. What if the best friend of your hero secretly wanted to kill him? What if the woman your central character loved deeply rejected him because he was poor, as was the case with Jay Gatsby? What would happen if the king's daughter—judged the most beautiful woman in the world—were kidnapped? Read the *Iliad* and find out.

Formulating what-if questions can generate story ideas quickly. We live in a universe of contingencies: One small event can trigger a long series of events that can change people's lives and even change history.

FOR FURTHER REFLECTION

Good storytelling is fueled by questioning. Embedded in the word *question* is the word *quest*: Posing a question is the first step on a quest to discover things we long to possess and would be willing to sacrifice much in the process of attaining. Think of the quest for the Golden Fleece, the Ark of the Covenant, the Holy Grail, or the Fountain of Youth. All of these quests may well have begun with the question, *What if ... ?*

.....................................TRY THIS.....................................

Formulate a dozen what-if questions, and then, each day, write a page-long plot-synopsis for one of them. Here are a few to get the cognitive wheels rolling:

- What if a chemical spilled into a reservoir causes wide-spread paranoia or amnesia?

- What if a solar storm knocks out all communication satellites?

- What if the present penal system were replaced with a pharmaceutical program that erased criminals' personalities and turned them into model citizens?

When you finish at the end of twelve days, choose the most promising synopsis and continue working on it.

ON MEMORIZATION

Memorization has gotten a lot of bad press because it is associated with un-imaginative or militaristic teaching—which is unfortunate, because memorization, used properly, can be a powerful learning tool. Of course, you need to feel the desire or the necessity to memorize—desire and necessity being the best motivators for learning. But you also need to be convinced of a good reason as well. One good reason is that memorizing a text, contrary to being superficial, draws you deeply into the subtleties of the work, thereby enabling you to create an effective modernization. Actors must master their lines before they can convey subtler aspects of the characters they portray. Another possible reason might be to be able to transfer the mood, the atmosphere, the suspense of the original into your modern retelling without having to keep referring to the source.

FOR FURTHER REFLECTION

Utilizing our memories keeps our minds agile and alert, and memorization is an excellent way of doing that. The more you memorize, the better you'll get at it. Start by memorizing things you love—poems, anecdotes and jokes, facts and figures about topics that intrigue you, vocabulary from the foreign language you've been trying to learn, important moments in a historical period. Committing information to memory allows you to compose without interrupting yourself to look things up.

..................................TRY THIS....................................

Memorize one of your favorite poems that is more than fifty lines. If you've not had much experience with memorizing, choose a poem with a distinct rhyme scheme or one that is linked to a sport or holiday, such as "Casey at the Bat" or "The Night Before Christmas." Afterward, write a journal entry describing the steps you took to commit the poem to memory.

DISCOURAGEMENT AS INSPIRATION

We always hear how important it is for aspiring writers to receive encouragement. Well, encouragement has some importance but maybe not as much as discouragement. Robert Fitzgerald thought that poets (and perhaps to a lesser extent all writers) "need the most discouragement possible." Fitzgerald isn't being cynical; poetry is the easiest thing to write badly, and unless would-be poets receive blunt criticism about their initial efforts—in effect, are discouraged—they may never master a very difficult craft. Any writer who folds up from discouragement might not have the mettle to make it as a writer. Discouraging criticism can hurt, especially if you're a beginning writer, but if you can grow a proverbial thick skin, discouragement—coupled with iron-willed determination—will help you to recalibrate, to take a long hard look at your apprenticeship and resolve to make a concerted effort to improve. This might take months, even years. No one has ever said that writing is an easy skill to master; on the contrary, it may be one of the most difficult.

FOR FURTHER REFLECTION

How thick is your writer's skin? Can you take candid, even harsh, criticism? Can you continue to write with fierce determination to succeed despite discouragement? One of the greatest impediments to success as a writer is being delusional about your level of skill. If you think you're better than you are, you'll never be sufficiently motivated to improve.

......................................TRY THIS......................................

Give a writing teacher or workshop leader known for her blunt, uncompromising criticism a sample of what you consider to be your finest work—a piece you've tried to publish but couldn't. When you get the manuscript back, lay out a plan not only for improving it but for improving yourself holistically—as a poet or fiction writer. Perhaps it may result in spending a year reading a lot more, studying poetic or fiction techniques a lot more, and of course writing a lot more. Track your progress in a notebook dedicated to your self-improvement as a writer.

JUNE 21
INCUBATION, OR LETTING IT SIT FOR A WHILE

Never be too hasty in sending off something you've written. Like a stew or soup, a draft of a story or essay or poem will benefit from simmering. As the Nobel Prize-winning novelist Doris Lessing says, "The more a story cooks, the better." Psychologists, in fact, have identified incubation as one of the stages of creativity.

It makes sense. When we write in a white heat, we're so close to the material—so subjectively involved with the story details—that we're unable to visualize the big picture. For that to happen, we need to give ourselves emotional distance, to see the draft more objectively. Time plays a major role here. After completing a draft, allow a week or so for the objectivity to kick in. Turn your attention to another writing project. Weed your garden, read a book, take a cruise.

Also, returning to a draft after a hiatus makes it easier to detect problems—in substance, continuity, or clarity. You will spot verbose passages, awkward phrasing, and inaccurate word choice. You may even be tempted to scrap the entire draft and start afresh. In this case, start afresh but don't scrap the draft; you never know what might be salvageable in the future.

FOR FURTHER REFLECTION

Drafts, like eggs, need to incubate on the proverbial back burner where the draft in progress can grow in the nurturing darkness of the subconscious. The creative process recruits the whole brain, not just its rational centers. It is important for writers—for all artists—to recognize this subliminal dimension of creativity.

...................................TRY THIS....................................

Compose a piece of flash fiction (a story of about five hundred words) and set it aside for seven days. On the eighth day, make note of the problems you detected, and revise accordingly. Now let the revised draft sit for another week, and then read it over critically. If you feel that it could benefit from another revision, revise. Learn to heed your inner voice when it tells you that the draft needs more work.

JUNE 22
STORYBOARDING

Storyboarding is most often associated with scriptwriting. Each scene in the movie being scripted is represented on a card, often consisting of a sketch plus summary text. The cards are then pinned in sequence to a large board where they are continually studied and modified as the final draft of the screenplay materializes.

Many authors structure their novels cinematically and will use some form of storyboarding. William Faulkner, who worked for a short time in Hollywood (returning in great haste to his native Mississippi), used a peculiar mode of storyboarding for his novel *A Fable*: He scribbled his storyboards directly onto the wall of his study. You can see them for yourself when you visit his antebellum estate in Oxford, Mississippi.

With storyboarding, writers are able to see their story progression from scene to scene, as well as flashbacks or flash-forwards or shifts in viewpoint.

FOR FURTHER REFLECTION
Visual stimuli can be helpful when it comes to plotting a novel, and storyboarding uses visual elements to help writers construct plots. The "thicker" (i.e., more complex) the plot, the more useful storyboarding can be.

......................................TRY THIS......................................

Purchase a stack of extra large (6" x 8") index cards and use them to create a storyboard for your novel. Each card should consist of a description of a story moment, together with a drawing that "sets" the scene. Tack the cards onto a large corkboard or tape them to the wall. Use arrows to indicate temporal or spatial direction (these will be especially useful in indicating flashbacks and flash-forwards). Use different colored cards to represent different viewpoints. Remember that you can easily change sequences by moving the cards around.

JUNE 23
KNOWLEDGE INTO WISDOM

To what end is knowledge? Some crave knowledge for its own sake; some, like Faust, would give away their souls for it. The Faust legend—powerfully captured by Goethe in his play *Faust* and by Thomas Mann in his novel *Doctor Faustus*—reminds us of the folly of lusting after knowledge, to become omniscient and godlike. Instead, we must learn to cultivate knowledge into wisdom, sort of like domesticating fire or nuclear power. A question we need to ask ourselves: To what moral ends do we wish to apply the knowledge we acquire? In the context of authorship, this can mean studying a moment in history more intensely than others in order to write a more precise account of that moment. Knowledge in itself is neither bad nor good; the uses to which it is put determine its value.

FOR FURTHER REFLECTION

Knowledge for its own sake has little value; it needs to be applied, to be used as a beacon for illuminating truth—of the human condition, of the natural world. To put it another way, knowledge—neutral information about things—needs to be tested out in the arena of human experience: Does the applied knowledge yield wisdom and human betterment, or does it lead to calamity?

......................................TRY THIS....................................

Take an inventory of all that you know about a specific topic or activity like bowl-ing or growing tomatoes. Now, write a paragraph explaining how you can apply some of those facts toward a worthy goal, such as a how-to essay on how to improve your bowling score, or how to ensure a rich crop of healthy tomatoes.

JUNE 24
ANGLES OF VISION

Whatever you write, you are writing from a point of view, a perspective, an angle of vision. That even extends to reportage. Reality is viewpoint-dependent. Some novels are told from the omniscient point of view, which sounds as if the narrator is God; actually, it's the author playing God, entering freely to examine the thoughts of every character, sometimes leaping into the future to hint at what is going to happen.

John Gardner reminds fiction writers of the importance of deciding upon which point of view to adopt early on. Will it be first-person narrator? Third-person narrator? Will the viewpoint shift from narrator to narrator in corresponding chapters? (See the entry for April 22.) In his thriller *The Footprints of God*, novelist Greg Iles shifts from first person (protagonist) to third person (villain). Melville's *Moby-Dick* is ostensibly told in the first person ("Call me Ishmael"), but the narrator eventually all but vanishes and the novel morphs into an omniscient angle of vision.

FOR FURTHER REFLECTION

Angles of vision shape the experience of the story, bringing the teller, the narrator, into the story as a character, even if that character is the omniscient author. For readers, the story is enriched by perceiving things through contrasting points of view, through the lens of very different personalities.

....TRY THIS....................................

1. Begin a three-character story (seven or eight paragraphs will do) from the first-person point of view (angle of vision); next, begin the story again, this time from the third-person point of view. Every two or three paragraphs shift the angle of vision from one character to the next.

2. Write a paragraph or so in which your viewpoint character is an environmentalist describing a logging operation. Next, describe the same logging operation from the point of view of one of the loggers.

SPIRITUAL SETTINGS

A story need not follow an overtly religious plot to have a spiritual aspect. A character's search for his roots (familial or cultural or both), or for a deeper sense of purpose, will likely generate a spiritual undercurrent, and if the setting happens to be one in which spiritual dramas have been played out traditionally—Damascus or Mecca or Jerusalem, say—then the spiritual undercurrent will become that much more prominent.

Ancient settings can evoke a spiritual aspect practically by default. These are times when gods and humans seemed to have interacted more—"the age of miracles" we like to say of this era. The Egyptian pharaohs possessed both godlike and human attributes. Writers have a wonderful opportunity, when setting their stories in ancient times, to intertwine gritty realism (think of Egyptian or Roman slaves being whipped as they hammer away in limestone quarries) with motifs of spiritual deliverance.

FOR FURTHER REFLECTION

In the ancient world, the natural and the supernatural intertwined. If you plan to set your story in the ancient world, you will want to find ways to convey this synthesis, perhaps by describing the way the people experienced the natural world, the heavens, and the interconnections between human and divine law.

..................................TRY THIS....................................

Learn as much as you can about a particular ancient sacred site, then prepare an outline of a story in which the site plays a significant role in the story. For example, outline a story about the circumstances surrounding a Druid ceremony taking place at the 4,000-year-old temple of Stonehenge (on the Salisbury Plain in southern England).

PILGRIMAGE

A pilgrimage is a journey undertaken for spiritual purposes, visiting one or more sacred sites. "The object of pilgrimage is not rest and recreation," Huston Smith reminds us. And as Phil Cousineau explains in *The Art of Pilgrimage: The Seeker's Guide to Making Travel Sacred*, "The pilgrim's motives have always been manifold: to pay homage, to fulfill a vow or obligation, to do penance, to be rejuvenated spiritually, or to feel the release of catharsis."

Writers are pilgrims virtually by default: They travel both figuratively (via the imagination) and literally in search of unanswered questions and higher truths and to recover that which has been lost—a sense of purpose, a renewed sense of what is sacred.

FOR FURTHER REFLECTION

Approach each writing project as an occasion for pilgrimage, a journey into the sacred heart of your subject. It is not enough merely to conduct "background research"; a writer must leave the conventional world behind in order to participate holistically in the truth-seeking that is to culminate in a book, be it a memoir, biography, or novel.

......................................TRY THIS....................................

1. In your journal, make a list of spiritual places you'd like to visit on a pilgrimage. Include shrines, monuments, cemeteries, archaeological sites, missions, and cathedrals.

2. Take yourself on a pilgrimage to a spiritual site, perhaps to a historic mission or cemetery. Before embarking, learn all you can about the site and plan to pay special attention to the things that interest you most about the site. For example, if you plan to visit the church of St. Clement Danes on Fleet Street in London, research the history of this ancient church. You will learn that the church was a pagan sanctuary in Roman times.

3. Write a story about an artist who develops a spiritual connection with her subjects. Imagine what happens when she paints a tree, a horse, a homeless person ...

TELLING STORIES: A HUMAN ATTRIBUTE

Nonwriters often marvel at the sheer volume of narrative production that books represent, and tend to regard such production as "genius"—beyond the accomplishments of most mortals. Well, the truth is that we are all predisposed to narrative. Rarely does a day go by when we fail to tell someone about "what happened" at work or in the neighborhood or (most commonly) while traveling. Our brains are *wired* for narration. Telling stories represents our collective effort to make meaning out of our lives and our relationship to the world around us. It also represents our ongoing struggle to find historical continuity. Part of how we regard ourselves is influenced by what we have done in the past—collectively as a nation, a culture and individually through our particular lineages.

FOR FURTHER REFLECTION

"We tell stories in order to live," writes the distinguished essayist and novelist Joan Didion. When we tell stories of our lives, we are, in a sense, shaping them into meaningful units; we are framing them, inviting others to pay closer attention to them. Much of what drives us to tell stories, to share stories with others, is our instinctual need to give some kind of permanence to our actions. From the cave paintings depicting successful hunts to the sagas of spaceflight, we yearn to immortalize ourselves through our best accomplishments.

......................................TRY THIS......................................

Take a moment to put into words your reasons for telling the stories you wish to tell. Are you writing stories that attempt to foreground social ills that interfere with your vision of an ideal society? Do you write to celebrate the power of love or faith? Perhaps you want to show how adventurous and fun-filled and mysterious life can be. Articulating your reasons for storytelling might help you to give your narratives a heightened sense of purpose.

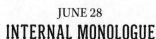

INTERNAL MONOLOGUE

You can give a story psychological depth by exploiting your narrator's inner voice through what is commonly called internal monologue. This is not quite the same thing as ordinary monologue—characters talking to or by themselves, as in a Robert Browning poem or a Shakespeare soliloquy (see the entry for May 7). Internal monologue is similar to stream of consciousness, except that the latter tries to emulate the unedited flow of thought, which tends to bypass conventional grammar and syntax. Internal monologue captures the rhythms and the fluency of interior speech while trying to maintain a minimal degree of grammatical coherence, and it filters out the gibberish.

One of the masters of internal monologue is William Faulkner, as we can see from the following excerpt from *Light in August*, in which we find ourselves in the mind of its central character, Joe Christmas:

> He seemed to watch his hand as if from a distance. He watched it pick up a dish and swing it up and back and hold it there while he breathed deep and slow, intensely cogitant. He heard his voice say loud, as if he were playing a game: "Ham," and watched his hand swing and hurl the dish crashing into the wall, the invisible wall, waiting for the crash to subside and silence to flow completely black before taking up another one.

FOR FURTHER REFLECTION

Internal monologue brings us deep inside the psyche of a character. Irrational impulses collide with visual perceptions and mundane concerns. We are reminded of the turbulence that is consciousness.

......................................TRY THIS....................................

1. Write a page of internal monologue from the perspective of one of your characters. Let your sentence structure reflect the flow of thought while at the same time building around a central concern.

2. Develop two dramatically contrasting streams of internal monologues, one for your hero, the other one for your villain.

NATURE SYMBOLISM

Thirty thousand years ago, one of our remotest ancestors crushed some colored rocks into a powder, added water and egg to create tempura pigments, and painted bison and other animals on the walls of his cave dwelling. Here was the first example of nature symbolism, which was then inseparable from religious symbolism. To represent is to make real, to embody.

We have always experienced an intimate relationship with nature—no surprise, since we are literally, physically a part of nature: The salinity of the sea matches the salinity of our blood; we share 98 percent of our DNA with chimpanzees; the menstrual cycle is almost exactly that of the lunar one. No wonder the most ancient religious rituals expressed an intimate relationship with the natural world.

FOR FURTHER REFLECTION

Nature has given us a treasure trove of symbols that enhance our insights into life's profundities. We use trees to symbolize our familial and biological relationships; we associate clouds with fantasy, soil with humility (from *humus*, the Latin word for soil), the wind with destiny, birds with freedom, and so on.

...................................TRY THIS.....................................

Write a poem or short story in which you employ symbols derived from the natural world. Remember that anything can be made to resonate symbolically. Examples: What symbolic associations can you give to the following?

- rain or snow
- mountains, valleys, canyons
- earthworms
- flies, mosquitoes
- granite, pyrite (fool's gold), or other minerals

JUNE 30
MENTAL FATIGUE

Writing takes a lot of mental energy, which is why three or four hours of it can feel like eight hours of physical work. To reduce the level of mental fatigue, you might do any or all of the following:

- **Take frequent breaks.** Doing a household chore (or part of one), taking a walk, watching television, fixing yourself a snack, taking a nap, or simply closing your eyes and listening to music can recharge your mental batteries quickly.

- **Shift projects.** For some writers (not all), it's a good idea to work on more than one project—the more dissimilar the better. If you're working on your memoir, shift to poetry or drama when you feel yourself running out of ideas or energy.

- **Shift from composing to researching (or vice versa).** Additional research can spark new ideas for your work in progress; writing can remind you of research areas you've overlooked.

FOR FURTHER REFLECTION

It is easy to become mentally fatigued when engaged in the kinds of concentrated thinking that writing demands. Instead of ignoring the fatigue (and risking quality of work as a result), stop working as soon as it feels okay to do so, and give yourself at least a short break. Ten minutes of doing physical chores, for example, can be enough to give you a second wind.

......................................TRY THIS.....................................

During your next work day, maintain a log of the time and duration of your breaks. Note which breaks you took because of mental fatigue and what you did during that break to relieve the fatigue. Over the next week, correlate your periods of mental fatigue with amount of time spent and type of activity (nap, snack, chores, exercise, etc.) you engaged in during the break. Finally, figure out what breaks relieved your mental stress.

FICTION AS ALLEGORY

Fiction has its roots in those most ancient of writings we generally refer to as myths or legends: tales of heroes who struggle mightily against great forces or dangerous enemies. Fiction writers today would do well to remember these ancient roots because whether their heroic characters are detectives or starship captains or war veterans struggling to overcome the trauma of combat, they ought to possess something of the marvelous—a rare (as opposed to magical) talent that sets them apart from mainstream humanity. In Plato's famous allegory of the cave,* in Book 7 of the *Republic*. For example, in which prisoners (representing all of humanity) are chained in a cave, one of the prisoners breaks loose and ventures outside where he is momentarily blinded by the light. Soon, he is able to appreciate the light for what it is, the higher truth, and now feels compelled to return to the cave to "enlighten" his former fellow prisoners.

FOR FURTHER REFLECTION

Allegory teaches moral lessons through concrete example in the form of a story everyone can relate to. Abstractions alone rarely persuade; they must be rooted in human experience; they must *demonstrate* the necessity of adopting their lessons before they can be believed.

...................................TRY THIS...................................

1. Write a short story in which a seemingly ordinary person, such as a stay-at-home mom or an office worker who prefers a domestic rather than an exotic life, suddenly comes to realize that she or he possesses very special (but not supernatural) powers—the power to be an effective leader during an emergency, for example.

2. Read Plato's allegory of the cave, and then write your own "updated" allegory of the cave set in a confined place such as a cellar or dungeon.

---

* Plato, through the mouth of Socrates, refers to it explicitly as "a parable of education and ignorance" (W.H.D. Rouse's translation, *Great Dialogues of Plato*; NAL, 1956).

JULY 2
GUSTAVE DORÉ'S ENGRAVINGS

Few illustrators have been as popular and as revered as Gustave Doré, who has produced breathtaking engravings of scenes from the Old and New Testaments, Milton's *Paradise Lost*, the fables of Aesop and La Fontaine, and other works. In "Jacob Wrestling With the Angel," based on the story in Genesis, chapter 32, in which Jacob refuses to let go of the angel "except thou bless me" (i.e., establish a covenant?), Doré is able to convey through the physical tug-of-war between mortal and immortal forces the more profound spiritual struggle taking place. Both Jacob and the angel are unrelenting. While Jacob is more muscular, the angel is stronger and taller, and so a stalemate is reached, resolved only with Jacob's request being granted. He has earned his blessing by demonstrating a show of strength needed to lead a people, the Israelites (in fact, the angel tells him that henceforth his name shall be Israel).

FOR FURTHER REFLECTION

Stories of struggles between mortals and immortals are as old as civilization itself. Notice how Doré places this archetypal struggle upon an earthly landscape at daybreak (they had wrestled all night according to the biblical story). Like the two wrestlers, sky and land (heaven and earth) come to a resolution.

......................................TRY THIS......................................

After reading the story of Jacob and the angel in Genesis 32, and then viewing the engraving at www.dore.artpassions.net, write a story from the point of view of Jacob. What is going through his mind as he encounters the angel at Peniel? Perhaps he is not immediately aware, in the darkness, that the stranger is indeed an angel. How does he find out? (Seeing his wings is too easy; imagine that, folded, they are nearly invisible in the darkness.) Consider setting the wrestling match in a modern, urban location.

CONTROVERSY

If you've been reluctant to tackle a subject because of its controversial nature, keep in mind that people are drawn to controversy. Whenever people depart from the norm, they are subject to criticism—and the greater the departure from the norm, the higher the controversy quotient. If we're dealing with celebrities, then the controversy quotient shoots up even higher. Dealing with controversy, after all, is dealing with conflicting value systems, and whenever there's conflict, there's story.

Whether you're working on your memoirs or on a novel, focus on the controversies, don't bypass or even slight them. It may be difficult and, in the case of nonfiction, there may be legality issues. Before you start writing about a scandal involving a public figure in your community, make certain that the facts are rock solid, fully documented, and verifiable.

FOR FURTHER REFLECTION

Controversy fuels reader-interest. However, it's important to recognize the line between news of a controversial nature and gossip. Of course, plenty of writers make a living dishing up gossip for the tabloids; but unless tabloids are your calling, keep in mind that the difference lies between what is beneficial to know and what is served up simply to satisfy morbid curiosity.

..................................TRY THIS...................................

Write a confrontation scene between two intelligent characters whose views of a subject are utterly contradictory. Because these two characters are intelligent, they are not going to resort to shouting matches or to name-calling or to saying hurtful things (the way of too much of the world, alas). Instead, show them being respectful of each other's views, but at the same time using reasoned arguments to persuade the other of what he considers the truth.

RESPONSIBILITY TO YOUR AUDIENCE

Arrogance is an occupational hazard among writers: The freedom we feel when we set words to paper ("I can write about anything and in any manner I please!") not only exhilarates us as the creative possibilities stimulate our imaginations (which is a good thing, of course—a big reason so many people want to be writers), but it can blind us to audience expectations and needs.

Of course, the opposite is also true: We can become so enslaved by our desire to please everyone, that we betray our own vision, our own unique way of seeing the world. Perhaps Erica Jong is over-reacting when she says that worrying about how readers will react to your work is "really dangerous and ultimately destroys you as a writer," but it does make sense to ensure that you do not compromise the integrity of your vision and voice. Arrogance becomes a problem when writers are indifferent or hostile toward the expectations of potential readers.

FOR FURTHER REFLECTION

Reflect for a moment on the way you think about your readers. Do you think about them at all? If so, are they little more than a vague abstraction, or do you actually envision individuals reading and responding to your work, much the way actors envision their audiences responding to their stage or screen performances? Are you able to draw the line between satisfying your readers and pandering to them? How you envision your readers can influence the way you write.

...................................TRY THIS....................................

Imagine that your future readers are present before you and that their question to you is, "Why should we lay down twenty-five dollars for your book? What will we gain from reading it?" List the reasons you would give them that would justify their purchase.

INDISPENSABLE BOOKS
FOR WRITERS: POETRY

Poetry is the neglected genre of the modern world—a sad irony, considering that literature came into being through poetry. The Sumerian *Epic of Gilgamesh* written at the dawn of civilization; the Homeric poems, the *Iliad* and the *Odyssey*); the sacred epic poems of Hinduism, the Mahabharata and the Bhagavad-Gita; the Song of Solomon; the Psalms, and portions of other books from the Bible; Ovid's *Metamorphoses*; *Beowulf*; Dante's *Divine Comedy*; Chaucer's *Canterbury Tales*; Shakespeare's plays and sonnets; Milton's *Paradise Lost*—all poetry.

If you haven't read much poetry, here is a list of poets who deserve to be read along with the great poetic masterpieces mentioned above. Reading these works will undoubtedly enrich your appreciation for the role that poetry can play in capturing the subtleties and complexities of the human condition.

- Walt Whitman, *Leaves of Grass*
- Emily Dickinson, *Complete Poems*
- Robert Frost, *Complete Poems*
- Langston Hughes, *Complete Poems*
- T.S. Eliot, *Complete Poems and Plays*

Prose writers, not just poets, need to read poetry; prose writers *learn* from poets. Novels like Joyce's *Ulysses* or Proust's *Remembrance of Things Past* are noted for their poetic prose—language that is rhythmic, rich in metaphor, multilayered in meanings.

FOR FURTHER REFLECTION
Poetry represents the noblest, most artistic use of language. For that reason, poetry can teach writers of any genre a great deal about the power of language to generate layers of meanings and associations. Such language versatility plays an important role in fiction and nonfiction

.....................................TRY THIS....................................

1. Write an essay in which you reflect on the wisdom you've gained from reading a single poem, or a group of poems by a single poet.

2. Just for practice, compose a poem in the manner of one of your favorite poets. Later on, revise the poem in your own manner.

JULY 6
"WRITE BADLY"

Quite likely, your first reaction to this strange bit of advice is, "Now there's a suggestion I can follow with no trouble at all!" And that is precisely the point of it. The advice comes from the popular writing teacher Brenda Ueland, who instructed her students to write the worst possible story they could. The logic of this is almost diabolical. When you write badly, you become painfully aware of your bad moves: the awkward and verbose sentences, the imprecise word choice, the incoherent story or idea progression. The lesson is similar to the one parents use to ensure that their children do not get hooked on cigarettes: Go ahead, light up! Take deep drags! (And the unmentioned final act: Get so nauseated you'll never want to touch another cigarette again.)

Scott Rice, an English professor at San Jose State University, conducts an annual "worst writing awards" competition (which he named the Bulwer-Lytton Contest, after the Victorian novelist credited with that clichéd opening sentence, "It was a dark and stormy night."). Rice received thousands of entries from writers who strove to produce the most wretched prose imaginable—so wretched it was hilarious. Here's an example from contestant Ann Rhodes Conley:

> The waitress's eyes shone like the fabric of his cheap, threadbare trousers, and even as she sloshed hot coffee on them, muttering an absent-minded "Oops!" in apology, Duffy knew that someday she would be pouring java in his home.

FOR FURTHER REFLECTION
Writing badly improves our ability to recognize those problems that contribute to bad writing; it is a way of making you so aware of commonplace problems that you'll be sure to avoid them more quickly than you might otherwise.

..................................TRY THIS..................................

1. Write a truly awful opening paragraph to a Western, mystery, or science-fiction story.

2. Write a short-short story in which you do your best to break every rule of good writing that you've been taught. Afterward, go over the story carefully and identify each of your "transgressions."

CONTRASTING CHARACTERS

If you're working on a novel, take a close look at your principal characters: Do they possess strong distinguishing features? Do they represent distinct differences in personality, tastes, worldviews? You add to a story's richness by creating a broad spectrum of character types.

Think back on some of your favorite novels and recall the personality differences of the main characters. In George Eliot's *The Mill on the Floss*, for example, the siblings Tom and Maggie Tulliver couldn't be more different from each other. Tom is unadventurous, matter-of-fact, while Maggie is irrepressible and hungers for new experiences. Each sibling represents a facet of mid-Victorian English society on the threshold of great change.

FOR FURTHER REFLECTION

Stories, in a sense, are enhancements of the real world; nowhere is this more evident than the different kinds of characters we encounter, even in short stories. Readers enjoy—and learn from—different personality types and the consequences of personality on destiny.

......................................TRY THIS......................................

1. Outline the traits of the major characters in two or three novels you've recently read. Jot down as many physical and behavioral characteristics as you can locate. Keep these character-contrast sheets handy to remind you of the importance of drawing up your own distinctive characters.

2. Write a skit in which two characters with dramatically different personalities and tastes clash over a difference in opinion. For an example of characters with clashing personalities, study the arguments between Felix and Oscar in Neil Simon's *The Odd Couple*.

JULY 8
BRINGING SCENES TO LIFE THROUGH DETAILS

Readers are eager to enter the fictional worlds you create for them, but you need to help them along by providing them with enough details to bring a setting or an event to life in their imaginations. Every detail you add *animates*: the dust that wagons or horses' hooves stir up on a dirt road; the humming of mosquitoes on a humid August night in the Midwest; the spasmodic movements of infants, and the way their faces wrinkle when they cry to be nursed. In her novel *The Bonesetter's Daughter*, Amy Tan writes how, during the Full Moon Festival, a Chinese restaurant "was jammed with a line flowing out the door like a dragon's tail," and how the children "used chopsticks to play percussion on teacups and water glasses." Fictional reality is a rushing river of details, without which your story is little more than a lifeless shell.

FOR FURTHER REFLECTION

Vivid, specific details provide the magic that brings writing to life. To enliven your story with details, place yourself into the fictional milieu you are trying to conjure up. Don't be content to think generalities ("The cellar seemed creepy"); rather, imagine yourself navigating in semidarkness through thick cobwebs and dusty shelves covered with rodent droppings. Being imaginative is an active, not a passive experience.

..................................TRY THIS....................................

Use your writer's notebook to practice describing various settings: a run-down neighborhood, a fog-shrouded beach town, a children's playground, an airport terminal during a holiday. For each setting, try to represent most or all of the five senses in your description.

REVISING FROM SPIRIT

F. Scott Fitzgerald once wrote a note to himself, "Revise from spirit." In other words, instead of trying to salvage bits and pieces from a draft that failed to meet his standards, he opted instead to begin anew, but with a keen sense of the original creative impulse that made him begin the project in the first place. Revising from spirit means revisiting that original impulse, recovering the enthusiasm needed to make the story come to life, only this time having a clearer sense of the possibilities as well as being more alert for the pitfalls.

Beginning anew, especially if one is talking about the draft of an entire novel, sounds drastic at first: "all that wasted effort" you might think, except that there is no such thing as a wasted effort when it comes to drafting.

FOR FURTHER REFLECTION
Beginning a second draft "from spirit" operates on the faith that you will be able to incorporate the strengths of the first draft while avoiding the problems. It may be necessary, however, to set the project aside for a while in order to reconsider it from a fresh perspective. Revising from spirit prevents one from becoming bogged down with a draft that probably would not work out if it were just tinkered with.

..................................TRY THIS....................................

To get the feel of revising for spirit, start with a short work, such as a poem or short-short story. After writing the draft, set it aside for at least two weeks. After rereading it carefully, put it away and produce a new draft without ever consulting the original.

DREAM SEQUENCE

Dreams possess their own internal logic, and that includes the way they un-fold—seemingly randomly, free-associatively, our waking brains tell us; but psychologists may uncover an underlying, rational explanation for that progression. The subconscious is very clever at condensation, so that what might seem like a meaningless sequence could well be a logical pattern super-condensed, like a computer Zip file.

Dreams can also be, psychologists tell us, disguises or masks: They cleverly cover up a too disturbing or painful experience with a more agreeable symbolic façade, much the way a fanciful fairy tale can represent an uglier reality—the big bad wolf (frightening enough!) representing an adult predator of children.**

Writers from ancient times, not just from the dissemination of Freud's theories, have been influenced by dream sequence. Think of Oedipus before the Sphinx, Hamlet confronting the ghost of his father, Macbeth's dreamlike confrontation with the witches—which also brings sorcery and prophecy into the picture—truly a witch's brew of enthralling storytelling.

FOR FURTHER REFLECTION

Every story is magical in the way it lets a made-up world interact with the real world. Readers, especially children, love "losing themselves" inside of a book for that reason. Thinking of a story as a waking dream will remind you that narrative progression can proceed down the yellow brick road of surprise and delight.

.....................................TRY THIS....................................

Think of your story or novel as a yellow brick road down which your Oz-like hero chances upon one surprising situation after another. Write a synopsis for each one of the five or six strange confrontations your hero encounters along the way.

** For a psychological study of fairy tales, see *The Uses of Enchantment*, by the child psychologist Bruno Bettelheim.

SPIRITUAL EXPERIENCE

In his essay "On Experience," Ralph Waldo Emerson tells us that the definition of "spiritual" should be "that which is its own evidence." It's a tantalizing insight, one that subtly links spiritual experience to democratic experience (recall the famous "that which is self-evident" clause from the Declaration of Independence). Part of the reason why it's difficult to convey our spiritual experiences to others is that they're both self-evident (assuming others have experienced something similar), and they resist conventional language for experiencing them.

But if you're determined to share such experiences with others, it would be a good idea to talk to as many people as possible about their experiences, being attentive to their ways of describing, say, out-of-body sensations, or becoming connected to God through prayer.

FOR FURTHER REFLECTION
Spiritual experience takes us into the deepest recesses of the human psyche. What we find there are the common bonds of human striving and values. Without question, scientific reason, together with the need for reliable evidence to support assumptions, is one of the hallmarks of the modern era, but it is important to recognize the role that spiritual experience also plays in the modern era. Without a spiritual dimension, life loses its luster. Experiences like beauty and mystery, destiny and hope, tend to evaporate.

..................................TRY THIS..................................

1. Using Emerson's definition of "spiritual," list as many spiritual moments as you can recall.

2. Develop one of the moments you listed for number one into a personal-experience essay, poem, or short story.

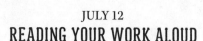

READING YOUR WORK ALOUD

Good writing approximates conversation. That is, the rhythms of speech (formal, semiformal, or colloquial, depending on the writer's purpose) are reflected without being reproduced too literally. Rhythm, which is governed by the way sentences are constructed and varied with relationship to one another (some short, some long; some assertive, some reflective), contributes to readability. Prose rhythm facilitates comprehension and makes the writing seem more human, less mechanical. A good way to train your ear for creating the illusion of conversation in your writing is to read your work aloud, either into a tape recorder or to someone who is willing to pay attention to the way your prose "flows." You yourself will often discover problems in sentence construction, repetition and such, by vocalizing. That's because we've spent more time practicing our habits of speech than our habits of prose.

FOR FURTHER REFLECTION

Readers are sensitive to the rhythms of written prose. If the sentences in a paragraph have little variation, they will interfere with the reader's ability to concentrate on the subject matter. We writers want our prose style to be transparent enough to facilitate understanding (or the ability to experience a story world vicariously), but not so transparent that the prose seems bland and artless. An effective way to check for prose style is to read your work aloud. Does it engage a listener's attention quickly? Does it call attention to stylistic rough spots?

......................................TRY THIS....................................

While reading a page of a work in progress aloud to a friend, both of you take separate notes in which you respond to possible rough spots in the prose style. Afterwards, compare notes; see if you've reached a consensus voice. Next, revise the page and read it aloud again, checking to see if the rhythmic elements have been improved.

JULY 13
SYMBOLIC FOODS

Because food is so elemental to basic living and to culture, it is not surprising to learn that many foods symbolize a great deal of human experience—religious, psychological, aesthetic. Bread, of course, is the archetypal food, rich in religious connotations. In Greek mythology, Demeter (Ceres in Roman mythology, from whose name the word *cereal* is derived) was the goddess of the grain harvest and of fertility.

Writers can learn a great deal about human nature and different cultural traditions by learning about the symbolic value certain foods have for a particular culture.

FOR FURTHER REFLECTION

Is there some truth to the saying, "We are what we eat"? Do the animals we consume make us more animalistic? Are vegetarians prone to pacifism? Sometimes, it works the other way around. Thoreau, having spent several months in wilderness, encounters a woodchuck and has a sudden urge "to eat him raw."

Whether fact or fable (most likely the latter), the idea makes for good horror stories, vampire stories especially, with its underlying assumption that the ingestion of blood has the power to animate the dead.

...................................TRY THIS....................................

Learn about the symbolic value some foods have in a given culture. Write an essay in which you trace the lore, legends, and symbolic associations that one of the following foods possesses: olives, pomegranates, oranges, bread, grapes.

TAPPING INTO LOCAL HISTORY

Everything and every place has a history, and any history is intrinsically worth exploring, especially if not too many have done so. This is sometimes the case with communities or landmarks that have not yet captured national attention.

If you're an aspiring writer of nonfiction who is fascinated by the historical background of, say, the first grocery or drug store chain; or of your church, mosque, or synagogue; or a distinctive institution like a theater, zoo, or museum in your community, then you may have an excellent opportunity to break into print with a photo-story for a regional publication.

FOR FURTHER REFLECTION

Fascinating story and article material may be right in your own proverbial back yard. Of course, you need to do a little investigating to see what is out there. Quite likely, you will discover a lot more than you realized! Every institution, from mom 'n pop stores to flea markets to theme parks, has a history that locals would enjoy learning about and that local periodicals would like to publish.

...................................TRY THIS....................................

Write a local-history feature about one of your favorite haunts—a flea market, a restaurant that has served the community for generations, a local theater, a city park or playground. After completing a draft, write a query letter (these days e-mail queries are often welcomed) to the editor of a local magazine or newspaper summarizing your piece in a way that would arouse the editor's curiosity.

THE ART OF KEEPING A POCKET NOTEBOOK

Pocket notebooks are ideal for the writer on the go who does not wish to be hampered by having to carry larger notebooks under her arm. Pocket notebooks are much smaller, of course, but the idea is to jot down just enough of an idea to prompt you when you get home.

Because note taking on the go means that you're writing while attending to other business, you need to practice taking notes quickly, accurately, and, in some cases, unobtrusively. It isn't exactly good manners to start scribbling in a notebook while conversing (unless you pass yourself off as a reporter!) or at a social gathering. Write in abbreviations; record only what you need to trigger your recollections later on. Keep in mind that a few choice words can conjure up a flood of associations.

FOR FURTHER REFLECTION

It is possible to jot down ideas while doing other things. In fact, doing other things can trigger ideas. One of the "occupational hazards" of being a writer is that your mind becomes accustomed to finding ideas everywhere and at any time. It can be frustrating, but the joy of coming up with new ideas overrides the frustration. The only challenge is to find a fleeting moment to jot down your thoughts without being impolite or risking your safety. Regarding the latter, it's best not to write in your pocket notebook while you're driving—even if stopped for a light. In such cases, make a strong mental note to do your journal jotting as soon as you're at your desk.

......................................TRY THIS....................................

1. The next time you set off on a nature walk, take a pocket notebook with you and record as much of what you observe and listen to and smell and touch as you can.

2. Select several of the pocket-notebook jottings from your nature walk and work them into a full-fledged outline for an essay.

LANGUAGE AND THOUGHT

Language and thought are profoundly intertwined; work to enhance one and you automatically enhance the other. To put it another way, in order to think deeply, we must have language to give that thinking substance. Neglect language and thought becomes impoverished. That is why the party of Big Brother in Orwell's *1984* works so hard to diminish language via "Newspeak": language stripped of color and subtlety. Every new edition of the *Newspeak Dictionary* is thinner than the one preceding it. By impoverishing the thinking ability of its citizenry, the totalitarian regime of Orwell's nightmare world is better able to maintain its oppressive power.

FOR FURTHER REFLECTION

The deeper and more precise one's thinking and observing become, the more one's vocabulary will grow. It's inevitable: Language is necessary for nuanced thinking; nuanced thinking, in turn, recruits ever more precise language and explanation. Writing is such a valuable skill for everyone, not just for those wishing to become professional writers, because it requires us to exercise our linguistic and cognitive skills to such a high degree of proficiency.

...................................TRY THIS...................................

To demonstrate to yourself the influence of language on thought, do a free-write in your journal on a subject you know something (but not a lot) about, but wish to learn more. Perhaps the Dead Sea Scrolls is such a subject. Write everything you already know about them; then, write down questions you'd like to have answered about them. Next, spend the next few days researching the subject, taking copious notes. Maintain a list of new concepts, along with new vocabulary, that you have learned during the course of this research.

JULY 17
LISTENING TO ANIMALS

It isn't necessary to be a Doctor Dolittle to discover that animals have much to say; and if you listen carefully and pay attention to their actions along with their voices, you'll learn a lot about animal nature and how they often shed light upon our own nature. In *Walden*, Thoreau is always listening carefully to his "brute neighbors"—like the crafty loons or the startling partridges:

> Whichever side you walk in the woods the partridge bursts away on whirring wings, jarring the snow from the dry leaves and twigs on high, which comes sifting down in the sunbeams like golden dust, for this brave bird is not to be scared by winter.

But the creature whose sounds enchant Thoreau the most is the owl …

> Near at hand you could fancy it the most melancholy sound in Nature, as if she meant by this to stereotype and make permanent in her choir the dying moans of a human being—some poor weak relic of mortality who has left hope behind, and howls like an animal, yet with human sobs … I find myself beginning with the letters gl when I try to imitate it.

FOR FURTHER REFLECTION

Animals speak with the voices of the wild, of primal nature. We've always been rooted to nature as well, which is why we feel a bond to animals when they howl at the moon or sing in the trees or growl from the shadows. Perhaps because we ourselves are part of the animal kingdom, we're able to sense a deep and ancient bond with other creatures.

....................................TRY THIS....................................

1. Write a parable about a child who is able to communicate with animals, or with certain animals.

2. If you're a bird watcher—and bird listener—then write an essay on the musical language of birds. Focus on perhaps four or five species of birds; describe their habitat, behavior, and the character of their birdsong. Also consider reflecting on the more subjective quality of their music and how that music affects you.

WRITERLY MEDITATION

Meditation is to thinking as wisdom is to knowledge; effective meditation involves a fusion of body, intellect, and spirit, the sort of fusion writers need to achieve in their work—that is to say, a fusion of logical story progression with emotional buildup (not only *How will Jill win Jack's heart?* but also *What does the emotional roller-coaster ride both Jill and Jack are experiencing feel like to the reader?*). Being able to fuse logic with emotion in a story seems to demand more than just formulaic planning: Writers must experience these emotions themselves to some degree, or at least try to experience them vicariously—and that is where meditation comes in. Deep, sustained, directed thinking allows us to tap into dormant emotions as well as heightens our ability to tap into the emotions of others. This ability is known as empathy; it is one that all writers should cultivate.

FOR FURTHER REFLECTION

Writerly meditation is holistic thinking—thinking that fuses logic with imagination. Unlike certain kinds of spiritual meditation, which advocate emptying the mind, writerly meditation advocates the opposite: *filling* the mind with ideas, making creative connections among those ideas, probing for complexity and nuance, envisioning the consequences of situations, wondering about the intricacies of human behavior and the mysteries of the natural world. This kind of meditation must be cultivated and practiced continually.

....TRY THIS....................................

Spend a few moments thinking deeply about a specific facet of the story or essay you're currently working on. For example, if you're writing an essay about bird watching, reflect on the underlying benefits that such a pursuit can provide over the years; or meditate on the different varieties of birdsong. Later, write down some of the thoughts that occurred to you.

MEMORY AND ATTENTIVENESS

We marvel at those who appear to possess excellent memory—actors, for example, or literature teachers who can quote long passages from Shakespeare or Milton. But as Samuel Johnson reminds us, the art of memory is the art of attention. Why "art"? Because memory, to serve well, cannot be mere passive recollection; one must willfully and intensely engage all of one's faculties in the act of retention, not just the external elements (the words, the appearances), but the emotional connections one must establish with the object of memorization. Memory, then, is a holistic experience.

What does this mean for writers? If you wish to evoke a special place that has had great significance for one of your characters (or for yourself if you're working on a memoir), then you will need to evoke minute sensory details. The attentiveness behind the effort to capture memories in detail can itself strengthen the ability to remember.

FOR FURTHER REFLECTION

The ability to recollect experience is invaluable for writers. Note taking will often compensate, but note taking has its limitations: You need to take time away from *writing* to go over your notes. The key to improving memory is to work on attentiveness: making a concerted effort to pay close attention to things; keeping all of your senses on the alert; being an active rather than a passive observer. Such attentiveness needs to be regularly practiced; it will go a long way toward improving your ability to remember things.

...................................TRY THIS...................................

Take a long walk with someone. During the walk, pay close attention to everything you encounter: trees, flowers, landforms, passing vehicles, construction projects, animals, insects—and to phenomena other than visual, such as changes in humidity and temperature, wind-borne odors. Include at least one interior setting (where you stop for coffee, say). Tell your walking partner to write down everything you observe, and use those notes as a measure of your retention skills.

CHARACTER MOTIVES

There are five interconnected questions we must ask of the characters we create:

- What do they want?
- Why do they want it so badly?
- How do they intend to get it?
- What stands in their way?
- How will they overcome those obstacles?

Work out the answers to these questions in sufficiently complex detail and you have a story. Underlying the drive to attain a goal and to overcoming the obstacles to that goal is motivation. Mountaineers may claim that they wish to climb a treacherous mountain "because it is there," but their motives are often more complex than that. It is up to you as a storyteller to probe those deep-rooted, underlying motives: to prove to a skeptical parent that he can do something exceptional? To triumph over a disability? To demonstrate exceptional prowess and courage in the eyes of the world? This last motive was what partially fueled the motive to land Americans on the moon—a feat that occurred on this very day in 1969.

FOR FURTHER REFLECTION

We want our characters' motives to be universal motives with which our readers can readily identify. This means taking time to think deeply about the motives that drive our own lives and the lives of those around us and being able to extrapolate our characters' motives from this resource.

......................................TRY THIS....................................

Prepare a "motives" page for each of your characters. Draw from your in-depth study of the motives you see at work in people you know as well as your own motives. The latter might be the toughest task of all, since we seldom take the time to pinpoint the motivational elements that make us want to do what we do.

ON CREATIVITY

Few words are as difficult to pin down as *creativity*, yet we see it used as if there were no question as to its meaning. The word has traditionally been used to distinguish fiction, poetry, and drama from factual writing; but many reject that simplistic dichotomy on grounds that factual writing demands just as much creative thinking as fictional writing.

Creativity happens when the artist fashions something that is sufficiently new or unexpected as to instill aesthetic delight in the audience—aesthetic delight, because the newness might be a sensation of wonder, of the uncanny, even of fright (as in horror fiction or films).

Some assume that creative thinking is antithetical to analytical thinking, but that is not the case. Think of Einstein's astonishing feats of creative *mathematical* thinking that produced his world-changing theories of relativity; of Buckminster Fuller's creative *geometric* and *architectural* thinking that produced the geodesic dome.

FOR FURTHER REFLECTION

Society values creativity because it allows us to see reality in new and refreshing ways. Creativity extends our sense of what is possible in the world; it epitomizes freedom of intellect, every bit as precious as democratic and religious freedom.

...............................TRY THIS...................................

1. Compose an essay in which you explore the different facets of creativity as you understand and have experienced them. Be sure to include colorful cases in point to illustrate these different facets.

2. In a meditative essay, reflect on the pleasures of creativity that you've experienced over the years.

TYPES OF OPENINGS

Writers often get hung up on story openings, worrying about whether they "set the stage" effectively. For first drafts, write an opening that sets the story in motion. Later on, you can then decide which type of opening to employ:

- **Reportorial opening.** A blunt statement of fact instantly sets up the fictional world as if it were the real world. Consider John Irving's opening to *The World According to Garp*: "Garp's mother, Jenny Fields, was arrested in Boston in 1942 for wounding a man in a movie theater."

- **Fairy-tale opening.** A "Once upon a time ..." opening that establishes scene and circumstance. Practical, effective for children's stories, but not very compelling for adult fiction.

- *In medias res* **opening.** This plunges readers directly into a situation. Reader reaction: What the heck is going on here? After a few pages, you provide the necessary information.

- **Mood or atmosphere opening.** Some writers want to establish a specific mood right away. In *Bleak House*, Charles Dickens immerses his readers in the oppressive atmosphere (both literal and figurative) of the London site of the High Court of Chancery:

    > Smoke lowering down from chimney-pots, making a soft black drizzle, with flakes of soot in it as big as full-grown snow-flakes—gone into mourning, one might imagine, for the death of the sun. Dogs, undistinguishable in mire. Horses, scarcely better; splashed to their very blinkers. Foot passengers, jostling one another's umbrellas, in a general infection of ill-temper ... Fog everywhere.

FOR FURTHER REFLECTION

Openings pull the reader into the story world. And while they should be written with care, writers need not fuss over them in the first draft. Wait until a few chapters are written in order to work out the best type of opening to get the story going.

............................TRY THIS....................................

Take one of your old stories and give it an entirely different kind of opening. Does the new opening change the mood? The pacing? Does it add new life to the story? If not, try another kind of opening.

CONVEYING YOUR WORLDVIEW CONVINCINGLY

Are you an optimist at heart? A pessimist? A hedonist? A Darwinian survival-of-the-fittest pragmatist? A romantic idealist? As a writer, you want to communicate your worldview clearly and compellingly. Readers of fiction and nonfiction alike wish to learn how a given philosophy or value system or worldview can be enacted in everyday life. Readers are pragmatists in that they want to see value systems played out, not just talked about. They want to see worldviews put to the test. Is your protagonist a woman who enters business administration in order to help end sexual harassment in the workplace? Along with dramatizing one or more incidents in which she herself had been a victim of harassment, you may want to show her clashing with fellow executives as well as clients who cannot shake off their sexist thinking. What clever ideas does she put into motion to help enlighten them—especially after one of her ideas backfires?

FOR FURTHER REFLECTION

Writers inevitably develop an elaborate worldview, one from which they draw for future writing projects. Every so often, it makes sense to take a long, hard look at that worldview to ensure that it is internally consistent and that it reflects your most current way of thinking.

...............................TRY THIS..................................

1. What are the key elements of your worldview? Write a four-page summary of them. Every so often, review your summary and add, delete, or modify it as needed.

2. Write a story that embodies one of your strongest-held beliefs. Render your ideas through action rather than merely have your characters expounding on your ideas in static conversation. For example, instead of having your main character talk about the importance of holding firm to one's beliefs despite widespread dissension, create a scenario in which your character is being attacked by a hostile audience for speaking his mind.

3. Write an essay that traces the evolution of one of your beliefs, from childhood to the present day.

ON VERISIMILITUDE

We say that a story possesses verisimilitude when it gives readers the sense that it has captured the situation with total authenticity. Like a *trompe l'oeil* painting in which the grapes look as though you could pluck them right off the canvas and eat them, or like *cinema verité*, which gives readers the impression that unedited reality is unfolding before their eyes, verisimilitude in fiction does not filter out the crudities, the disturbing details. Of course, filtering is always going on in ultra-realistic fiction, and that is the source of its power. Readers *know* they are reading fiction (and are thus being entertained). There's a quantum difference between, say, actually struggling to keep your sailboat from capsizing in a sudden violent storm and reading about the experience. Whenever we as readers are able to transport ourselves imaginatively into harrowing situations, we are experiencing art to the fullest.

FOR FURTHER REFLECTION

We construct our reality around our senses. We are also able to reconstruct reality through specific and precise sensory language—the language of verisimilitude. Stimulating as many of your readers' senses as possible in the process of telling a story helps readers to accept that story's reality.

............................TRY THIS....................................

Practice writing descriptions of objects using as many different kinds of sensory impressions as possible. Start by describing these objects in enough detail for them to come to life in the reader's mind.

- thick steaks broiling on a mesquite grill
- freshly baked pastries in a bakery window, from the viewpoint of a hungry, homeless person
- a forest path during or just after a rainstorm
- a dank, moldy cellar late at night

JULY 25
MEDIEVAL SETTINGS

The very mention of the word *medieval* invokes images of legends that combine spiritual quest with romantic adventure and knights and crusades. A great deal of modern fantasy writing is influenced by medieval lore and legends. It is an era infused by spirituality, as suggested not only by the Crusades and endless conflicts between religious sects, but by the prevalence of witchcraft, alchemy, and superstition.

Some mystery writers set their stories in the Middle Ages. One of the best-known is Ellis Peters, whose Brother Cadfael mysteries take us back to twelfth-century England during the reign of King Stephen. Notice how deftly Peters establishes the setting of her fifteenth Brother Cadfael novel, *The Confession of Brother Haluin*, in which the eponymous brother makes what he thinks is his deathbed confession of a terrible secret, but then does not die:

> The worst of the winter came early, that year of 1142. After the prolonged autumn of mild, moist, elegiac days, December came in with heavy skies and dark, brief days that sagged upon the rooftrees and lay like oppressive hands upon the heart. In the scriptorium there was barely light enough at noon to form the letters, and the colors could not be used with any certainty ...

FOR FURTHER REFLECTION
The medieval period offers writers a cornucopia of ideas for stories with settings that combine a variety of moods—spiritual, occult, fantastical—with intrigue, betrayal, and good old-fashioned murder and mayhem.

......................................TRY THIS....................................

1. Outline a mystery story set in a medieval monastery or convent.

2. Research the life of one of the saints, such as St. Clare of Assisi or St. Sebastian, and write an essay or short story in which he or she is the viewpoint character.

JULY 26
CULTIVATING MYSTERY

Even the most rational among us savor a moment of mystery now and then. Rationality and enchantment may be superficially at odds, but on a deeper level, there are commonalities. Consider astrology and astronomy: Both have evolved out of the sense of wonder we experienced by contemplating the stars. "What have the stars—the heavens—to do with us?" we asked. From ancient times through the Renaissance—that is, before the rise of modern empirical science—astrology provided answers: Certain configurations of planets and constellations signaled particular events on earth, anything from peace to disasters (literally "bad stars") and "star-crossed" romantic relationships. The reason astrology has persisted into the present day is that a part of us wants there to be some mysterious connection between the heavens and our mortal selves. Ironically, it is not the pseudoscience of astrology that provides evidence of such interconnectedness, but the "hard" science of astronomy. Astronomers have discovered that the chemicals comprising all life on earth were cooked inside first-generation giant stars that exploded and dispersed this heavier material, which eventually coalesced into second-generation stars like our sun. Carl Sagan put it most succinctly: "We are all star stuff."

Fiction writers should remind themselves that human nature is shaped by enchantment as well as reason. The pull of destiny, the experience of strangeness, the sense that supernatural forces govern our existence, the eternal struggle between good and evil, love and hatred underlie all great stories.

FOR FURTHER REFLECTION

The human condition is a synthesis of rationality and wonder, harsh reality and dreamlike enchantment. Fantasy stories, to ring true, usually posses elements of realism and inner logic. Realistic stories, similarly, possess elements that transcend rationality, such as spiritual or sinister undercurrents.

......................................TRY THIS....................................

Outline a mystery story that unfolds in a familiar setting like a college campus, factory, or golf course. Write about a night janitor in a computer-chip manufacturing facility, say—one who discovers a document, slated for the shredder but somehow misfiled, that hints at a plan to sabotage competing computer-chip manufacturers.

MODES OF STORYTELLING

"Modes" in this context refers to the vehicle that carries the story forward. Typically, it's a narrative unfolding in real time. But there are other modes that have proven to be effective conveyors of story. One is the letter. Entire novels have been fashioned out of letters (they're known as epistolary novels)—Samuel Richardson's *Clarissa* is an example; a more modern example is A.S. Byatt's *Possession*. Sometimes novelists will use the journal, diary, or notebook as the story vehicle. Daniel Defoe's *A Journal of the Plague Year* is an example. One of the most fascinating applications of the journal format is Daniel Keyes's *Flowers for Algernon*, in which the mentally retarded protagonist, Charlie, captures the progress of his rapidly developing intelligence, induced by an experimental drug, through the changes in Charlie's journal-writing style.

Another popular mode of storytelling is the frame-story mode, in which we get stories within stories. A good example of this is Emily Brontë's *Wuthering Heights*, in which the housekeeper Nelly tells the story of Catherine and Heathcliff to the lodger, Mr. Lockwood.

FOR FURTHER REFLECTION

The vehicle you choose for presenting your story will also suggest the manner in which story content is disclosed. Letters, diaries, journals and notebooks, logs, reports, uncovered lost manuscripts, and the mind itself as a sort of raw transcription of a character's mind (the so-called stream-of-consciousness narrative), all can serve as versatile story vehicles.

.....................................TRY THIS....................................

1. Develop a synopsis for a novel in letters or in a series of diary entries. The first step will be to create a slate of entries that would suggest a story progression.

2. Try your hand at writing a story in which the survivor of a natural disaster, like an earthquake, hurricane, or tsunami, tells the story of what happened to him. To enrich the plot, include a present danger that the survivor (and the person to whom the story is being told) must face.

PERFECTING READABILITY

Here is a simple bit of advice that will take you far: Work toward making your writing as easily readable as possible. Such advice is easy to misinterpret, however: What is meant by "easily"? The short answer is, using as few words as necessary, arranged in the most straightforward sentences that will communicate exactly what you want to say. If you use convoluted sentence structure and overinflated diction to convey a simple idea, readers will be annoyed and frustrated at not being able to process the writing quickly: You're demanding, in effect, that your readers spend more reading time than they need to, and readers do not like their time wasted.

"But what if my ideas are complicated?" you may ask. That's all the more reason to strive for readability. Even complicated ideas can be explained gracefully and clearly without sacrificing accuracy. On the other hand, you may need to spend more time explaining those complicated ideas—but that's a separate issue from writing style.

FOR FURTHER REFLECTION

It is hard to overestimate the importance of readability. Beginning writers sometimes assume for some strange reason that one's writing style should be complicated if the ideas being discussed are complicated. Quite the contrary; every writer's goal should be to do everything stylistically possible to convey complex ideas and situations clearly and straightforwardly.

......................................TRY THIS.....................................

Take a concept from a subject you have specialized knowledge in and explain it as simply and as clearly as you can to an audience of laypeople. For example, if you have some expertise in pottery making, write a page or two in which you explain the process of glazing. Be attentive to your word choice (especially jargon) and sentence structure. Define terms where necessary for this audience.

NATIVE AMERICAN SYMBOLISM

The traditions of the many Native American nations—Algonquin, Apache, Blackfoot, Cherokee, Cheyenne, Chippewa, Comanche, Hopi, Iroquois, Kiowa, Navajo, Seminole, Sioux, Zuñi, and dozens more—are rooted in spirituality and kinship with the natural world. One finds, not surprisingly, a wide range of religious symbols in the daily lives and rituals of these native peoples whose cultures and ways of life we have marginalized in the process of pursuing our manifest destiny directive (a symbolic system of a very different sort, inimical to any culture for whom the ownership of land, of "private property," had once been inconceivable).

In Native American cultures, the natural world and the spiritual world are inextricably intertwined. Eagle feathers embody flight; horses embody the life-force; bluffs and mounds symbolize gathering sites, hence togetherness, in both life and the afterlife.

FOR FURTHER REFLECTION

The beauty of Native American symbolism lies in the way it reflects spiritual connectedness with the natural world and the forces of nature. We find profound spirituality and reverence combined with earthy and sometimes fanciful poetry.

....TRY THIS...................................

1. Prepare one or more journal entries in which you describe the natural world as inhabited by spirits such as might be found in Native American legends.

2. Study the symbolism of one particular Native American nation, and write a story in the manner of a tale told in their tradition. For example, a Choctaw and Chickasaw story, "The Sacred Bluff," begins like this:

   > Long, long ago, the ancestors of the Indians lived in a distant country, far away to the northwest. They hunted game in the forests and built their towns on the river terraces where the floods could not reach them. ... But at last the time came when their fire was old and they could no longer live in that place. They must find a new country somewhere ...***

*** Plato, through the mouth of Socrates, refers to it explicitly as "a parable of education and ignorance" (W.H.D. Rouse's translation, *Great Dialogues of Plato*; NAL, 1956).

CONCEPTUAL BLOCKS

Conceptual blocks can be challenging because they demand extended time—and patience—reasoning out thorny problems in plot construction, character behavior, historical milieu, geographical knowledge, and botanical knowledge (e.g., the nature of regional habitats). The easy answer is do more research; but often the problem lies in what to research, what to extract from the research, and how to incorporate it into the story.

One way to overcome such conceptual blocks is to do research beyond the immediate scope of your subject. For example, if you're working on a mystery novel set in San Francisco after the Gold Rush, you may want to research, along with the low-life culture of the Barbary Coast (topless bars, gambling dens, and the like), the aristocratic culture of Nob Hill. Ideas begin to spark when surprising connections can be made between one set of circumstances and another.

FOR FURTHER REFLECTION

"Inability to write," Victoria Nelson reminds us in her book, *Writer's Block and How to Use It,* "means your unconscious self is vetoing the program of your conscious ego." In other words, there's something going on subconsciously that is telling you to expand or revise your original approach to your work in progress. If you're not writing, try listening to that inner voice, which may offer you important advice on something you've overlooked.

...................................TRY THIS...................................

The next time you feel the tug of uncertainty about where you're headed with your book or article, head for the library—your own or the public library. Begin by reading more about the history of your subject, even though you've researched it before. There are always new areas to explore with additional scrutiny. Keep an eye out for obscure facts, things you might have overlooked the first time around. Chances are, you'll find something useful and the writing should resume.

JULY 31
HARD WORK

How hard are you willing to work to achieve success as a writer? Before you can answer that, you need to know what "hard work" means in the context of authorship. It means spending hours at the keyboard framing or outlining an idea, creating detailed profiles of principal characters, and digging for background information (not just surfing the Net but talking to experts, reading specialized books and periodicals).

And then there's drafting: discovery draft, first draft, second draft, any number of additional drafts before the final draft; then comes the copyediting and proofreading. Knowing what kinds of work writers face, and a rough sense of the time it takes to do this work—anywhere from weeks for short pieces to two or three years (or longer) for books. Also, knowing that there is never any guarantee that you'll succeed with a project is important. Failure is always a real possibility. But just adopt George Bernard Shaw's attitude toward failure: "Nine out of ten things I did were failures," he confessed. "So I did ten times more work."

FOR FURTHER REFLECTION

When it comes to writer's work, think "labor of love": what better way to work hard than at that which nurtures the soul, fills our needs to express ourselves creatively, and offers the dual gift of entertainment and edification to the world?

...............................TRY THIS...............................

1. Jot down your reflections on writer's work—how you feel about the labor of inventing, drafting; the false starts, the revising and polishing, and the proofreading? Which tasks do you least enjoy and why?

2. After a month of steady writing, return to the reflections you recorded for number one. Has your attitude toward writer's work changed? What do you suppose accounts for it?

THE HERO'S JOURNEY

Part of what it means to be a hero, in the largest sense of the word, is the need to embark on a journey—a quest, an obstacle course, a descent into the maelstrom or the unknown to achieve an urgent goal—whether it is to find sufficient evidence to bring a serial killer to justice or to find an antidote for a mysterious plague.

In *The Hero With a Thousand Faces*, the mythologist Joseph Campbell identified three stages to the archetypal hero's journey:

- **Departure:** The hero-to-be receives a "calling" and embarks (sometimes reluctantly) on an adventure that, it is hoped, would benefit his people. A dragon, in effect, needs to be slain.

- **Initiation:** It's never easy for the hero-to-be, who must overcome many traps, enigmas, and whatnot to achieve victory. To become heroic, he must undergo a transformation of sorts. Think of Moses's transformation on Mt. Sinai.

- **Return:** Heroism means daring action for the sake of others; hence, the now-transformed hero-to-be, in order to become fully a hero, must return to the community in order to share the fruits of victory. Moses must share God's commandments with the people.

As you can see, the paradigm of the journey can serve as a template for storytelling of all kinds.

FOR FURTHER REFLECTION

A hero is one whose valor and deeds are extraordinary enough to be memorialized. The myths and legends of ancient cultures are mostly tales of heroic acts, and modern storytelling has evolved from them. Modern fictional heroes have their roots in these ancient tales.

....TRY THIS....................................

1. Prepare a synopsis of a short story organized into the three stages—departure, initiation, return—of the hero's journey.

2. Write a fantasy or real-world short story based on the synopsis you prepared for number one.

JACQUES-LOUIS DAVID: "THE DEATH OF SOCRATES"

The story, in Plato's dialogue *Phaedo*, of Socrates' decision to accept the Athenian court's sentence of execution (by drinking hemlock) rather than to renounce his teachings, is one of history's best-known examples of the triumph of individual integrity over unjust laws. The French Enlightenment painter Jacques-Louis David powerfully captures Socrates' resolve in one of his most renowned works. You may view the painting online via the Metropolitan Museum of Art Web site (www.metmuseum.org/works_of_art). David depicts Socrates as a great teacher, one who goes on teaching until the very end—indeed, who uses the circumstances of his death as a final lesson for his disciples.

FOR FURTHER REFLECTION

Writers are, in essence, teachers: Regardless of genre, they convey an angle of vision, an insight into life that illuminates some small corner of the human condition or the natural world. And Socrates is the quintessential teacher, not only because of his wisdom but because of his uncompromising integrity.

......................................TRY THIS...................................

Write a story or play in which you bring Socrates to life as a teacher. Before doing so, you may want to study Plato's dialogues (*Euthyphro*, *Apology*, *Crito*, *Phaedo*) covering Socrates' trial, in which he expounds on his idealist philosophy and his role as a teacher. You might even consider putting Socrates in the modern world, being tried in a modern court.

WINGING IT

Writers tend to be intuitive sorts. Yes, it's sensible to work with an outline or synopsis, especially for book-length projects, but sometimes too much planning ahead can impede output. If you find yourself plodding along or feeling that writing is more of a chore than an adventure, consider winging it, flying by the seat of your pants, putting yourself out on a limb, having faith in yourself.

We learn from our day jobs the importance of planning ahead, of keeping the risk factor at a minimum. With writing, as with most any kind of creative work, intuition and cautious planning ahead are often at odds. So much of creative writing involves spontaneous discovery and following one's hunches. Sure, we can fall flat, but part of the fun of writing is seeing where it all leads. The payoff quite often compensates for the setbacks.

FOR FURTHER REFLECTION

"Winging it" means taking flight from the tried and true, even if you're not sure where you're headed with the new idea. It means to explore new ways of telling a story, of turning a phrase. Keep in mind that readers are explorers too, and they will be delighted to embark on new narrative and verbal pathways.

......................................TRY THIS....................................

For the next few days, add "winging it" entries to your journal. These entries might be ideas for stories containing protagonists who are experts in fields you know little about—a county medical examiner, a circus acrobat, an FBI agent, an astronaut, an archaeologist with a deep knowledge of Egyptian hieroglyphics. Outline the story you'd like to write in each case, and then begin researching the area of expertise in each case. Once you decide to develop one of these stories, you'll need to commit to weeks of in-depth research (perhaps months if the story will be developed into a novel).

AUGUST 4
WRITING AND SPEAKING

It is important for writers to be mindful of how efficiently your readers can process meaning from your words, sentences, and paragraphs. Too many obscure words can disrupt a reader's emotional involvement. Long and complex sentences can cause readers to lose track of narrative progression. Rows of sentences constructed too similarly, or containing too many repeated words and phrases, will create a monotonous effect and lull your readers to sleep.

Because we speak more often than we write, we generally have a greater facility with spoken language. Paying closer attention to our speech habits can be helpful in conveying thoughts on paper more effectively. (See also the entry for July 12.)

FOR FURTHER REFLECTION

Our speech habits can serve as a reliable template for checking our writing habits until we gain more experience as writers. The more one writes, the more one develops an "ear" for the best word for the context, sentence rhythm, and texturing.

......................................TRY THIS....................................

Write a one-page mini essay describing a favorite travel destination. When finished, read the essay aloud in your normal conversational voice, ideally into a tape recorder so you can play it back and study it for stylistic rough spots. Keep tabs on the problems you find. A few days later, write another mini essay, and once again dictate it into your tape recorder to check for problems. Did fewer problems crop up this second time? If not, maintain the habit of writing and recording mini essays until you notice improvement.

AUGUST 5

INDISPENSABLE BOOKS FOR WRITERS: DRAMA

Aside from reading Shakespeare, few people read drama, but dramatic literature is every bit as rewarding as nondramatic. True, the character taglines can be somewhat annoying at first, but, as with reading subtitles in foreign-language films, it soon settles into a subconscious routine.

Modern plays that have earned their reputation as masterpieces of dramatic literature include the following:

- Anton Chekhov, *The Cherry Orchard*
- Henrik Ibsen, *A Doll's House*; *An Enemy of the People*
- Bertolt Brecht, *Mother Courage and Her Children*; *Life of Galileo*
- Arthur Miller, *Death of a Salesman*
- Samuel Beckett, *Waiting for Godot*
- Jean-Paul Sartre, *No Exit*
- Tennessee Williams, *The Glass Menagerie*; *A Streetcar Named Desire*
- Edward Albee, *Who's Afraid of Virginia Woolf?*
- Beth Henley, *Crimes of the Heart*
- David Mamet, *Glengarry Glen Ross*

FOR FURTHER REFLECTION

One of the pleasures of reading drama is that we can stage the play ourselves, in the theater of our own minds. Drama, in a sense, is distilled fiction: The characters must carry the story through dialogue and action, in relatively restricted settings.

................................TRY THIS................................

1. List your favorite plays—the ones you have seen produced on stage. Now read these plays. In your journal, describe what you've gained from reading the play that you didn't gain from seeing it performed.

2. Try your hand at writing a scene that could fit into one of the plays you've recently read and loved.

WRITING RITUALS

Think of a ritual as ceremonial preparation: patterned physical movements that enable us to enter a state of mind ideal for the experience we seek. Religious rituals, such as lighting candles or burning incense, help us to enter a sacred inner space as well as help consecrate an exterior space.

Writers, too, can benefit from rituals, so long as the rituals do not displace the writing! The proverbial sharpening of pencils and cleaning up the desk seem more like symptoms of obsessive-compulsive disorder and can displace valuable writing time; on the other hand, sharp pencils and neat desk space can facilitate the writing.

More productive writing rituals include jotting down ideas in your journal, going on walks to compensate for long hours of sitting, allotting time to read no matter how busy you are with other things, treating yourself to a gourmet dinner at a classy restaurant every time you finish a writing project.

FOR FURTHER REFLECTION

We are predisposed to ritualizing portions of our lives to help make our lives more meaningful, to dispel tediousness, to give us emotional ballast in order to get through the often difficult task of completing a story or essay or chapter of a book. Writing rituals are nearly as important as the writing they help bring to fruition.

......................................TRY THIS....................................

1. Make a list of your daily or weekly rituals, minor and major. Now select one or more of them and write an essay about their origins and why you continue to practice them.

2. Write an essay about the different kinds of writing rituals you and other writers adopt. Which are the most productive? The least productive?

STRUGGLE AND REWARD

Stories must contain conflict, we're always told, and that is true, but there are many kinds of conflict, from warfare to confrontation with natural forces to inner struggle with one's own clashing desires and ambitions. *Struggle* is an especially good word to keep in mind when planning a story; it suggests a valiant effort to endure adversity, to push one's goals forward, to confront daunting counterforces. *Struggle* speaks to the human resolve to triumph despite the obstacles, whether physical or psychological.

Struggle also implies a *sustained* effort to overcome opposition. In other words, a struggle that is too swiftly resolved will disappoint readers. And in order to convincingly sustain a struggle, the conflict has got to be formidable, even overwhelming at first. Formidable conflict, in turn, demands not just muscle to overcome it, but cleverness as well.

FOR FURTHER REFLECTION

The more arduous the struggle, the sweeter the reward—which is to say that when setting up a conflict situation, be sure not to let your protagonist reap her reward without a valiant struggle, one that includes dark moments and dead ends, moving relentlessly toward a climactic moment.

..................................TRY THIS....................................

Outline a story idea in terms of the struggle your viewpoint character must face in order to achieve her significant reward. The struggle should be daunting—and perhaps somewhere along the way seem insurmountable.

DETAILS AND EMOTIONS

When King Lear, holding his dead daughter, Cordelia, in his arms, wonders aloud, "Why should a dog, a horse, a rat have life and thou no breath at all?" it isn't necessary for Shakespeare to tell us that Lear is grief-stricken. In fact, if he did, we would accuse him of overdoing it. When it comes to eliciting certain emotional responses from the audience, the cardinal rule is let the facts speak for themselves.

Early in the last century, the poet-critic T.S. Eliot, in an essay on "Hamlet and His Problems," called attention to the correlation between a situation presented in a literary work and the emotional impact it can impart, so that the writer need not "spell it out" for the reader, which would be tantamount to explaining a joke. Eliot referred to it as the objective correlative—"a set of objects, a situation, a chain of events which shall be the formula of that particular emotion, such as that when the external facts, which must terminate in sensory experience, are given, the emotion is immediately evoked."

FOR FURTHER REFLECTION
Instead of hitting your readers over the head with explicit descriptions of emotional reactions ("Tears poured from her face and dripped onto the floor as Jane watched her eldest son sail off to war"), it is more effective to allude to the emotion indirectly ("Jane dug her nails into her arm as she watched her son board the battleship").

......................................TRY THIS...................................

1. Write a scene in which you convey your main character's emotions indirectly through dialogue or action rather than through explicit description of the emotional response.

2. Describe a landscape in a way that generates a feeling of bleakness or sublimity, without resorting to words like "bleak" or "sublime."

THE OPENING SENTENCE

Many a writer finds herself stymied by the opening sentence: It's got to be perfect! Why? Because everything will build from this first sentence, right?

Wrong.

Oh, it's certainly possible that if you've worked out a detailed storyline before you've begun drafting that that might be the case. But even then, unanticipated twists and turns in plot or character development could radically alter those plans—and if you're hell-bent on "sticking to your outline" or refusing to give up a scrupulously planned opening sentence, then your story could suffer. Better to be flexible.

Approach every word, sentence, paragraph, page as contingent upon potentially numerous revisions over the weeks and months ahead.

FOR FURTHER REFLECTION

Writing down the first sentence can give one pause, understandably: What if that sentence starts you off on the wrong track? Well, writing is largely tentative, no matter how much preliminary planning you do. It is not uncommon for writers to complete an entire draft of a novel only to realize that they need to begin afresh. No matter how carefully you fashion that opening sentence, likelier than not, you'll be replacing it several times over.

...................................TRY THIS...................................

1. To demonstrate to yourself just how tentative opening sentences can be, write ten versions of an opening sentence to a story you've been planning to write. Rank them in order of effectiveness.

2. Write ten versions of an opening sentence to a story you've already begun or even finished.

DREAMS AND MAGIC

Magic and fantasy have always been important ingredients for storytelling, but these days they seem to be in especially high demand. Day-to-day reality can be tough-going: demands in the workplace, financial concerns, parenting and marital responsibilities, civic duties—these need to be offset by recreation and a little whimsy now and then. Good storytellers are always in demand because writers who can fulfill the desire to escape from the mundane into the magical are always in demand. Think of it: The stories you create are gateways to new realms of possibility for countless readers.

FOR FURTHER REFLECTION

Fantasy parts the curtains that daily life sometimes keeps drawn. When the imagination takes reign, the human spirit soars. Rationality is vital, no question, but it can also be oppressive. As a writer, you want always to keep a channel open to the possibility that "reality" may involve more than conventional rationality can accommodate. There is something to be said for acknowledging the role of mystery in our lives. It is clear that without mystery, art would be impoverished.

......................................TRY THIS....................................

Outline a story that centers on a particular kind of magic. For example, you might give the hero of your story the ability to levitate—but only in special circumstances (e.g., he has to enter a trance or waking dream state first). Work out a predicament whereby he must use his levitation powers to escape from an evil captor.

EXPERIENCE AND INSIGHT

An experience becomes valuable and worthy of being shared by milking it for its underlying wisdom. Oliver Wendell Holmes, Sr. writes that "A moment's insight is sometimes worth a life's experience." What is the point of having experiences if we don't learn from them? As writers, we need to probe the experiences we've already acquired—a process that requires some preparation. A good way to begin is first to identify the experiences and describe them in as much detail as possible. For example, you might recall a time in elementary school when you came face to face with the school bully. Unlike the other kids, you were determined not to be intimidated by him and wound up being popped in the nose. Most people would stop there, but because you're a writer you will add the following:

- a re-creation of the specific things said and actions taken that led to the confrontation

- a detailed description of the bully: What was he like in other situations? When did you first encounter him?

- what happened immediately after he rammed his fist into your face

- the long-term effects of the incident; e.g., the changes in the way you related to other kids and perhaps to teachers

And, most importantly:

- what the incident taught you about human nature

FOR FURTHER REFLECTION

Any experience is a learning experiences—some more than others, perhaps—but even minor experiences offer some insight into people or the world. A good writer considers the implications of any experience.

...................................TRY THIS...................................

1. In your journal, create two columns. In column A, list an experience; in column B, describe this experience in a sentence or two. On occasion, return to this entry and add details to it if you can.

2. Begin drafting a story around one of the experiences listed in number one and the lesson your main character has learned from it.

AUGUST 12
SELF-CRITIQUING YOUR DRAFTS

Writers almost always benefit from receiving detailed feedback from those whose judgment and objectivity they can trust. However, it isn't always easy to find such a reader. In that case, consider critiquing your own drafts. Be careful, though: Self-critiquing isn't as easy as it might seem. First of all, any draft you're going to self-critique should have had time to "cool." What will feel like a fine accomplishment as soon as you've finished may make you cringe a few weeks down the road. Second, you need to approach your draft as though you were an editor and ask, *Will my readers like this story? Is it innovative yet not too innovative? Is it the right length? Is the story both entertaining and edifying—i.e., does it convey a substantive theme or insight into human nature?*

FOR FURTHER REFLECTION

Self-critiquing is an important skill to master, but it takes time to perfect, so avoid being hasty. To be a good critic of your own work, you ought to have spent some time in workshop groups in order to acquire a set of critiquing strategies. One of the pitfalls of serving as your own critic, of course, is being too easy or too harsh, assuming either that editors are idiots or that you are wasting your time trying to write.

......................................TRY THIS....................................

Make two copies of one of your completed stories and give one copy to someone who can offer you reliable feedback. Use the other copy for your own critiquing. Now compare the two critiques to see if yours is as useful as that of your reader's.

REGIONAL FOODS

Integrating regional foods into a story helps establish authenticity. Readers enjoy learning about customs peculiar to different regions of the United States and other countries, and despite the homogenization of regional or ethnic foods, one can still experience different types of food or styles of cuisine in different parts of the country.

- blue crabs: Chesapeake Bay region
- lobster: Maine
- hominy: the deep South
- sourdough bread: San Francisco
- baking powder biscuits: Minnesota (thanks to Garrison Keillor for perpetuating this one!)
- chili: Texas (but folks in Ohio, especially Cincinnati, might protest)

FOR FURTHER REFLECTION

Foods capture the distinctive character of a region, a good reason for writers to do their share in emphasizing regionalism in their work whenever feasible. The United States has become so homogenized, thanks in part to restaurant-chain franchises and to mass-media advertising, that regional cuisine has sadly gone by the wayside. One must venture into rural areas or to historic villages (like the Shaker and Amish communities) to find region-specific cooking nowadays.

...................................TRY THIS....................................

1. Research the foods that traditionally have been linked to your region. If you live near a historic village, explore its own distinctive cuisine; purchase one of their cookbooks, if possible.

2. Write an essay on an unusual regional dish, based on the research you've conducted for number one.

SHAPING HISTORY

Joyce Carol Oates pointed out in her 1970 National Book Award acceptance speech for her novel *Them* that writers, in their struggle to make sense of the age in which they live, "are also creating it," are shaping history. What else, after all, is history if not *writing* about what has happened in the past? It's a sobering thought, is it not? All that we know of history we know because of writers making sense of past events. It also means that every new book about a historical event changes history to some degree, either by building upon it based on newly discovered artifacts or documents or by new interpretations of old artifacts and documents.

History, then, is what historians—i.e., scholars who research historical periods and then write books based on their research—make of it.

FOR FURTHER REFLECTION

All writers of nonfiction partake in the shaping of the history of their subject matter to some degree. An essay on the topic of zoos will inevitably add to the history of zoos, even if zoo history is not the principal topic. For example, if you're writing about improved containment areas for elephants, you are at least implicitly calling attention to less-than-satisfactory containment areas in the past.

......................................TRY THIS....................................

1. Prepare an outline for an article you would like to write. Include information about the history of your topic.

2. In your journal, reflect on the way the history of a subject you have some familiarity with has changed since you were a child. What, specifically, had contributed to the changes?

AUGUST 15
LETTERS TO THE EDITOR

Writing letters to the editor of your local newspaper is an excellent way to practice conveying your views on current issues succinctly and forcefully, not to mention quickly getting into print and being read by thousands of people. These days, though, you need to act quickly, on the same day as the article you're responding to, and by e-mail. But even before you begin writing, take some time to reflect on the news item. It might even be a good idea to take notes and do some book browsing or Web surfing to locate testimonials, statistics, or other ammunition you might want to allude to in your letter.

Even if your letters do not get selected for publication, the practice of commenting incisively on issues—of stating a clear point of view and supporting it as forcefully and as convincingly as you can, will prove intrinsically valuable.

FOR FURTHER REFLECTION

Writing letters is good practice for two reasons: It helps you to keep your audience firmly in mind, and it challenges you to articulate your thoughts concisely. Aside from letters to the editor (which really are open letters to the entire community), letters are addressed to one person, and being aware of that fact can imbue your writing with a degree of authenticity, in some cases of fervor and intimacy, that brings the writing to life.

......................................TRY THIS.....................................

Comb through the news section of this morning's newspaper and select an article that you agree or disagree with strongly. Write a letter to the editor, no longer than two hundred words, expressing your view. Give as much support to your assertions as you can within the length limit allotted.

CONNOTATIONS

Words not only possess standard definitions, they also can trigger predictable associations, or connotations, in readers' minds. Poets are especially sensitive to the possible connotations of words. Flowers—notably roses, lilies, daisies, daffodils, and sunflowers—possess highly connotative meanings that extend far beyond their botanical definitions, thanks in large part to poets. Consider the connotations of "sick" or "worm" or "secret" in William Blake's "The Sick Rose":

> O Rose thou art sick.
> The invisible worm
> That flies in the night,
> In the howling storm:
>
> Has found out thy bed
> Of crimson joy:
> And his dark secret love
> Does thy life destroy.

First, of course, we have the literal rose that is sick because it is being consumed by the parasitic worm. But the tone of the poem as a whole tells us that this poem is not a botanical treatise, but rather a chilling observation of human corruption resulting from sexual predation and its consequences.

FOR FURTHER REFLECTION

A given word can have both public as well as private connotations. *Home*, for example carries associations of comfort, security, warmth, and stability for a great many people. But it is also likely that for many others, home can carry more private associations—a place of confinement, let's say, or of provincialism. By being aware of the potential for private connotations of words, writers can generate layers of meaning to stories, and especially to poems.

......................................TRY THIS......................................

1. Read several poems by one or more of your favorite poets and focus mainly on those words that generate emotional associations for you. In your journal, describe these emotional associations.

2. Write a poem incorporating words that generate not only public connotations but private ones as well.

LISTENING TO GHOSTS

Literature is inhabited by ghosts of all kinds: not just ghosts that haunt houses and castles, but ghosts that haunt people's minds, ghosts that speak to us from the ruins of ancient civilizations. What we listen for are the sounds of history and legend emanating from what people who have lived centuries or even millennia ago have left behind.

Ghost hunting is serious business, even in this day and age—or maybe because of this day and age. People are inundated with the rational; they crave the unknown, the supernatural. People pay good money to tour haunted houses, like the Winchester Mystery House in San Jose, California—a house owned by the rifle baron's widow who feared ghosts so much she kept adding on extra rooms to her home to contain them. The house contains dozens of rooms that lead nowhere.

If you have a fondness for ghost lore, there are many areas to explore for story material. Seek out the mystery houses in your area; research the histories of homes of well-known persons that may have become public landmarks.

FOR FURTHER REFLECTION

You don't have to be a sorcerer or mystic to write a good ghost story—just imaginative. Assuming that ghosts are real, that they do indeed haunt houses or hotels or loiter around graveyards, what kinds of sounds would they make to call attention to themselves?

...................................TRY THIS...................................

1. Write a story about someone who has found a way to communicate with ghosts, or with a particular ghost who, let's say, is trapped inside a house that it really does not wish to haunt.

2. Write a poem or short story in which your speaker or narrator is a ghost.

AUGUST 18
EXTRAPOLATING

The fine art of extrapolation involves studying what has been happening in the past and using that trend to predict how the future might unfold. As you might guess, extrapolating is a science-fiction writer's stock-in-trade. When conjuring up a propulsion system that would permit interstellar travel, for example, a writer might extrapolate from propulsion systems already in existence or on the drawing boards. The writer would be obliged to factor in the far vaster distances involved, of course. How could a propulsion system, one at least theoretically possible today, be augmented to travel a thousand times faster (i.e., instead of ten miles per second, *ten thousand* miles per second—which would still amount to little more than 5 percent the speed of light)?

FOR FURTHER REFLECTION

A well-thought-out extrapolation will add plausibility to even the most far-out science fiction. Of course, one need not be a science-fiction writer to make good use of extrapolation skills. For example, if you write thrillers, you might conjure up clever new kinds of espionage gadgetry, as in the James Bond adventures.

..................................TRY THIS....................................

1. Develop an outline for a story set in the near or distant future in which you imagine objects and situations extrapolated from current ones. For example, imagine what computers will be like in the year 2075 and how society will have been affected by such machines.

2. If science fiction isn't your cup of Cardassian tea, develop an outline for a spy thriller in which brain-implant technology exists that enables mind reading or mind control.

AMNESIA TALES

Psychiatrists insist that long-term amnesia is a rarity, if even that. As Jonathan Lethem notes in his Introduction to *The Vintage Book of Amnesia*, a collection of stories an essays on the subject of memory loss, "Real, diagnosable amnesia ... is mostly just a rumor in the world"; yet the bookshelves are filled with novels about amnesia victims who typically regain consciousness (from an accident or traumatic experience) not knowing who they are and spend the rest of the story trying to put the fragments of flashbacks back together (with the help of friends and relatives they can't remember). These are marvelously entertaining stories—examples of what Lethem calls "literary amnesia," and so we're willing to suspend disbelief.

FOR FURTHER REFLECTION

Memory loss makes for intriguing storytelling. The device is somewhat over-exploited, but a fresh approach will always be welcomed. It's best to become familiar with as much "literary amnesia" storylines as possible; Lethem's *The Vintage Book of Amnesia*, with stories and essays by Martin Amis, Donald Barthelme, Philip K. Dick, Thomas M. Disch, Karen Joy Fowler, Shirley Jackson, Haruki Murakami, Oliver Sacks, Robert Sheckley, and Jonathan Lethem himself (among several others), is an ideal place to start. See also the entry for May 19.

...................................TRY THIS...................................

Outline a plot for an amnesia story, but look for opportunities to do something innovative. Maybe instead of your viewpoint character waking up and not knowing who or where he is, consider a situation in which he begins to experience memory loss gradually and inexorably, and struggles desperately to find the cause, and a remedy. Or perhaps your viewpoint character's original memory is being manipulated or replaced by someone else's ...

AUGUST 20
MOTIVES FOR WRONGDOING

When we think about motives, we tend to think about honorable ones—the desire to help the poor and oppressed, the desire to succeed, the desire to be the best there is at a certain sport or skill. But as writers, we need to think about the things that motivate the villainous. The implication here is simply that even the most dastardly human beings are still human beings. It is only natural for the public to portray terrorists, rapists, and murderers as subhuman, as mindless and heartless monsters, as *evil* (a word that tends to shut down the very possibility of in-depth understanding), but writers need to think more deeply about the forces that drive some persons to commit monstrous crimes. Literature is what it is, we might argue, because of the willingness of authors to penetrate beyond media-generated caricatures to arrive at a more truthful picture of human nature.

FOR FURTHER REFLECTION
Motives are rarely simple; they may have been shaped by many forces—physical disability, poor nutrition, parental abuse, isolation, brainwashing, drugs, psychological trauma, or a combination of things. Society, understandably, demonizes persons exhibiting criminal behavior—which is all the more reason why writers must probe more deeply. Human nature is all-too-easily caricatured, but caricatures tend to discourage truth-seeking.

...................................TRY THIS...................................

Develop a profile of a villain. Include both a superficial perception of this person along with an in-depth analysis of him. Include in your analysis information about the person's childhood and adolescent experiences, relationship with parents and siblings, schooling, and anything else that may have impacted his life.

ON INSIGHT

We gain insight into something or someone when we have discovered (or intuited) the causes underlying the manifest appearance or behavior. Clearly, writing is all about insight, gazing past the surfaces of reality to explore its underlying dynamics and to build stories around them.

Idealistic as it may sound, there needs to be a greater willingness to think insightfully and carefully—as opposed to thinking in a rapid "no-nonsense," "decisive" manner to meet the demands of a society driven by commerce. That is why books and in-depth commentary (as opposed to sound bites) are so necessary.

People may champion so-called bottom-line thinking as much as profit margins, but usually it's because our consumer society demands it. Job security is not easy to come by. Making ends meet, supporting a family, building a nest egg—these must come first. Yet the hunger for insight into the nature of things persists.

FOR FURTHER REFLECTION

Insights lead to ideas for poems, stories, essays. Can insight be trained, cultivated? Absolutely, but it takes time and determination. You need to *want* to deliberately improve your capacity for insightful thinking—and even more fundamentally, you need to be convinced that insightful thinking is crucial to the health of society.

...................................TRY THIS...................................

Over the next several weeks, develop a list of issues, culled from the news, that would benefit from insightful commentary—in other words, commentary that aims to prevent misconceptions and, in turn, prevent ill-will among disputing parties.

AUGUST 22
THOUGHTS ABOUT STORY PACING

An important part of the art of storytelling is pacing the story properly. You do not want story development to drag because of ponderous static reflection, background detail, or psychological probing; on the other hand, you do not want to hurry things along too quickly. Remember that readers want to experience the story world vicariously. A rushed plot will spoil the illusion of real life unfolding.

The best way to pace a story effectively is to study the plot progression of a master of suspense. Pay attention not only to the series of events that unfold in the story but the time it takes for each. You will note that some events take more time than others, depending on the role they play in the overall story, or in their complexity. Superficial as this sounds, it will also help to keep a record of the number of the pages the author devotes to each dramatic incident.

FOR FURTHER REFLECTION

Pacing is integral to plotting. Think of it as the heartbeat of storytelling. Action scenes increase the pacing; breath-catching intervals relax it. Such modulation of the story's rhythm adds pleasure to the reading experience.

....................................TRY THIS....................................

Check the draft of one of your recent stories for its pacing. Is there too much or too little dramatic tension? Too much or too little "relief" (to give your readers as well as your characters a breather)? Finally, revise the story to improve its pacing.

COMMON SENSE

Common sense has its ups and downs. Sometimes it offers the best solution to thorny problems; other times it tends to oversimplify and distort. Regardless of its shortcomings, though, common sense is good to exercise in everyday situations. One doesn't have to understand psychopathology, for example, to give comfort to a friend suffering from emotional distress. A few kind gestures—like taking the time to listen to what the distressed person has to say or letting the person know that her feelings and viewpoints are important—can work wonders.

Writers will find that drawing from common sense can be quite useful. When writing fiction or memoir, for example, showing characters tackling gritty life experiences in a down-to-earth way will add authenticity to the story.

FOR FURTHER REFLECTION
Practicality goes a long way in everyday life. Calling in a therapist or resorting to prescription drugs when a child misbehaves or has an emotional outburst may well be overkill. Sometimes the simpler solution—like confining the child to his room (and making sure the child understands the connection between bad behavior and the resulting punishment)—can be the most effective recourse. Similarly, with writing, simple and straightforward language will almost always be more effective than complex or embellished language.

. . . . TRY THIS . . . .

What are your practical, common-sense views of things? In your journal write a paragraph on any or all of the following topics:

- budgeting your expenses

- planning a vacation

- getting your children to make a habit of reading, studying, and being sensitive to the feelings of others

REALITY-IN-FANTASY

What makes fantasy such a popular genre? Why do so many readers love to escape into a land where magic is a fundamental reality and where witches and demons exist? One possible answer is that it fulfills a deep longing for supernatural forces, a universe in which the supernatural can somehow co-exist with the natural. And who can say with any final authority that they cannot? Recall Hamlet's famous lines to Horatio: "There are more things in heaven and earth, Horatio, than are dreamt of in your philosophy."

But for the fantasy world to seem authentic, it must possess an internal reality. Even magic, ironically, must be governed by consistent rules and regulations to be convincing; otherwise, any conflict situation could simply be dispelled by the wave of a wand.

FOR FURTHER REFLECTION

No matter how filled with wonders the natural world is, we wish to be able to transcend it, to embrace a reality that contains magic and supernatural beings. Fantasy is more than a place to escape to, however. It is a place we strive to incorporate into our lives, into the so-called real world.

......................................TRY THIS......................................

Outline a fantasy story set in the real world. Perhaps your hero is a magician who has been exiled from his world because he had misused his magical powers, and is forbidden to practice his magic here. Now conjure up a crisis that can only be solved with magic.

RENAISSANCE AND MODERN SETTINGS

The modern era is an extension of the Renaissance, the "rebirth" of philosophical inquiry, artistic expression, political and social advances that characterized ancient Greece. The Renaissance also marks the birth of modern scientific inquiry, when for the first time, experimental evidence developed to the point where it trumped revered authority. Such was Galileo's great legacy, whose simple demonstrations toppled nearly two thousand years of Aristotelian claims that had never been questioned simply because they were Aristotle's.

The Renaissance also marks the time of major religious reforms. It is the age in which Martin Luther nailed his *Ninety-Five Theses* on the church door in Wittenburg, giving birth to Protestantism; the age in which King Henry VIII created the (Anglican) Church of England. It is an age in which Galileo struggled to reconcile his extraordinary telescopic discoveries with his religious beliefs. These scenes of scientific discovery and religious reform (hence the term "Reformation" and its Catholic backlash, the "Counter-Reformation") have given the Renaissance its special character.

FOR FURTHER REFLECTION

The turbulent, spiritual landscapes of the half-millennium long modern era, which came into being in the latter half of the fifteenth century, is filled with potential story material—stories about the lives of the great painters and sculptors, the early scientists and political theorists. The greatest ones have been written about extensively, of course—Leonardo da Vinci, Galileo, Michelangelo, Machiavelli—but there are many more important individuals obscured by the shadows of these great men whose stories also deserve to be told.

......................................TRY THIS....................................

Conduct research into one or more of the lesser known philosophers, artists, scientists, or political theorists who lived during the Renaissance. Write a biographical essay about this person, targeted for young adults, perhaps.

AUGUST 26
THOUGHTS ON MAGIC

Love of magic seems to be a universal human attribute. A good stage magician can hold us enthralled for hours. But magic can refer to more than sleight of hand or sorcery; we also associate magic with celebrations and ceremonies, with certain holidays (the magic of Christmas; the sorcery of Halloween). Magic in this context suggests the inexplicable wonders our emotional and spiritual lives, wonders that transcend the rational and the everyday. These are wonders we do not *want* to be explained away.

Writers are dabblers in wonder, simply by virtue of transforming words into imaginary worlds. Writers imbue their characters with certain powers that make them fascinating—the ability to read lips, say, or to do complex mathematical calculations in their heads.

FOR FURTHER REFLECTION

Magic in varying degrees is elemental to all art. As writers, we ought to think about the ways in which magic might manifest itself in our fiction and poetry. Magic is not incompatible with reality; in fact, magic (say, in the form of strange discoveries, rare natural phenomena, serendipitous encounters) can add spice and wonder to reality.

......................................TRY THIS....................................

Compose a story steeped in gritty reality—a homeless person struggling to survive in Boston or Montreal during the winter, let's say. Inject an element of magic into that grim scenario. For example, have your homeless character discover, quite by accident, that she has the ability to predict which stocks are going to rise and fall the next day.

MOVING THE STORY FORWARD

An engaging story progresses steadily toward a central objective, despite the obstacles (conflict). Danger may lurk around every corner, intensifying to a fever pitch at times (we call this suspense—the greatest source of aesthetic pleasure in reading mystery, horror, and other genre fiction). Once the forward movement of the story is established, you can bring in backstory. Any time the plot progression goes slack, or doesn't seem to be heading anywhere, readers will become annoyed: It's a little like being awakened from an enchanting dream.

The prolific novelist William F. Nolan (*Helltracks*; *Logan's Run*) reminds fiction writers that "each scene or chapter must move our narrative forward along a rising arc of drama. Characterization and incident should always contribute to this forward movement."

FOR FURTHER REFLECTION

Stories must progress; that is, the plot unfolds in stages until it reaches a crisis moment when a showdown becomes inevitable. Our actual lives contain this kind of story progression, but usually the progression is spread over large spans of time and is frequently interrupted by irrelevant matters. In a work of fiction, on the other hand, the author "edits out" the gaps and irrelevancies.

....TRY THIS....................................

Write a story synopsis in which you set up strong "road blocks" (conflict situations) that threaten to keep your hero from reaching his goal. These conflict situations should be threatening enough to (a) create a real sense that all will be lost, and (b) keep your hero from achieving too quick or easy a victory.

AUGUST 28
FORMAL VS. INFORMAL STYLE

We adjust our manner of speaking depending on whom we're addressing. For example, we address our supervisors differently from the way we address our children; we use different levels of formality when addressing strangers or close friends. Writers, likewise, adjust their levels of formality depending on the audiences they're targeting.

Every social situation calls for a particular level of formality. In some cases, certain protocols of usage must be observed, as is the case when reporting to a teacher, to a commanding officer in the military, or to a head of state. Fiction writers need to be aware of such differing levels of usage: How people speak to one another depending upon their respective places in the social hierarchy contributes to the realism of a story.

FOR FURTHER REFLECTION

Think of language as a painter's palette, where different groups of pigments represent different types of language use or levels of formality. If you're writing a story about farmers interacting with other farmers, you will draw from one group of language pigments; if you're writing a story about evangelists, you will draw from another group of pigments. And if you happen to write a story about farmers interacting with evangelists, you'll find yourself mixing the pigments together.

......................................TRY THIS....................................

Write a short story in which the two principal characters are from different levels in the social hierarchy. For example, write a story about a dedicated piano teacher trying to work with a rebellious but brilliant student who learned much of his manner of speaking from the streets.

AUGUST 29
WORKING WITH RELIGIOUS SYMBOLISM

Symbols are embodiments of abstract concepts, of experiences too complex to describe easily. A symbol like the Egyptian ankh, for example, embodies life and vitality. In Taoism, the Yin Yang circle embodies the harmonious co-existence of opposites, like day and night, good and evil, life and death. Spin the Yin Yang and the opposite hemispheres meld together. One could write for hours on the subtleties represented by the Yin Yang; but the symbol itself conveys the idea in a nonverbal flash.

Writers of all genres use religious symbols to communicate complex ideas in a concrete way in the shortest possible space. Some of these symbols are ancient and pagan, like the ring, which symbolizes the cycle of life and death, of time, and of connectedness—for example, the ring as a link in a chain of events, or as a link between the human and the divine.

FOR FURTHER REFLECTION

A religious symbol concentrates many complex beliefs and associations into one concrete object of veneration, or icon. The experiences religious icons convey could (and do) fill whole books, which is why such symbols are so powerful. By tapping into religious symbols (ancient or modern), writers, in effect, tap into the belief systems of an entire people.

..................................TRY THIS....................................

Write a story in which the viewpoint character lives out the complex associations derived from a single religious symbol such as the Yin Yang circle, the Star of David, or Hinduism's dancing Shiva.

AUGUST 30
DEALING WITH FAMILY INTERFERENCE

Writers mostly work at home, and that can pose a problem, especially if the writer has children. To ensure against quarrels or having the kids or the spouse feel neglected, the writer in the family needs to negotiate (not mandate like some dictator) ground rules. Another approach is to open your study to the kids. Introduce them to your work, explain your project to them in ways they'll both understand and appreciate. You might even invite them to hang around and watch you working (about as unexciting as can be imagined for most children); it makes them feel more a part of you and gain more of an internal understanding of why you need to work uninterrupted. The opposite approach, making your study off limits, giving it the impression of being The Forbidden Zone, might prove just as effective superficially, but doesn't do much to foster family togetherness.

FOR FURTHER REFLECTION

Perhaps the best way to handle family interference is to let them interfere in the sense of making them feel welcome in your inner sanctum. There's a memorable photograph of JFK at work in the Oval Office with four-year-old John-John frolicking at his feet. Children can better intuit how best to behave around a working parent once they feel that they're included rather than excluded.

...................................TRY THIS....................................

Write a letter to your family—or to one person in your family—explaining why it is important that you are not disturbed while working. The explanation should be decisive yet still convey your love and caring.

CULTIVATING SELF-DISCIPLINE

Inspiration is a good feeling to have, no doubt about it, but relying on inspiration can do a writer in. Inspiration just doesn't happen often enough. Many prolific novelists are well aware that inspiration has more to do with what happens once the writing is underway than when it hasn't gotten off the ground. To write every day, you need self-discipline: the determination to be your own boss and to demand no less than your best effort. The writing you produce has a way of being its own source of inspiration; the act of writing itself inspires you to beget more writing.

Easier said than done, no question. How does one *attain* self-discipline? There are many ways: You can reward yourself every time you finish a page of writing, for example. Food is usually a good reward: Today's page, for example, might be your ticket to a coffee break, or to lunch. Another strategy is to promise your significant other that you will show him or her your day's output. Sometimes, though, you just have to swim upstream: You drag yourself to the keyboard whether you want to or not. Inevitably, the writing habit will take hold, and you'll become so absorbed in the story you're telling that your problem will be to know how to *stop* writing. Such a transformation could take anywhere from three weeks to a month, though. Be patient with yourself.

FOR FURTHER REFLECTION
The freedom of the writer brings with it the responsibility for self-discipline. That is why getting into the habit of writing is necessary. Writing then becomes not so much a product of discipline as a product of compulsion or need.

..................................TRY THIS....................................

1. Write a page on this topic: "Things that distract me from writing." For each distraction you mention, explain why it distracts you and what you might do to keep it from distracting you in the future.

2. Conduct a survey to determine how other writers practice self-discipline and what they consider to be their greatest distractions. Summarize your findings in an article.

ASTROLOGY AS ALLEGORY

Some may find it strange that in the twenty-first century, with four centuries of scientific understanding behind us, millions of people continue to follow their horoscopes, that astrological signs continue to be popular topics of conversation. However, recalling that astrology is rooted in ancient religion, we realize that astrology, for many, embodies the desire to believe that the universe is controlled by forces beyond rational understanding.

Astrological forecasts can serve as springboards for allegories for writers. For example, if the forecast for Capricorns happens to be, "Resist any business venture proposed by anyone who is a Gemini," you might plan an allegory in which your main character (say, one who embodies Vulnerability) falls into a trap by a scam artist (say, one who embodies Deception).

FOR FURTHER REFLECTION
Astrology is a kind of mythology for a world in which the supernatural has been driven out like the plague; yet despite (or perhaps because of) our technological culture, the hunger for spiritual experience remains as acute as ever.

...................................TRY THIS....................................

1. Begin work on a story that takes place in a universe where astrological forces are beyond dispute, where the movements of the stars and planets actually do govern people's lives. What would it be like to live in such a universe?

2. Read the astrological forecasts that appear in the daily newspaper (or in the daily tabloids). Select an especially intriguing forecast for a particular sign, and build an allegorical short story around it.

GIORGIO DE CHIRICO: "ARIADNE"

One of the first "surrealists," artists who rejected so-called objective reality as the ultimate reality and instead sought a deeper sense of reality in the human imagination, Giorgio de Chirico drew heavily from dream symbolism and dreamlike juxtaposition of objects that, from a rational point of view, do not belong together, like trains and goddesses (in the shape of a reclining statue, no less). De Chirico challenges our conventional habits of association, not simply to make everyday objects seem strange but to remind us that human perception *constructs* nature, and doesn't passively and objectively record "things as they are." For us writers, this is a liberating revelation: It reminds us that we can creatively arrange the things of the world to suit our artistic purposes. You may view "Ariadne" and other de Chirico paintings via the Web site of the Metropolitan Museum of Art (www.metmuseum.org).

FOR FURTHER REFLECTION

Artists rationalize that reality is inevitably shaped by the order that we impose upon it, so why not allow our imaginations to impose order? There is something to be said, in other words, for the way in which the subconscious mind orders things. It may seem incoherent to the rational, waking mind, but that judgment is biased because we collectively privilege rational order over irrational. Surrealists were the first to challenge such determinism.

......................................TRY THIS......................................

In free-association mode, create a list of widely differing objects—the greater the differences the better. Now create scenarios in which some of these objects wind up together.

GROPING FORTH

There are times when it seems as if we're writing in the dark, groping our way forward, hands extended, trying to maintain some kind of equilibrium. What twists and turns do you want your characters to face in order to make your story "a page turner"? You might plan the big picture with relative ease, but the moment-by-moment progression can be vexing. Trust your spontaneity! It may be hit-and-miss, but so what? Being a writer means learning to feel comfortable with such tentativeness. Be patient; there's no rush! Stories can be frustratingly slow to materialize, and there will be false starts. The greater your persistence, the better you'll get at it.

FOR FURTHER REFLECTION

Being too cautious a plotter at the first-draft stage can rob your story of what might be called "creative surprise." Practice conjuring up unexpected twists and turns in the story you want to tell. Yes, there will be times when the ideas you discover as you go along will have to be tossed, but the brilliant flashes of insight you derive from spontaneity will more than compensate.

...................................TRY THIS...................................

As quickly as you can, churn out a synopsis of a mystery or psychological thriller. Once you conceive the basic idea (e.g., Jekyll and Hyde-type doctor stalks a former female patient whose life he saved), write without pausing to think out the plot twists and turns. You can always revise later; the point here is to trust your spontaneity to come up with unexpected twists that you might have missed had you been too careful too soon.

THE WRITER IN SOCIETY

What is the role of the writer in today's society? When you notice the thousands of titles on every imaginable subject filling a bookstore or library, it is apparent that nonfiction writers play a vital role in giving us in-depth information on current affairs, history, science, politics, business, philosophy, and the arts; that fiction writers probe the depths of the human heart through stories that illuminate and entertain; that poets capture subtleties of perception and phenomena that often escape the perceptions of most people. Writers, we might, say, comprise the collective mind of civilization in all its multicultural and multidisciplinary variations. And if that is true, we must all work together to keep the culture of books and reading alive and healthy, especially for younger generations for whom the attractions (or shall we say distractions?) of high technology—from video-phones to interactive videogames—are leading to serious declines in reading, according to recent studies conducted by the federal Education Department and the Labor Department.

FOR FURTHER REFLECTION

Writing helps make the complexities of society comprehensible and goes a long way toward heightening understanding of human nature, of tolerating and appreciating cultural differences. Writers can truly improve society by enabling people to experience vicariously (and thereby gaining deeper understanding of) those areas of human experience that would otherwise be alien to them.

.................................TRY THIS....................................

1. Each time you finish reading a novel, biography, work of history or current affairs, write a journal entry explaining how the book has changed your understanding of society.

2. Research the life and times of one of your favorite authors; then, write an essay in which you reflect on the ways that author's works influenced his or her society. An obvious example would be Harriet Beecher Stowe. "So you're the little woman who wrote the book that started this great war," Abraham Lincoln supposedly said to the author of the antislavery novel, *Uncle Tom's Cabin*.

SEPTEMBER 5
ON LITERATURE

Literature is writing that remains in the public consciousness, works that continue to be taught in schools generation after generation, works that do not go out of print. Relatively few works acquire the status of literature, although some works are forgotten and then rediscovered.

The word *literature* can be off-putting to some, and that's a shame. The greatest pleasures experienced by the imagination come from books of all kinds. Teachers from the earliest grades through college, and in all liberal arts disciplines, should always look for opportunities to remind students of the intrinsic value of reading, and maybe not lean too heavily on the word *literature*, with its implications of suffering through thick centuries-old tomes without adequate preparation.

If only all students could experience, at least once, the intense pleasure of reading books that poet-memoirist Melissa Green experienced as a child. As she writes in the preface to her memoir, *Color Is the Suffering of Light*,

> I fell in love with the language of books because it was won-drous, thrilling, tactile, alive; words had texture, shape, color, taste, dimension, weight, each like a sweet in my mouth. ... Words that were spoken at home were flat, judgmental, punitive, and cruel. I was amazed that language had such power.

FOR FURTHER REFLECTION

An endearing term for those who love it, *literature* can intimidate those who do not. If you are a parent or a teacher, one of the greatest gifts you can bestow upon children is the love of reading—more specifically, the love of reading *books*, for books are a physical embodiment of that love; they serve as a steady beacon from their bookshelf perches to remind everyone of the supreme importance of literature in our culture.

.....................................TRY THIS.....................................

1. Compose a short autobiographical sketch in which you describe your experience with literature over the years.

2. If you are a teacher, write an essay on how you help your students acquire the love of reading. If you are not a teacher, what strategies might you use if you were?

TALKING IT OUT

Writing gurus will sometimes advise you to refrain from talking out a story idea for fear that doing so will dissipate your enthusiasm for writing it. That might be the case if you haven't put anything down on paper, but if you have, and haven't fully worked out the story details, then talking it out might prove to be a prudent step. We are much more adept at translating thoughts into speech because events in our daily lives require it. Hence, if you were to talk out your story idea, you would probably find yourself conjuring up ideas on the spot more readily than if you were writing them down. And because conversation is about receiving as much as giving, comments that others make will inevitably spark additional ideas.

If you feel comfortable talking out your ideas, then consider using a tape recorder. Some writers will orally transmit only an outline or synopsis of their work in progress; others will "talk out" a rough draft from scratch, inventing as they go along. Still others will produce a detailed first draft, working from a skeletal draft or outline. If you're unsure how a tape recorder will best serve your needs, spend a week experimenting.

FOR FURTHER REFLECTION
Spontaneity goes a long way, and by talking out your ideas, you are engaging your innate ability to generate story content spontaneously. The experience can be exhilarating: We can amaze ourselves by how inventive we can be "off the cuff." And if you engage in this spontaneous oral invention frequently, you will become even more adept at it.

......................................TRY THIS....................................

Share your embryonic story idea with a relative or friend, encouraging her to ask questions or request elaboration or clarification. Keep pencil and paper handy!

STORY-BUILDING DIALOGUE

Dialogue not only brings your characters to life, it can effectively develop the story framework and convey important background information without interrupting story progression. To write authentic dialogue, you need to pay close attention to the way different people speak, to your own habits of speech, as well as to the way in which fiction writers handle dialogue. Consider this famous dialogue exchange between Desdemona and her husband, Othello, who has grown suspicious of his wife's fidelity, thanks to Iago's sinister machinations:

> Othello: ... Swear thou art honest.
> Desdemona: Heaven doth truly know it.
> Othello: Heaven truly knows that thou are false as hell.
> Desdemona: To whom, my lord? with whom? how am I false?
> Othello: O Desdemona! away! away! away!
>
> —IV.2

FOR FURTHER REFLECTION

As you build conflict between characters, you are automatically building story conflict. Sometimes character-based conflict is all that is necessary; other times, it is the means to an end. For example, if your villain has planted a bomb in a large metropolitan area, your hero will likely want to find a way, through conversation, to get the villain to disclose the bomb's location.

...................................TRY THIS...................................

Write a scene in which dialogue between two or more characters moves the story forward in a distinct fashion. For example, show the hero attempting to get the villain to reveal where he has hidden the kidnapped president of a country in order to extort a billion dollars from that country.

HANDLING PERSPECTIVE

The next time you watch an Alfred Hitchcock film, pay attention to the camera angles. You'll notice that to heighten suspense, the camera will look upward, as if to enhance the feeling of vulnerability. In *Vertigo*, the Jimmy Stewart character's acrophobia is made real to us by shooting climbing scenes from a downward angle, thus accentuating the distance from the ground.

Writers, too, can emphasize perspective by describing things from a great distance or by describing the angle of ascent, as in a mountain climbing scene. In *2001: A Space Odyssey*, Stanley Kubrick, director and co-screenwriter (with Arthur C. Clarke), emphasized the relativity of motion by switching frames of reference—e.g., a rapidly moving mother ship from the viewpoint of the seemingly motionless shuttle; a rapidly moving shuttle from the point of view of the seemingly motionless mother ship. In relativity, both are correct: All that matters is which frame of reference the viewer chooses.

FOR FURTHER REFLECTION

Description can capture the cinematic effects of perspective by calling attention to height, to distance, to the uncertainty of what lies ahead, or above, or below. The writer has the freedom to select any frame of reference as the preferred point of view, and to shift it whenever he deems necessary, as when a shift from one character's point of view to the next is called for.

....TRY THIS....................................

1. Write a short-short story from the point of view of an onlooker, someone who has an opportunity to observe the main characters closely without actually participating in their drama.

2. After completing the short-short story exercise in number one, retell the same story, only this time from the point of view of one of the principal characters.

MISTAKES

It's a fact of life: We learn from our mistakes, and it's no different for writers. The trick is to be able to recognize mistakes, be they relatively minor or superficial ones like awkward or unclear sentences, or more substantive mistakes like inconsistent characterization or incoherent plot progression. "My pencils outlast their erasers," observes Vladimir Nabokov. Such a confession from one of the greatest novelists of the twentieth century should reassure any writer that mistakes always occur, and they occur often.

It is by way of revision that writers are best able to recognize their mistakes. When finishing a draft, it makes sense to shift focus to another project than to plunge immediately into a revision. That way, you gain the necessary critical distance you need to see mistakes more clearly.

FOR FURTHER REFLECTION

We not only learn from our mistakes, we learn deeply from them. Making mistakes is inevitable in writing simply because writing represents complex, multilayered thinking. Also, with large projects, it's easy to keep track of subplots, character descriptions and actions, and the like. One needs to set aside large chunks of time to check for such inconsistencies.

...................................TRY THIS...................................

As you revise a draft, keep a list of the mistakes you catch—"mistakes" being insufficient attention to detail, faulty story progression, inconsistent description of events and characters, undesired repetition. Such itemization will help you identify mistakes in future drafts.

TRICKSTER FIGURES

Call them what you will—tricksters, jokers, gadflies, clowns, fools, court jesters—trickster figures add the spice of life to stories and plays. They have all sorts of roles to play: Some tricksters (like the clowns and fools that populate Shakespeare's plays) serve as the alter-ego of the monarch; others are mischievous, monkey-wrenching the order of things—bad news for the protagonist, who must outfox the trickster in order to reach his goal; good news for the story itself, which would not be much of a story if no one came along to make things difficult.

Tricksters need not be purely villainous; in fact, many, like Batman's nemesis, the Joker, or the Jim Carrey character in *The Mask*, are full of mischief and downright craziness.

Trickster figures appear in all cultures and have their roots in ancient religion and folklore. Joseph Campbell, in *The Hero With a Thousand Faces*, talks about the Yoruba (West African) trickster god, who personified the center of the world (i.e., the world's navel), and appears to different people in different guises, thus triggering a battle.

FOR FURTHER REFLECTION

Tricksters abound in literature and folklore as impish characters. They can be gods, demigods, jesters—in general, all-around pains in the posterior. In serious works, they serve to break through the façade of propriety to speak bluntly. Even then, they add a kind of lightheartedness and comic relief to stories.

....TRY THIS.................................

Write a synopsis for a story that includes one of the following trickster figures:

- a god in disguise

- a clown who sheds candid insights into situations perpetrated by the foolhardy but tyrannical king

- a con artist who attempts to use his guile to overthrow the monarchy

EMPATHY

Whether we write fiction, histories, exposés, treatises, or biographies, we are writing mostly about people. Even popular science writing places the scientists as much in the limelight as the science. Readers want to enter the minds and hearts of those whose works change the world for better or worse. They want to be able to *empathize* with them, to tap into their psyches and (perhaps on a less than fully conscious level) seek out the similarities and differences between such individuals and themselves.

The capacity to empathize with others goes a long way. First of all, the urge to find out "what makes 'em tick" adds fuel to the months and even years of researching and interviewing that may be needed. The more you learn about a person, the more your capacity for empathizing will become. You begin to pick up things between the lines so to speak; you begin to intuit things.

FOR FURTHER REFLECTION

Empathy—what former President Bill Clinton seems to possess to a high degree ("I feel your pain")—is as much a valuable attribute for writers as it is for world leaders. Can it be learned? Yes, but it takes a great deal of willingness to share experiences—disturbing and painful experiences sometimes. Perhaps one of the reasons why so many artists go off the deep end is that they have cultivated too much empathy. If you find yourself tapping too deeply into someone's experiences, back away.

....................................TRY THIS....................................

Write a series of journal entries that chronicle your efforts to empathize with others' emotional difficulties—a friend who has just broken up a romantic relationship; a relative struggling with the death of a dear friend; a co-worker who has just been handed a pink slip. In your entries, imagine yourself in that other person's shoes. This exercise will help you create realistic characters in the future.

SETTING UP AN E-FEEDBACK GROUP

It's great to be part of a writer's group in which you offer feedback on your fellow writers' drafts as well as receive feedback on your own drafts. But because of people's hectic schedules, it isn't easy to meet on a regular basis. E-mail to the rescue. Many writers are thankful for the Internet and e-mail because of the ease with which it permits rapid communication to anyone, anywhere. In a matter of minutes, instead of days or weeks, you can get feedback on a draft in progress via e-mail.

Of course, like any other system, e-feedback has its limitations. Being physically present when giving and receiving feedback adds a social dimension to the experience; it can make the feedback easier to assimilate. The social interaction makes the critiquing more enjoyable.

FOR FURTHER REFLECTION

The advantages of e-mail feedback outweigh the disadvantages, especially if writers live too far apart from each other, making get-togethers too time-consuming. But if e-feedback groups are going to work, they must follow certain rules of courtesy, privacy, frequency, and the like.

......................................TRY THIS...................................

Set up an e-feedback group with three or four other writers. Before giving each other feedback on drafts, however, decide on some ground rules: Who gets critiqued when? How frequently should the group interact? How many feedback exchanges per draft should there be?

SEPTEMBER 13
BIZARRE FOODS AND BEVERAGES

If you're a *Star Trek* fan, you know about Romulan ale and Klingon blood wine, and many other bizarre concoctions served in Ten Forward. Starfleet crew also chill out with a glass of synthehol—a nonalcoholic beverage that mimics the effects of alcohol but not its negative effects, including hangovers. (By the way, you can actually purchase some of these beverages in the Star Trek Experience gift shop at the Las Vegas Hilton.) In Frank Herbert's classic, *Dune*, the chief export of the planet Arrakis (Dune) is a spice that imparts supernatural powers when ingested, but is dangerously addictive. And thanks to J.K. Rowling's Harry Potter series, you can feast on weird-flavored jelly beans and chocolate frogs.

If you're a writer of fantasy or science fiction, think about extending your inventiveness with culinary possibilities. Margaret Atwood does so with great satiric effect in *Oryx and Crake*—a story about survival in a world destroyed by bioengineering gone wild.

FOR FURTHER REFLECTION
Writers working in all genres can instill both whimsy and realism into their stories with imaginary foods and beverages. They need not be invented from scratch, however. For example, you can give "steak" a new spin by having it come from dinosaur-like creatures—or from dinosaurs themselves if your characters travel back to the Jurassic Era.

...............................TRY THIS...................................

1. Develop a mini-cookbook consisting of imaginary foods and beverages.

2. Write a story in which you incorporate some of the foods and beverages you've invented for number one.

THE ART OF IN-DEPTH RESEARCH

Researching a topic involves a lot more than scooping up facts and figures off the Internet—although Internet research can be a good starting point. Most of the information you'll need to unearth will come from what are referred to as primary sources: original documents such as contracts, correspondence, diaries and notebooks, deeds, depositions, trial transcripts, as well as from the testimonies of experts, obtained through interviews. Such in-depth research can take years, so it is important to have a clear plan of what it is you wish to research, where you must go to access the necessary materials, and how you wish to incorporate your findings into your book. Even in the Internet Age, writers must plan to travel to specific libraries, museums, and other institutions where the materials are archived, since these documents seldom are digitized.

FOR FURTHER REFLECTION

"Sleuthing" is a favorite metaphor for in-depth researchers. The allusion to detective work is not inaccurate: Many researchers must probe with great persistence and ingenuity into obscure corners to locate important information. Yes, it can be time consuming and frustrating, but it can also be an adventure.

......................................TRY THIS....................................

Go on a sleuthing adventure in order to obtain little-known information for an article on a topic that requires examining primary-source materials. For example, if you wish to write an article about the private life of a war hero who grew up in your community, you will need to access that person's military record, personal correspondence, notebooks, public school and college records, and so on. Be sure to take detailed notes.

JOURNAL WRITING AND THE TRIUMPH OF INDIVIDUAL THOUGHT

In the opening chapter of *1984*, Orwell's masterpiece of individual rebellion in a society that strives to crush individualism, the protagonist Winston Smith attempts one of the most daring acts imaginable: He dares to write down his thoughts, barely out of telescreen range, in a blank journal he had just purchased on the black market …

> He dipped his pen into the ink and then faltered for just a second. A tremor had gone through his bowels. To mark the paper was the decisive act. … For whom, it suddenly occurred to him to wonder, was he writing this diary? For the future, for the unborn. … For some time he sat gazing stupidly at the paper. … It was curious that he seemed not merely to have lost the power of expressing himself, but even to have forgotten what it was that he had originally intended to say. For weeks past he had been making ready for this moment … Suddenly he began writing in sheer panic.

After having scribbled down mundane events such as the war newsreels he'd recently seen, and then turning his attention to the Two Minutes' Hate on the telescreen, Winston again picks up his pen and this time he finds himself printing in all capital letters, "DOWN WITH BIG BROTHER" over and over.

FOR FURTHER REFLECTION

The act of writing is a triumph of individuality, a celebration of our most precious asset: the freedom to think for ourselves, to assert our views about any topic no matter how disapproving society will be of them.

......................................TRY THIS....................................

Spend the next week or so writing down your most audacious thoughts; the more unacceptable you think they are, the better. Whether you ever find use for these thoughts is beside the point. The point here is to exercise the freedom you have to write whatever you wish.

USING STRONG VERBS

When it comes to powering up a sentence and moving a story forward, verbs can prove to be either lazy mules or thoroughbred racehorses. Consider, for example, the following sluggish sentence:

> Margaret had a strong suspicion that she was being followed.

It's the noun phrase "a strong suspicion" that suggests the action rather than the puny auxiliary verb, "had." But strong "racehorse" verb phrases are much better suited for the job:

> Margaret *strongly suspected* that she was being followed.

For some reason, noun phrases seem more impressive to novice writers—perhaps because they sound more "official," or simply generate more words, thereby sounding more authoritative. As a result, they may clog their narratives with lazy mules like these:

> Tony's final assessment of the committee's report was that it would be beneficial if it underwent another revision.

One has to read through that officialese (as it's sometimes called) several times to get at the meaning; but turn the sluggish nouns into strong verbs and the meaning gallops through:

> Tony concluded that another revision would improve the committee's report.

FOR FURTHER REFLECTION

Sentences that employ strong verbs achieve three goals at once: They improve clarity, enhance readability, and inject more energy into the writing. It takes a while to develop a knack for using strong, lively verbs, however.

......................................TRY THIS....................................

Pull out an old story or essay and scrutinize it for its use of verb phrases. Where sluggish noun phrases predominate, revise by turning them into verb phrases.

ON SILENCE

Silence, as we learned from a Simon and Garfunkel folksong, is a sound. Silence is also palpable—it can be felt. Most of all, silence is a special space a writer can enter and either meditate or dance around in. Silence is "the nothing that is," as mathematician Robert Kaplan describes the zero. "For zero," Kaplan writes, "brings into focus the great, organic sprawl of mathematics, and mathematics in turn the complex nature of things." Silence, too, brings into focus the complex nature of things. Silence marks the beginning and the end of sounds, gives shape to rhythm and meter in poetry and song.

FOR FURTHER REFLECTION

There are different kinds and degrees of silence, ranging from the semisilence of a town at night, with only the sound of a breeze or the occasional distant barking of a dog, to the silence that follows a loud and steady sound, to the silence that follows a shocking discovery or remark as one might encounter in a film or stage play. Then there's the reverential silence one encounters inside a church or mosque, and finally, much less common than the other silences, the total silence of, say, the interior of a desert or a cave, where the only thing you can hear is the sound of your own breathing. Any of these silences are conducive to deep meditation.

......................................TRY THIS....................................

Write an essay on the different kinds or degrees of silence as you have experienced them. Along the way, reflect on the importance of silence, and where one might journey to seek out the best kinds.

QUESTIONS AND QUESTS

It is no accident that *question* and *quest* are etymologically linked. By asking questions we embark on a journey of knowledge. The questioning quest is never-ending, because the more we search for answers, the more we find ourselves posing new questions. The legend of Faust reminds us that the desire to know everything takes us out of the role of humanity altogether and turns us into demigods willing to sacrifice our souls for omniscience. But the desire to continue our knowledge quest is not Faustian; it is supremely humanistic. Were it not for that undying quest, we would still be foraging for berries and huddling in caves.

Writing is a quest. We write to create new ways of understanding human nature and human society. We write to teach others what we learn from our personal quests. Writers are archetypal heroes who venture apart from their fellow human beings to discover new truths and then return to the fold to share their discoveries.

FOR FURTHER REFLECTION

Life can be described as a multiplicity of quests—perhaps leading toward one supreme quest. In any case, every time we begin a new writing project, we embark on a new quest to uncover a new set of perplexities about the human condition and to articulate them in sufficiently precise and powerful language.

................................TRY THIS..................................

Begin a new story or poem, but think of the work as a quest to discover something important about people or about the state of the world. Divide the work into the archetypal stages of separation, initiation (or discovery) and return. (See also the entry for August 1.)

DANGEROUS KEEPSAKES

Keepsakes are full of positive connotations: objects that rekindle happy memories of experiences and people we want to keep alive. But sometimes, a keepsake can have more complicated associations: a romantic relationship that had gone terribly wrong; a once-trusted friend whose words and deeds have grown sinister as a result of new disclosures; a potentially life-changing opportunity that had somehow slipped by.

Such keepsakes serve as effective prompts for stories. Invite a relative or friend to share her memories that a particular keepsake conjures up, and likelier than not, the stories will pour forth—not just wispy, nostalgic memories in the case of dangerous or disturbing keepsakes—but emotionally complex stories leading to other stories.

FOR FURTHER REFLECTION

Objects that conjure up negative experiences and moods can be just as valuable to a writer as those that conjure up positive experiences and moods. Think of Dorian Gray's portrait, from Oscar Wilde's novel, which becomes ever more hideous as the years go by, while Dorian himself remains unscarred by his vices and the passage of time.

...................................TRY THIS....................................

1. Make a list of keepsakes that generate complex associations for you. Beside each, write a sentence or two describing some of these associations.

2. Return to your list keepsakes (and its complex associations) prepared for number one and use it to outline a short story or personal-experience essay.

REKINDLING ENTHUSIASM

It's only human nature to lose enthusiasm for a writing project that initially excited you and motivated you to rush to the keyboard every morning. Perhaps you've encountered a snag in characterization or hit a road block in your attempt to obtain necessary background information. Or perhaps the writing task is more difficult and frustrating than you first imagined. Or initial feedback from readers may have been harsh. Other demands on your time may also be usurping your energy. First of all, try to pinpoint the problem. Writers sometimes have trouble rekindling enthusiasm because they cannot identify the source of the difficulty. Next, work out a strategy to help you overcome the difficulty.

One strategy might be to take some time to read what others have written on the subject. A fresh change on perspective can re-energize your own project quickly.

FOR FURTHER REFLECTION

Writing projects are often as difficult as they are exiting to pursue. One has to be ready to struggle with discouragement and loss of enthusiasm; these setbacks simply come with the territory. To prevent discouragement from becoming debilitating, writers resort to any of a number of motivation rekindlers, from taking a long walk to shifting to another writing task to treating oneself to a chocolate sundae.

...................................TRY THIS....................................

Set up a what-to-do-in-case-of-discouragement plan to keep working on your writing no matter what. Some things to include in your plan:

- A one-page explanation of your reasons for embarking on the project and why you think it's a worthy project. Reminding yourself of your original goals and reasons will help you weather harsh criticism (including your own).

- A timeline for completing the project. Maybe you haven't allotted yourself enough time to do the necessary research and outlining of the project. If that's the case, simply extending your timeline could help get rid of the discouragement.

- An overview of the toughest parts of the project. Identifying them may help you grapple with them more successfully.

REFLECTIONS ON INTUITION

All artists need intuition to create; writers are no exception. To put it simply, being intuitive means being able to make good use of hunches, gut feelings—about the way people behave in certain situations. Intuition is generated when deep thinking is coupled with playfulness, a willingness to forget the rules and let your imagination lead the way. As Coleridge listens to a wind harp, which he describes, in "The Eolian Harp" as "a soft floating witchery of sound / As twilight Elfins make," he suddenly makes this intuitive leap:

> And what if all of animated nature
> Be but organic Harps diversely fram'd,
> That tremble into thought, as o'er them sweeps
> Plastic and vast, one intellectual breeze,
> At once the Soul of each, and God of all?

FOR FURTHER REFLECTION

Sometimes we get too close to a problem or concept we're trying to understand. Intuition will enable us to view it holistically, to help us get past the piecemeal trees in order to envision the entire forest. In this sense, intuition and creativity go hand in hand: the more adept we become at exercising our creative thinking through storytelling, poetic imagining, and essay writing, the likelier our intuitive skills—our ability to see the big picture without resorting to conventional stages of reasoning—will serve us.

...................................TRY THIS...................................

1. Compose a poem in which you make at least one intuitive leap from the particular to the general—as Coleridge does in comparing a wind harp to all of nature.

2. Prepare a profile of a character who has powerful intuitive skills, and pit him against a character who lacks such skills.

TWISTS AND TURNS

An exciting story is one that gives readers a roller-coaster ride. The first shocking "plunge" into the story serves to hook the reader; each sharp twist and loop and dip compounds the excitement and builds anticipation for what will come next.

Readers, like roller-coaster riders, love the twists and turns. A story, after all, is a kind of thrill ride. The action does not have to include scaling mountainsides or swimming through shark-infested waters; a domestic or psychological drama can have its twists and turns too: unexpected revelations that resolve crises hitherto considered unresolvable.

FOR FURTHER REFLECTION

Stories are most enjoyable not only when their outcomes are unpredictable but when the narrative path contains unpredictable twists and turns as well. Readers expect to encounter surprises—unpleasant as well as pleasant—along the path toward a climactic revelation. Imagine how much less enjoyable *The Wizard of Oz* would be if Dorothy did not encounter anyone (let alone the likes of the Scarecrow, the Tin Man, and the Cowardly Lion—or, for that matter, the Wicked Witch of the West) along the Yellow Brick Road leading to the climactic revelations before the Wizard.

...................................TRY THIS...................................

In your journal, outline a story, giving special attention to twists and turns—to unexpected disclosures or incidents. Err on the side of excess here: Journal writing, remember, is for discovery and practice, to get the feel of what it's like (in this case) to plot a story that will keep the reader glued to the page.

SEPTEMBER 23
"KNOW THYSELF"

These words mark the beginning of wisdom. Without self-knowledge, without insight into our needs and interests, our temperaments, our strengths and shortcomings, we will stumble about uncertain as to which paths to pursue. Of course, the pursuit of self-knowledge is a task in itself, involving much exploration and testing. Even limited to the writing profession, it may take awhile to determine what kinds of writing we would enjoy most and be most skillful in pursuing.

Self-knowledge is two kinds. One is "soul searching"—not necessarily a spiritual exercise, although it could be practiced as such. Usually, it simply means meditating deeply on the nature and causes of our thoughts and actions. Another kind of self-knowledge involves applying what we have learned about the human mind—either from books and courses or from a therapist.

"Gain better self-knowledge" should be part of every writer's mission statement because the better we know ourselves the better we can understand the motives and actions of the characters we put into our stories.

FOR FURTHER REFLECTION

Knowing oneself may be the most difficult knowledge-acquisition challenge of all. Where to begin? What are we really looking for? What do we do with the knowledge when we find it? Psychologists point out that merely acknowledging an impulse ("Yes, I'm aware of the fact that I harbor a great deal of hostility from my job and look for ways to vent that hostility") is a major step toward controlling it.

...................................TRY THIS....................................

Prepare a journal entry in which you describe some of the things you don't know, or know very little, about yourself. For example, are you uncertain about how you would perform in a stage play? Have you ever decided not to participate in an activity simply because you had no idea if you could handle the task?

SEPTEMBER 24
ON EVIDENCE

Everyone has opinions; not nearly as many have sufficient evidence to make their opinions pass muster, to be reinforced by evidence, to stand up against counter-arguments. Science has triumphed because its very foundation rests upon such testing—through laboratory demonstration, through mathematical modeling, through an ongoing effort to prove its assertions *wrong* (the falsification principle). During the Renaissance, modern science developed when empirical evidence replaced authorial decree. No one had questioned Aristotle's claim, for example, that heavier objects fell faster than lighter ones until, nearly two thousand years later, Galileo proved it with his famous experiment.

Evidence plays a fundamental role in all writing. In nonfiction, of course, assertions must be backed by reliable data, testimony, analysis; they must weather counterarguments. Evidence also plays a role in fiction. If you're writing a political thriller, for example, and part of the drama is played out in the Pentagon, you will need to "prove" to your readers, by way of "inside" background information, that the setting is authentic.

FOR FURTHER REFLECTION

The truth is universally honored; yet many are not aware of the extent to which a claim must be backed by evidence before it can be accepted as truth. Moreover, as Carl Sagan once pointed out, "Extraordinary claims require extraordinary evidence." For example, if you're going to claim that you were visited by aliens, you had better come up with more than a photograph, which can be easily faked.

......................................TRY THIS....................................

1. Dramatize a scene in which a person who claims to be abducted by aliens tries to convince a scientist that his experience actually happened.

2. Write a story in which an evolutionary biologist tries to convince a creationist that human beings evolved from lower life forms; or, in which a creationist tries to convince an evolutionary biologist that human beings are not biologically linked to the rest of life on earth but were divinely created.

FASHIONING DREAMSCAPES

Sigmund Freud may have been the first person to demonstrate from a scientific perspective the importance of dreams in one's life as well as in society generally, but dreams have always played a significant role in human history. All of us can tap into the eerie, disorienting, phantasmagorical, yet somehow intensely real world of our dreams in order to re-create dreamscapes on paper.

When it comes to fashioning such dreamscapes for our stories and poems, artistry must oversee the otherwise rudderless, chaotic character of the dream vision. Thus, T.S. Eliot, in *The Waste Land*, in describing the Unreal City,

> Under the brown fog of a winter dawn,
> A crowd flowed over London Bridge ...
> `And each man fixed his eyes before his feet.
> Flowed up the hill and down King William Street,

creates the sensation of being in a dream, but also the sensation of witnessing disoriented, virtually disembodied, individuals cut off from one another.

FOR FURTHER REFLECTION

Dreams have profoundly influenced modern art and literature and continue to influence them. Poets, novelists, and memoirists should all be students of dreams. It isn't necessary to read Freud (although that would certainly help), but simply to pay close attention to the role that dreaming plays in our psychic lives.

......................................TRY THIS....................................

For the next couple of weeks, collect your dreams, or fragments of dreams, in your dream journal, if only to get the feel of capturing dream images in language. Later, shape these images into coherent stories.

SEPTEMBER 26
WRITING AS AN EXPRESSION OF FAITH

Artists are explorers of the inner universe, much the way that scientists (including psychologists) are explorers of the outer one—the universe that obeys external, natural laws. The inner universe, the one in which the human drama is played out, is the universe of ambitions and passions, loves and hatreds, adventures and mysteries, quests and rituals. It is like a witch's cauldron, this inner universe, bubbling over with so many ingredients that it defies understanding. Like other artists, writers tap into that cauldron and try to make artistic sense of some small portion of it. It is a supreme act of faith in the human condition. In *A Stay Against Confusion: Essays on Faith and Fiction*, novelist and essayist Ron Hansen talks about "faith-inspired fiction," which "squarely faces the imponderables of life" in the quest for the truth about the human condition. We might go one step further by saying that all writers, not just religious ones, are engaged in expressions of faith when they write stories that hope to shed light on that infinitely complex, turbulent inner universe.

FOR FURTHER REFLECTION

Think of the power that words possess: They can be molded into stories, poems, plays, biographies; they can become histories and explanations of the most complex scientific and philosophical concepts. We humans define ourselves as a species through language, which rests on the profound faith that words are windows to the truth of ourselves and the universe.

......................................TRY THIS.....................................

It has been suggested, among postmodern thinkers, that language doesn't really capture reality "out there," but only other language-constructions of reality, which include thought-constructs (thoughts being a kind of proto-language not yet shaped into writing). Write an essay in which you reflect on the truth of this claim.

SEPTEMBER 27
"ONCE UPON A TIME"

Who doesn't feel the tug of imaginative escape at the sight of those four magic words? With them, a child's mind shifts instantly from mundane reality to magical reality, the reality of the imagination in which anything becomes possible. We are prisoners of time and circumstance, which is why we hunger for stories. They give our imagination wings and remind us that a vast world of other times, other places, make up "reality."

It's not surprising that "once upon a time" conjures up fairy tales; that is how many of them begin. Fairy tales, being quintessential stories, should be read by all aspiring storytellers because their story properties are so easily discernable.

FOR FURTHER REFLECTION

"Once upon a time" transports us—adults and children alike—into another world, and it's a world we are almost always ready to venture into and remain in for as long as possible. "I dwell in Possibility," Emily Dickinson begins one of her poems. For her, poetry represented not only escape from the bondage of mundane reality, but a continuously unfolding world of her own making, where she could enter and remain for as long as she wished.

....................................TRY THIS....................................

Write a journal entry in which you extend the possibility of conventional reality. Begin your entry by answering the question, "What would my life be like if I could read people's thoughts?" or, "If a genie gave me the power to perform one miracle, what miracle would I choose, and how would I put it to use?"

SEPTEMBER 28
WIT

Wit, in the eighteenth-century sense of the word, is sort of a cross between razor-edged intelligence (as in the expression "sharp-witted") and tongue-in-cheek cleverness. The term also suggests a certain degree of sophistication and daring.

It makes good sense to think of writing as an exercise of wit: keen perception with a dash of cleverness. In the memorable words of Alexander Pope in his "An Essay on Criticism":

> True Wit is Nature to advantage dress'd,
> What oft was thought, but ne'er so well express'd;

FOR FURTHER REFLECTION

Wit—or what we today might call high-spirited cleverness—can take writers far. Wit combines intelligence with personality, perception with vigor. Wit can manifest itself in many ways, from clever repartee to sarcasm to pun-filled wise-cracking. Shakespeare's characters, heroes and villains alike, are often paragons of wit—from Iago's ironic warning to Othello to be wary of jealousy, for "'Tis that green eyed monster that doth mock the meat it feeds on" to Falstaff's sack-saturated witticisms in *Henry IV*.

....................................TRY THIS....................................

1. Compose a letter to a close friend (you need not send it), in which you combine intelligence with a lively, animated style. Don't be affected, however. Think urbane, sophisticated—but not stuffy.

2. Write a profile of a character possessed of great wit (intelligence + cleverness + animated personality). Give her an important mission to accomplish, and place this person in a situation were her wit would be needed to achieve success.

SEPTEMBER 29
METAPHORS

Metaphors enrich our understanding of the nature of things and help us to grasp abstract ideas. They accomplish this by showing how one thing is like another (usually something more familiar, easier to grasp). Thus, by describing the propagation of sound through air or light through space as *waves*, we are identifying the familiar movement of water waves with the relatively unfamiliar movement of light waves. If we say that the flag *whipped* in the wind, we are likening the action of a whip to the movement of the flag.

According to George Lakoff and Mark Johnson in their book *Metaphors We Live By*, metaphors lie at the heart of our thinking and reveal much about our conceptualizing processes. For example, we apply orientational (up/down) metaphors to describe emotional states; thus, "The first fairy tale was u*plifting*, but the second one made me feel *low*."

FOR FURTHER REFLECTION

Metaphors are among a writer's most versatile stylistic devices. A strong metaphor can convey a concept with greater efficiency than an abstract explanation by itself. It is easier to envision the behavior of cosmic rays, for example, if we say that "they bombard the earth like billions of subatomic-sized bullets" than if we say "they irradiate the earth with ultra-high frequency gamma radiation"—even though the latter description may be more precise.

. . . . TRY THIS . . . .

Maintain an inventory of the different types of metaphors that you and other family members use. Refer to *Metaphors We Live By* for examples of the different categories of metaphorical thinking we engage in.

SEPTEMBER 30
READING YOUR WAY THROUGH WRITER'S BLOCK

Reading is a good way to recharge one's writing batteries. When you're writing, you're using language your own way, borne out of years of habit. When you're reading, suddenly you're immersed in someone else's manner of using language. The similarities probably outweigh the differences, but it's the differences that are refreshing, that can stimulate your sense of rhetorical and stylistic possibility.

Sometimes, a short stint of reading can go a long way—as little as twenty minutes with a short story or essay—can change your state of mind and lead to a fresh perspective on your work in progress.

Reading in areas directly related to your own project is always a good idea too, but sometimes it can bog you down even more. The best time to turn to project-related reading is after completing your work for the day. A good night's sleep between the reading and the writing can prove beneficial.

FOR FURTHER REFLECTION

By reading, we shift to the other side of language, as it were—not unlike shifting from performer to audience member. The new perspective on prose composition that reading offers can lead to fresh insights into the prose composition we create for others.

....................................TRY THIS....................................

During your next writing regimen, work in three reading breaks that you take when you feel blocked. If you don't experience any blocks, then take the breaks after reaching a certain kind of closure, such as finishing a chapter or a dramatic incident. Select your reading from a different genre each time. Take notes on how much time you spend reading, what you've read, and how (if at all) it has helped you to gain fresh impetus on your work in progress when you return to it.

FABLES

Fables typically are allegories in which some or all of the characters are animals whose behavior and deeds (both wise and foolish) serve to highlight the behavior and deeds of people. The greatest fabulist of the ancient world, of course, was Aesop. In tales such as the "The Tortoise and the Hare," children learn wisdom while being greatly entertained. Such fables are not just for children; novel-length fables such as Richard Adams's *Watership Down*—in which the characters are rabbits—have great appeal for adults. One of the most famous twentieth-century fables is George Orwell's *Animal Farm*, an anti-Stalinist satire that shows how Marxist ideals become corrupted by tyrants. After the death of Old Major (the worldly wise boar who instigated the animals' rebellion against mankind—"Only get rid of Man and the produce of our labor would be our own"), the pig Napoleon (representing Stalin), together with dogs (representing the secret police), oppress the other animals, perverting the most precious commandment, "All animals are equal" into "All animals are equal but some are more equal than others."

FOR FURTHER REFLECTION

Fables serve as an objective and powerful lens through which we can best observe human folly. They are excellent vehicles for conveying moral values, as in Aesop's tale of the tortoise and the hare. They are also fun to read and attract the attention of audiences both young and old.

......................................TRY THIS....................................

1. Write a fable in which you make an unusual animal your main character. That is, instead of opting for a cat, a dog, or a bird, try telling your story from the point of view of a snake or a giraffe, or some extinct animal such as a pterodactyl.

2. Read Henry David Thoreau's fable-like description of the battle between red ants and black ants in the "Brute Neighbors" chapter of *Walden*. Then write your own account of a confrontation between two similar species—say, between squirrels and chipmunks or ducks and geese. Give your fable a distinct moral purpose.

DIANE ARBUS: "MASKED WOMAN IN A WHEELCHAIR, PA"

"What I am trying to describe," Diane Arbus says in reference to her photographs, "is that it's impossible to get out of your skin and into somebody else's." Impossible, yes, but art can come closest to achieving that kind of deliverance. Arbus's photographs are powerful because they are able to convey what it is like to be the person photographed, however eccentric or freakish that person seems to be. Arbus photographs the way a novelist writes: by erasing the barriers that keep people from understanding one another.

In our stark confrontation with the "Masked Woman in a Wheelchair, PA," we behold a sad and complex irony: The woman is both hiding from us and exposing herself to us. The mask is hideous—but we quickly come to realize that it's more than just a Halloween fright mask; rather, the mask unmasks what the woman is experiencing within: elderly, disabled, cast aside from the rest of humanity.

FOR FURTHER REFLECTION

We all wear masks; in fact we wear a mask for every occasion. The mask we don when we're with a family member is not the same mask we don when we're with associates in the workplace. We don masks to hide our feelings or to project certain facets of our psyche. Perhaps the mask we don for a Halloween costume party reflects our desire to manifest a facet of our psyche that the mask represents: a Casanova type if we've been monogamous; a superhero (like SpiderMan?) if we're placid and self-effacing most of the time; or, like the woman in Arbus's photograph, a demonic being rather than the disabled nonentity left to wither away in a wheelchair. You may view Arbus's "Masked Woman in a Wheelchair, PA" at www.personal.psu.edu/users/a/m/amc327/images/Assignment8.pdf.

.....................................TRY THIS.....................................

1. List your masks, and then write an essay about why you wear them.

2. Write a story about a man who likes to dress as a woman (or vice versa) for Halloween. Explore the psychological impulses behind your character's desire to do so.

OCTOBER 3
SENSUOUS BRAVURA

The poet-critic J.D. McClatchy, writing in the *New York Times Book Review*, explained that "the pleasure we take in poems ... comes from their sensuous bravura," that is, the poet's courage to emphasize the sensuous nature of things or ideas we don't ordinarily notice, or don't ordinarily notice as having the capacity for sensuousness. Because poetry calls our attention to (and here McClatchy quotes Rilke) "the side of life that is turned away from us," most people miss out on experiencing life in its full sensuous nature. It is the job of poetry (and of all art) to illuminate what is hidden—and this demands no small amount of bravura on the part of the poet.

FOR FURTHER REFLECTION

Artists, writers included, must look at the sensuous wholeness of objects and people. The observations on nonartists tend to be superficial, highly selective; that is, they see only what they wish to see. To see the world artistically, we must learn to penetrate beneath the glittery surfaces of things. There is much beauty and mystery to behold underneath: surfaces beneath surfaces, like the organs of the human body, or the parts of a machine. These, too, deserve to be celebrated.

..................................TRY THIS....................................

Find a biology textbook, one with the full-color mylar overlays of the various internal organs of the human body, and write an essay on "the hidden beauty of the human body." Or limit your scope to just one set of organs, such as the lungs, or the intestines, or the heart. Remember that every organ has its own internal components as well, which you should include in your description.

THAT'S ENTERTAINMENT!

All writers are entertainers, and that includes writers of nonfiction. As the neologism "infotainment" implies, one derives pleasure from being informed by enhancing the bare facts with colorful anecdotes or imaginative figures of speech such as analogy or hyperbole. In *Connections*, a study of the way inventions in history have triggered chain reactions of social and technological change, James Burke entertains as he explains by emphasizing cause-effect relationships between events we had never before suspected were relatable—as in the connection between the invention of chimneys and the evolution of privacy. Before the chimney was invented, Burke explains, there was one central hearth, smoke from which exited through a hole in the roof. Everyone slept huddled around that central hearth during winter months. But by the thirteenth century, winters became much colder, and a more efficient way of heating had to be developed. "The understanding of the physics of updraught and downdraught in the use of chimney breastwork and hood, which are what enables the fire to both keep going and give out heat and at the same time carry away smoke and sparks," Burke explains, enabled the heating of multiple rooms. Burke then writes,

> The primary effect of the introduction of these new rooms was to separate the social classes. ... Special state apartments were constructed, and separately heated. Bathing became more common. ... The new heated bedrooms, where people slept away from the general community, and often naked, altered as well the attitude of love. It now became a personal, private, romantic activity.

(See also the entry for November 18.)

FOR FURTHER REFLECTION

Readers love to be informed in an entertaining manner. Fiction, we might even say, is philosophy, psychology, history, and sociology dressed up in dramatic scenarios. We learn best when ideas are played out on the stage of everyday experience.

...................................TRY THIS...................................

Take a subject you know well and retell it in a way that makes for entertaining reading. For example, if you know something about baseball, write an essay about batting technique that would fascinate young readers.

THE FUTURE OF BOOKS

In this digital age, one can only wonder what the future of books as we know them will be like. E-book technology is advancing. A rectangular pad about the size of a book, but in no way resembling a book (it has a screen instead of a cover and pages), can store as many as nine hundred downloadable books; one simply changes pages by pressing a button. Does the convenience of storing the equivalent of a small library in a single apparatus outweigh the feel, the physical presence, and the permanence of traditional books? One might argue that a book is more than what it contains: It is an aesthetic object, a keepsake—also a reference tool that we can interact with through underlining and marginalia (see the entry for June 12). Physical books are eminently sharable with family and friends.

There is no disputing the benefits of electronic information accessing, but we should be careful that we do not toss out the proverbial baby with the bathwater, as libraries did with their catalog cards in the 1980s. Public and university libraries are finding it increasingly difficult to afford the space and the maintenance required of their collections; but if we truly love physical books, we must find ways to finance their protection.

FOR FURTHER REFLECTION

It is painful to contemplate a world without physical books because, in many ways, they are like people—"my little kinsmen on the shelf," as Emily Dickinson put it. Digital texts are not books. However, because information accessing is so necessary these days, we can have both.

......................................TRY THIS.....................................

Interview the librarians at local public or college libraries. What is the outlook for future maintenance and acquisition of physical books from their perspectives? Write an article based on the information you obtain.

WILD AND CRAZY IDEAS

Some writers quickly discard any ideas that seem outlandish, irrational, or downright crazy; however, that might not be a wise option. Many original ideas that strike a chord with the public may seem outré at first; a writer must never pass judgment too hastily. Trying to second-guess public taste at any given moment can prove to be an act of futility. The best solution is to retain an idea if you like it despite its weirdness.

Moreover, wild and crazy ideas are fun to conjure up for their own sakes. Why does everything have to be gauged according to taste or market potential? Art thrives on experimentation and daring.

FOR FURTHER REFLECTION

History is filled with ideas that seemed outrageous at the time; and had their creators took public reaction to heart, we'd still be traveling cross country by stage coach and lighting oil lamps at night. Who would have guessed that a memoir about a mental patient who motorcycles across the country to reconnect with the part of himself lost to electroshock therapy—a book that was less of a memoir than a philosophical inquiry to boot—and not surprisingly rejected by 120 publishers, would be accepted by the 121st and become a major bestseller for nearly a year when it appeared as *Zen and the Art of Motorcycle Maintenance*?

Moral of the story: If you strongly believe in your work, and it represents your very best achievement, it will see print sooner or later.

.....................................TRY THIS....................................

Take your wildest and craziest short-story or essay idea and work it into a complete first draft. Set it aside to incubate for a couple of weeks, and then revise as you see fit, taking care to retain its craziness.

SEX

In an essay on Tennessee Williams, the distinguished novelist and cultural historian Louis Auchincloss complains about the way in which society tends "to perpetuate a system of boxes" regarding human nature, particularly sexual human nature. "Yet," he explains, "sex is an energy that pervades all of our imagination and most of our acts and that manifests itself in every human relationship"—a wisdom that Auchincloss sees pervading the plays of Tennessee Williams: "The presence of lust or love in every episode and piece of dialogue in his plays is what gives the warmth and glow even to his brutes and villains."*

While it may be true that sex has been overexploited in the arts, one does not need to be a Freudian psychologist to realize that sex is the powerful undercurrent driving all facets of human behavior. On the other hand, if you feel squeamish about depicting explicit sexual situations, then don't. Indirectness can be just as effective.

FOR FURTHER REFLECTION

We're all too well aware that, as the cliché goes, "sex sells." But sex used merely for sensationalistic ends can ruin an otherwise good story. If you're going to write about romantic relationships, often the best way to handle sex is through indirection, by way of building sexual tension, innuendo, erotically charged language and gestures.

......................................TRY THIS...................................

Write a scene in which a man and woman begin to experience sexual attraction for each other, but write it in a way that is suggestive rather than explicitly sexual.

---

* Louis Auchincloss, "Tennessee Williams: The Last Puritan," in *The Style's the Man: Reflections on Proust, Fitzgerald, Wharton, Vidal, and Others.* Scribner, 1994:135.

OCTOBER 8
TECHNICAL DETAILS

Every field of knowledge has its technical side, its areas of specialization that include specialized diction—its jargon. If one of your characters is a professional person, his use of jargon now and then will add to the realism of the story. But using jargon is tricky: first, you need to understand it yourself—at least, as much of it as you feel is necessary to give the impression that the character in question is indeed an expert in his field. Then you need to use the jargon in a way that doesn't confuse your readers. One way to do this is to have another character interrupt the expert to request an explanation.

One genre that virtually exults in jargon (much of it imaginary) is science fiction. *Star Trek* fans can even resort to technical manuals, such as *Star Trek: The Next Generation Technical Manual* by Rick Sternbach and Michael Okuda, which has chapters devoted to spacecraft structure, command systems, computer systems, warp and impulse propulsion systems, tactical systems, flight operations, and so on.

FOR FURTHER REFLECTION

Technical details add realism and believability to a story in which the expertise of one or more characters is called for. Are you writing a story about a private detective? Then you had better learn a thing or two about the way private detectives operate in relationship to police detectives. Reading P.I. novels is a good start, but it's not enough. You need to gain some firsthand knowledge about them, know what kinds of cases they typically work on, how a typical investigation unfolds, and so on.

..................................TRY THIS....................................

Spend a few weeks learning all you can about the profession of your main character. Start with books, but also try to "shadow" a professional in the field to be able to pick up the way jargon is used naturally on the job. Afterwards, incorporate some of this jargon into your story.

INCUBATION

Hens sit on their eggs to keep them warm enough—that is, they incubate them—so that the embryo develops into a healthy chick. Think of a newly completed first draft as an egg to be incubated. "Incubation" in this context refers to gaining critical perspective on the newly created work. The act of creation is often turbulent, disorderly, not always following logical precepts. Such is the alchemy needed for the work to assume a shape beyond the original idea that brought it into being.

How long should the incubation period last? The variables are complexity of the work and temperament of the writer. Some first drafts—e.g., of memoirs—have taken such an emotional toll on the writer that she must recuperate for a couple of weeks or more before attempting to rework the manuscript. Many writers will shift to another work in progress after completing a first draft; this tends to speed the incubation period along.

FOR FURTHER REFLECTION
Patience is a virtue when it comes to turning a "raw" first draft into a successful story or essay. It takes time to acquire critical distance, especially with book-length projects. The best way to acquire critical distance is to turn your attention to another project.

......................................TRY THIS....................................

After completing a draft of your next story or essay, let it incubate for one full week (longer if it's the draft of a novel or memoir). When turning to it again, begin by rereading it, slowly and carefully, taking notes as you go along. Now put the manuscript aside for another week. When reading it a second time, chances are you will find yourself taking many more revision notes.

UTOPIAN VISIONS

Do you fantasize about utopia, a harmonious, well-ordered society that has somehow gotten rid of war, crime, and poverty, and has perfected its economy, laws, and educational, health, and political systems? It is one thing to envision improvements for such programs, but (you may wonder) isn't it naïve to envision *perfect* programs? Even Sir Thomas More (or Saint Thomas More), who coined the word *utopia* (in his book by that title), hinted at the impossibility of such an ideal state ever being attained. The word is an embedded pun; it is derived from the Greek root *topos*, meaning "place" and either the prefix *eu-* which means "harmonious" or "ideal" or the prefix *ou-* which means "not"—thus, an ideal place or no place.

More may have been skeptical about his utopian vision, but the point of describing his perfected island society in *Utopia* was to demonstrate what humanity could and should strive toward.

The genre of fantasy grew out of the kinds of utopian visions that More and others wrote about during the Renaissance. Of course, for there to be a story, the utopian community needs to be threatened by some evil force—and sometimes that force comes from within: A benevolent leader is somehow tempted into forsaking his integrity.

FOR FURTHER REFLECTION

Utopias make for wonderful stories provided you include a powerful threat to its existence. It is human nature to dream of a totally harmonious existence, free of all the destructive forces that corrupt society; alas, it is also human nature to be drawn into those very corrupting forces.

......................................TRY THIS......................................

Dream up an idea for a utopian fantasy. Give it either a real-world setting (on some uncharted island, perhaps) or a fantasy setting in some alternate universe where magic reigns. Now introduce a formidable evil threat to that society.

INTIMATE EXPERIENCES

One of the many pleasures of memoirs and character-oriented fiction is to learn something about the intimate lives of people who interest us. It isn't that readers are busybody gossips; it's just that they're naturally interested in those facets of private life that often remain hidden or glossed over. Human intimacy lies at the heart of human nature.

People experience different kinds of intimacy, of course. In addition to the romantic variety, there's also spiritual intimacy (as in the case of a penitent confessing his sins), medical intimacy (as in the case of an ER surgeon struggling to save the life of a gunshot victim; or a nurse trying to keep a burn victim as comfortable as possible). Intimacy can also be experienced with animals. Think of Jane Goodall's work with chimpanzees. In the beautifully conceived but little-known film *Day of the Dolphin* (based on a novel by Robert Merle), George C. Scott plays the part of a scientist who learns to communicate with dolphins through his intimate relationships with them.

FOR FURTHER REFLECTION

Do you feel a bit skittish writing about human intimacy, especially sexual intimacy? You're not alone. Sure you can work around it, but doing so may compromise the three-dimensionality of your characters. Human beings are most human, one can argue, when they are intimate—sexually as well as spiritually.

....TRY THIS....................................

1. Describe, in your journal, an intimate experience in a medical, spiritual, or romantic context.

2. Write a story about the way a romantic relationship is formed out of a nonromantic type of intimacy.

"SO WHAT?"

Every so often writers need to pinch themselves to ensure that they aren't writing merely to display their egos or to hear the sound of their own voice. In other words, writers need to ask the "bottom line" question: *So what?*

We ask the "so what?" question of works in progress to remind us that our writing won't get very far if it doesn't offer something of value beyond a superficial conflict situation. We writers want to avoid writing in a vacuum or writing without thinking deeply about societal or historical contexts for the stories we want to tell. A good story should, in its own special way, broaden readers' understanding of human nature, the times in which we are living, or the story's historical milieu.

FOR FURTHER REFLECTION

The "so what?" question, asked repeatedly throughout composition, can help writers avoid superficial or directionless storylines. However, it isn't necessary to begin with that question. Conceiving of substantive characters in fascinating social contexts should come first. Interesting people and places have a way of leading to satisfying answers to the "so what?" question.

.....................................TRY THIS....................................

Develop a conflict situation over an issue that has widespread importance for our society. For example, when a woman in her first trimester of pregnancy learns that her baby has a high chance of being born with a genetic disorder, she wishes to proceed with the pregnancy, but her husband insists that she terminate it.

FOOD WRITING

Do you love to invent your own recipes and entertain with food, or contemplate the cultural dimensions of food? If so, then you ought to consider writing essays and books about your culinary experiences. Literary food writers like Anthony Bourdain, Ruth Reichl, Michael Pollan, James Beard, and the most distinguished food writer of them all, M.F.K. Fisher,** have raised the genre to high art. Ruth Reichl, for example, has edited an anthology, *Endless Feasts: Sixty Years of Writing From Gourmet*, for the Modern Library. Houghton Mifflin publishes an annual anthology, *Best Food Writing*, edited by Holly Hughes. There are even food-based memoirs, like *Miriam's Kitchen* by Elizabeth Ehrlich, the story of a young Jewish woman's rediscovery of heritage through the preparation of traditional Jewish meals learned from her mother-in-law, a Holocaust survivor. Recipes are included.

FOR FURTHER REFLECTION

Food can open a fascinating portal into a culture, a way of living. It's not just the food itself, but the preparation, and the special occasions for serving it. So much of life's little pleasures are tied to food—enough food lore to keep poets, essayists, memoirists, and fiction writers busy for a long time.

...................................TRY THIS...................................

1. Write an autobiographical essay that is structured around the foods you most enjoyed at different stages in your life.

2. Write a poem in which you capture the pleasure you experience eating a certain kind of food—an artichoke, an ear of corn, a potato chip (perhaps dipped in guacamole), an uncommon fruit such as a persimmon, or a common fruit like a plum.

** Biographical essays of Beard and Fisher appear in the *Endless Feasts* anthology.

"STRANGE BUT TRUE"

Readers love to learn about the offbeat, the unusual, and downright weird things that have happened in history but have been overlooked *because* they were offbeat, unsavory, or weird: stories about mental institutions, satanic cults, people with horrific diseases or afflictions. Memorable biographies, stage plays, films, and essays have been written about such individuals. Among the most famous is the story of the original Siamese twins, Chang and Eng Bunker (1811–1874), who, despite their being conjoined at the torso, lived out their relatively long, productive, and fulfilling lives (they married and had several children apiece). Then there's the popular 1979 Broadway play, *The Elephant Man*, by Bernard Pomerance, based on the not-so-fulfilling life of Joseph Merrick, who was grotesquely disfigured by elephantiasis, struggled (with the help of a friend) to escape his fate as a sideshow freak and be accepted as a human being with dignity. The neurologist Oliver Sacks has written a series of eloquent essays, collected as *The Man Who Mistook His Wife for a Hat*, based on case histories with individuals who have suffered from catastrophic injuries or illnesses. The title essay, for example, describes a gifted musician whose brain injury led to the loss of his ability to distinguish between one object and another—and during one fleeting moment, that is at once funny and heart-breaking, he reaches for his wife's head and tries putting it on his head.

FOR FURTHER REFLECTION

Stories about people with bizarre afflictions command our morbid curiosity as well as our sympathy—a powerful combination of emotions that explains why such stories, if written with authority and compassion, are in high demand.

......................................TRY THIS......................................

1. Prepare several profiles of strange persons about whom you would like write an essay or even a book-length biography. Draw from circus histories, medical histories, or psychological case histories.

2. Develop one of the profiles you prepared for number one into a full-length biographical essay.

LOGS

A log is a detailed record of activities. Scientists will keep logs of experiments; airline pilots and ship captains keep logs of their flights and sea voyages; artists often record the time it takes them to finish a painting or sculpture, describing the materials they use and the way those materials are applied; architects and construction supervisors will record every stage and expense of their building projects. Many writers will keep a close record of all activities associated with their writing projects, especially book-length ones.

A writer's log is important for several reasons. For one thing, you may need to backtrack on some of the research you've conducted; your log will have noted the sources (including URLs if accessed from the Internet); if writing a novel, you may want to maintain a record of each work session, a daily summary of your progress, a record of specific revisions, timelines. Logs are also useful for recording writing-related expenses (paper, writing implements, mailing envelopes, notepads, print cartridges, paper clips, cellophane tape) for income-tax and budgeting purposes.

FOR FURTHER REFLECTION

A writer's log supplements a writer's journal or diary. Reserve your log for record-keeping matters and your journal for raw ideas, character profiles, observations, reflections, daydreams, and rough drafts.

......................................TRY THIS....................................

Keep a log for your next writing project. Maintain separate sections for research data, number of pages completed, time spent during each writing session, outlining, and revising.

OCTOBER 16
EXAGGERATION AND UNDERSTATEMENT

Literary exaggeration, or hyperbole, can prove to be a versatile tool, especially if you have a knack for humor. A famous example occurs in Andrew Marvell's carpe diem poem, "To His Coy Mistress," in which the speaker tries to convince his lady friend that it would make more sense to surrender to his amorous advances now than tarry. He makes his point more emphatic by resorting to hyperbole. If we had all the time in the world, then

> An hundred years should go to praise
> Thine eyes, and on thy forehead gaze,
> Two hundred to adore each breast,
> But thirty thousand for the rest.

The best way to learn to use hyperbole is to study its present masters like Dave Barry. Consider the following example from *Dave Barry's Bad Habits*:

> I bet you don't read the *National Enquirer*, or any of the other publications sold at supermarket checkout counters. I bet you think these publications are written for people with the intellectual depth of shrubs, people who need detailed, written instructions to put their shoes on correctly.

The reverse of hyperbole is understatement, a kind of negative exaggeration. If it's a blisteringly hot day and you react by saying, "It seems to be getting a bit warm," you're using understatement. Woody Allen has perfected a form of understatement, which we might call comic reversal of high expectations: "I have taken to violent choking and fainting," he writes in *Without Feathers*. "My room is damp and I have perpetual chills and palpitations of the heart. I noticed, too, that I am out of napkins."

FOR FURTHER REFLECTION

Exaggeration and understatement occur in ordinary conversation. For literary purposes, they can be honed to deliver satiric bite. Humor writers rely on exaggeration and understatement frequently in order to generate quick laughs.

......................................TRY THIS....................................

Use your journal to practice hyperbole and understatement. Here are a few prompts to get you started:

- a driver weaving through traffic while talking on a cell phone
- goings on at a Halloween party
- anticipating a tooth extraction

"I GOT RHYTHM"

There is something almost biological about rhythm. Maybe it has something to do with heartbeat and breathing; maybe it has something to do with the rhythms of nature, of which there are many: the phases of the moon, the ebb and flow of the tides, the movement of clouds across the sky, even the way flowers and trees sway in the breeze. Other creatures certainly possess rhythm: birds (both in their singing and in their flying), butterflies, the sinuous movements of snakes, the movements of schools of fish, the dreamy swaying of jellyfish and the tendrils of sea anemones. Of course, art is all about rhythm—not just in music (drumbeats, ballerina pirouettes, and so on), but the rhythms one sees in paintings and sculptures. The most important thing about rhythm, at least from a writer's perspective, is the role it plays in holding the reader's or listener's attention.

If you read and write poetry, you understand the importance of rhythm, the combination of stressed and unstressed syllables, the pauses that add emphasis and connotations to words and phrases. Prose also has its rhythms. They're not as pronounced as the poetic ones, but sentences need to be sufficiently varied to permit ease of reading. Construct too many sentences the same way, and they'll seem choppy, mechanical.

FOR FURTHER REFLECTION

Rhythm is as important in writing as it is in all the other arts, in nature, and even in our own physiology and behavior. Life pulsates; we are most alive when we satisfy our instinct for rhythmic gratification.

.................................TRY THIS....................................

Compose a number of short poems, each one expressing a distinctive rhythmic character. Construct one poem predominantly with anapests (two unstressed syllables followed by a stressed, as in "'Twas the NIGHT before CHRISTmas and ALL through the HOUSE ..."; another poem with trochees (a stressed syllable followed by an unstressed, as in "HOLD me, KISS me, LOVE me"); and yet another poem based on a rhythmic pattern of your own devising.

OCTOBER 18
DWELLING IN UNCERTAINTY

Some people find uncertainty intolerable; most writers, however, dwell in uncertainty at every stage of a writing task. It may sound a little perverse, but
uncertainty is a healthy state of mind, especially during the planning stages.
"In order to invent," writes Brewster Ghiselin, "one must yield to the indeter-
minate … to certain ill-defined impulses which seem to be of the very texture
of the ungoverned fullness which John Livingston Lowes calls 'the surging
chaos of the unexpressed.'" If you insist upon a definite path for your story,
definite characters with definite personalities and definite goals, you run the
risk of brittleness. Because stories have a way of evolving as if they possess a
will of their own, resisting that kind of evolution might make your story seem
unimaginative, predictable. Note the word *might*: some writers work best when
they have everything mapped out beforehand and feel as if they're going off the
deep end if they deviate even slightly. If that sounds like you, then forget about
dwelling in uncertainty. But at least give yourself the opportunity to discover
what your tolerance for uncertainty is like.

FOR FURTHER REFLECTION

Metaphors of direction—paths, roads, points of the compass, guiding lights,
and so on—have their limitations when it comes to creating stories from scratch.
Creative writing is more like exploring a cave than like painting by numbers.

................................TRY THIS....................................

Begin writing a story with only a general topic in mind—say, the end of a love
relationship. Your opening sentence should set up the situation quickly—something like, "Martha could tell just by the way Gary shut the door on his way out
that he would not be coming back that evening." Without any further planning
or consulting sources, write the story spontaneously, letting ideas fall into place
from one sentence to the next.

OCTOBER 19
SOUVENIRS

Derived from the French word for *remember*, souvenirs can be tawdry kitsch or an emotionally stirring keepsake—a fluffy pair of dice to hang on your rearview mirror to remind you of that rowdy Vegas weekend or a piece of the Berlin Wall that was torn down in 1989, symbolizing nearly thirty years of Communist oppression.

Souvenirs remind one of vacations, of adventures, of experiences that have enriched our lives, of happy moments. Most importantly for writers, they work as heuristic devices—prompts to get the writing going. A facsimile statuette of a Greek goddess purchased on Crete; a Hopi kachina doll purchased on a reservation in Arizona.

FOR FURTHER REFLECTION

Souvenirs encapsulate experiences that often are worthy of shaping into stories, essays, poems. Even if you think that the souvenirs you possess lack such story-generating power, they most likely can at least generate scenes, incidents that could someday find their way into a larger discourse. When it comes to fiction writing, even the most seemingly trivial souvenir could stir the imagination and suggest much more than the literal experience with which it is associated.

......................................TRY THIS......................................

1. Go through the souvenirs you've collected over the years, without judging their story potential. Just gather them together. Be flexible, too, as to what should count as a souvenir.

2. Once you have your souvenirs gathered together, give careful consideration to each item for its story potential. Conduct some online research if necessary. Finally, select one souvenir—or a group of closely related souvenirs—and use it as a springboard for an essay on some facet of the culture it represents.

OCTOBER 20
ON INSPIRATION

What a wonderful feeling it is to feel inspired. Inspiration not only uplifts us and fills us with faith and optimism, it energizes us and makes us feel as if we can achieve whatever our hearts desire. Are you inspired to write the great American novel? Then say to yourself, *Yes! I can do it!* And then start working on it that very moment.

Serious writers do not wait for inspiration to strike, however—no more than they wait around for inspiration when it comes to doing their day jobs. Inspiration is most fruitful when it is worked into a pre-existing work routine. If you do not have such a routine, make one. You will get better mileage from a flash of inspiration when you're already in the habit of writing on a regular basis. As a matter of fact, those who write regularly are most often visited by the inspirational Muse. Readiness is all.

FOR FURTHER REFLECTION

There are two varieties of inspiration—passive and active. The former kind is seldom effective: If you're simply waiting around for a Muse to serenade you, you'll probably have a long wait. But active inspiration is generated by working at your writing. The harder you work, the more inspired your writing will become.

..................................TRY THIS....................................

Generate some active inspiration by getting a short story going this moment. Rather than wait for one of the Muses to whisper a plot outline in your ear, plunge directly into a story situation in which your protagonist meets one of the following individuals:

- a former lover

- someone who, five years ago, vowed: "If I ever see you again, I'll kill you."

- a magician reduced to homelessness and panhandling

Work steadily; after about half an hour, active inspiration should keep you going until you finish the draft.

INVENTION

"Invention" (Latin *inventio*), one of the stages of discourse in ancient rhetoric developed by Quintilian for the training of orators, refers to a systematic way of generating ideas or what to say about ideas. But invention can be spontaneous as well as systematic, depending on an orator's or writer's individual temperament.

One of the best known invention devices is the journalist's 5Ws and the H: Who, What, Where, When, Why, and How. This set of prompts is especially useful when outlining a writing project of any kind (not just a news report). "Who" conjures up the characters in your story; "What," suggests the story (conflict) situation; "When" and "Where" suggest the setting and time frame; "Why" suggests the characters' motives for their actions; and "How" conjures up ways in which the characters might reach their goals.

FOR FURTHER REFLECTION

"Invention breeds invention," Emerson reminds us. That is, the more inventive we are with language, with plotting, with character development, the more adept we will become at being inventive. This translates into the most important advice one can give to an aspiring writer: Keep writing!

....TRY THIS....................................

1. Use the 5Ws/H invention strategy for planning a story or essay.

2. Write the story or essay you've outlined using the 5Ws/H strategy, only take care that you don't let the outline show through the prose. In other words, you may want to defer character motivation until the very end of the story; or you may, for plot purposes, disclose the details of the setting only gradually.

FORM AS FUNCTION

Stories follow a pattern of some sort: Typically, they open with a problem or mystery, which the viewpoint character sets out to solve. The matter is urgent because the problem keeps getting worse: In a mystery, for example, people keep getting murdered. Things get even more urgent (and scary) when the danger hits close to home: The viewpoint character's close friend becomes the next target, say—or even the viewpoint character himself, who barely escapes with his life. This pattern of problem-leading-to-incident-leading-to-incident-leading-to-climax-and-resolution is what enables the story to function as a mystery or horror story or romance. Pattern determines content, in other words. The more overt the pattern, the more formulaic the story will seem. This is not necessarily a bad thing; mystery and horror fans expect this, at least semiconsciously.

FOR FURTHER REFLECTION

The pattern of a story adds to the aesthetic experience. Writers need to be careful, though: If the pattern is too conspicuous, the story will seem artificial. If there is no discernable pattern, the reader will feel adrift at sea, and lose the sense of anticipation. The best way to proceed is to tell the story you want to tell, in the way you want to tell it, and then worry about form later.

......................................TRY THIS......................................

1. Outline a short story, being very mindful of pattern; that is, of story sequence, rising curve of conflict, climactic moment, resolution.

2. Write the story you've outlined for number one. As you work on the draft, try to "mute" the pattern so the seams do not show.

IDEALISM VS. REALISM

It has been suggested that one is either an idealist or a realist (a variation on "one is either a Platonist or an Aristotelian"), but of course the complex situations we encounter in daily life makes that adage seem a bit simplistic. There are times when we're wildly idealistic and times when we see the world in an unrelentingly pragmatic, rational way, even though our temperament may orient us toward one or the other. In any case, it's useful for writers to think about the effect that each attitude has on personality and behavior. Optimists tend to be adventurous, willing to try new things, to take risks, to put a lot of hope in potential; realists tend to settle for what is tried and true, always weighing the odds and making the safest bets. Most realists do not gamble. The odds of picking the winning numbers, they argue, are so great that there is virtually no difference between betting and not betting.

FOR FURTHER REFLECTION

Idealism (or optimism) and realism alike can suggest characters that exhibit one or the other personalities or worldviews. Jay Gatsby is the perennial romantic idealist and optimist, for example: Even though Daisy had long ago rejected him and married another, he still believed he could have her. In Gabriel Garcia Márquez's *Love in the Time of Cholera*, the hero's love for a woman he cannot attain lasts for fifty years. Love, paradoxically, is rooted in both ideal and realistic universes.

...................................TRY THIS...................................

1. Are you an idealist or a realist? Write a journal entry in which you answer that question.

2. Outline a short story in which a realist, through some fascinating series of circumstances, becomes an optimist—or vice versa.

"TELL IT SLANT"

"The Truth must dazzle gradually / or every Man be blind," Emily Dickinson concludes one of her poems ("Tell all the Truth but tell it slant"). Dickinson knows that truth is best apprehended through indirection and example rather than by gazing into its blindingly bright essence.

Creative writing is like dramatized philosophy. The themes that emerge from stories and poems are the dazzling truth that shines through the concrete situations. When a story's theme becomes too obvious, we say that the story is contrived or "preachy." If fiction writers want to sermonize, we think to ourselves, they should write sermons instead.

Another kind of indirectness in truth-telling is adhering to a set of story-telling conventions, or paradigms. In *The Structure of Scientific Revolutions*, Thomas Kuhn explains the role that paradigms play even in scientific work. Paradigms allow science to progress, but unless they are subject to modification, science cannot progress.

Kuhn's thesis has relevance for writers. To tell a story, writers need to master storytelling conventions, but they also need to stretch them to embody the new insights, the new variations on the themes they wish to convey.

FOR FURTHER REFLECTION
Searching for new ways to disclose the truth of things is what writers have in common with scientists and detectives. The more insight we gain into human nature and the natural world, the more necessary it becomes for writers to discover new ways of embodying those truths artistically.

..................................TRY THIS..................................

Outline a story in which your main character's true nature emerges indirectly, through her "behind the scenes" thoughts and actions, which contradict the public ones.

OCTOBER 25
AUTUMN LEAVES

Autumn speaks to writers. It is the season most associated with learning because of the beginning of the school year. It marks the "new season" for shows and concerts; it is also a time of fading, but a fading that is rich in paradox. Leaves are suddenly ablaze in color, as if celebrating their summer flourishing just before they wither and fall away.

In a sense, autumn embodies the other seasons: It is a time of renewal, like spring; its "Indian summers" indeed are filled with bright sunshine, although such moments diminish steadily; and its evenings and nights usher in the chill of winter, compounded by the winds that denude the trees.

FOR FURTHER REFLECTION

Autumn is the ideal season for study and contemplation, and for writing. Memories seem to heighten as the summer light weakens and the shadows lengthen. The intense colors of autumn seem an ironic counterpoint to the tamer greens and blues of the summer months.

························TRY THIS····························

1. Maintain a list of autumnal images and associations. Descriptions of colorful leaves might top your list, but also include changes in weather, in clothes, in light and shadows, in foods, in the rhythm of daily life; perhaps certain changes in mood or personality as well.

2. Compose a series of autumnal poems. Read Keats's ode, "To Autumn" for inspiration:

> Season of mists and mellow fruitfulness,
>   Close bosom-friend of the maturing sun;
> Conspiring with him how to load and bless
>   With fruit the vines that round the thatch-eves run;
> To bend with apples the moss'd cottage-trees,
>   And fill all fruit with ripeness to the core …

OCTOBER 26
ON SORCERY

Art, because it arises from human longings, enhances everyday reality as it draws from it. Art is the mirror held up to nature, as Shakespeare famously tells us in *Hamlet*. Yes, art reflects reality, in other words, but reflections are enhancements. A mirror image is like a photograph: It is "faithful" to reality in one sense, but utterly unlike it in another sense. This transformation from intrinsic reality to "captured" reality, we could argue, is a kind of sorcery.

Another way to think about sorcery in the context of art is in the way art helps us find magic and beauty in the real world. Once we read a moving novel about the power of love, we seek out such power in our own relationships—or we find ways to enhance our romantic relationships.

FOR FURTHER REFLECTION

Art enchants and bewitches us; it represents the animation of imaginative thought, our quintessentially human ability to take the raw stuff of nature and magically transform it into story. Art can also add a dash of sorcery to our everyday lives, a case of reality imitating fiction. What greater sorcery can there be than this?

....................................TRY THIS....................................

1. Write a poem about the sorcery you detect in the everyday world.

2. Outline a story in which your main character, dissatisfied with the way his love life is progressing, decides to add some sorcery to it. What kind of sorcery does he resort to? Does it work or does it backfire? What are the consequences?

INTERIOR DRAMA

We associate storytelling with the unfolding of external events, but stories also unfold internally, through psychological stages. In such stories, conflict is generated through obstacles that block the viewpoint characters' ability to see things as they are. Of course, a teacher or therapist may supply "external" action, as is the case with the William Gibson play *The Miracle Worker*, the story of how a gifted teacher, Mrs. Sullivan, struggled to get the deaf and blind Helen Keller to make connections between concepts and their physical manifestations.

Interior drama is sometimes called psychodrama, but that term is somewhat misleading in that it suggests psychological aberration. Of course, stories about mentally disturbed individuals are fascinating, but interior drama can place us inside the mind of any kind of character. In Faulkner's *The Sound and the Fury*, we experience reality through the eyes and thoughts of Benjy, a thirty-year-old man with the mind of a five-year-old.

FOR FURTHER REFLECTION
The mind, like the ocean, has unfathomable depths. Even after more than a century of psychoanalytical research, the mysteries of consciousness and unconsciousness defy understanding. At the same time, enough has been learned about the dynamics of the mind to make for compelling internal dramas.

......................................TRY THIS....................................

Compose an interior drama from the perspective of one whose mental state is characterized by one of the following symptoms

- paranoia
- delusions of grandeur
- one of the phobias, such as a fear of heights (think of the Jimmy Stewart character in Alfred Hitchcock's *Vertigo*)
- obsessive-compulsive behavior
- seasonal affective disorder

WRITING SATIRE

Satire is sarcasm raised to the level of literary artistry. It pokes fun at hypocrisy, short-sightedness. It can be heavy-handed, even bitter in its attack, or it can be a gentle ribbing. Jonathan Swift (1667–1745), one of the greatest satirists in English literature, wrote satire of the first kind. Other satirists have used comedy as their vehicle—Charlie Chaplin, Lenny Bruce, Lily Tomlin, George Carlin, Woody Allen, and Nora Ephron being among the best-known examples. But whether serious or comic, satire aims primarily to alert readers to the ethical shortcomings of practices that, on the surface, seem altogether ethical. In his 1976 film *Network*, playwright and screenwriter Paddy Chayefsky satirizes the extent to which television executives will go to keep the ratings high, despite (or, ironically, because of) their commitment to serving the public interests.

FOR FURTHER REFLECTION

Cleverness combined with humor and a keen insight into human folly can work a powerful alchemy that can sometimes out-persuade even the most carefully developed logical arguments. The reason is that satire combines argument with wit, which in turn generates a keener emotional response; and it is part of human nature to be persuaded as much by our emotions as by our intellect. Satire combines the two.

......................................TRY THIS...................................

Test out your satiric wit by writing a story that pokes fun at some aspect of contemporary culture. Here are some possibilities:

- celebrity hounding
- what people *say* they value most in a presidential candidate vs. what they *secretly* value most
- courtship rituals

OCCULT SYMBOLS

The supernatural world is rich in symbolism. Think of Halloween with its skulls, cobwebs, black cats, and grinning pumpkins. Colors have symbolic significance for many beliefs, much of it based on associations with natural phenomena. Thus, red is associated with blood, orange with fire, green with fertility, yellow with sunlight, silver with lunar forces.

Writing is a kind of occult, shamanistic activity in the way it enhances the reality of symbols. The writer-as-shaman uses words to conjure up new realities for readers. Thus, writers of supernatural horror fiction serve up *two* occult experiences: generating symbolism through mere storytelling (e.g., the witch's gingerbread house in "Hansel and Gretel" symbolizing the evil that lurks under the surface of goodness) as well as taking full advantage of ready-made horror symbols, like crypts and dungeons, ghosts, gravestones, and howling wolves.

FOR FURTHER REFLECTION
Good and evil can be readily captured through conventional, universally recognized symbols like haloes, serpents, glowing red eyes, devil's horns, and such. Writers can also cook up their own symbols that can be made to represent good or evil or something ambiguous—a locket, a jewel, an artifact, a bone …

......................................TRY THIS......................................

1. Make a list of objects (lamps, old photographs, trophies, clocks) that might carry symbolic value in an occult story.

2. Work up a horror story that includes conventional symbols of good and evil along with symbols of one or the other, or both, that you have invented.

PREVENTING WRITER'S BLOCK

It is one thing to overcome writer's block, quite another to prevent it from occurring. Is it actually *possible* to prevent it, the way a flu vaccination can prevent one from getting the flu? Wouldn't it be better simply to deal with a block if and when it happens? It would be all right, but not necessarily better. The ideal is to work through a project without giving writer's block a chance to strike.

One way to prevent writer's block is to keep writing *something*, no matter what it is. Write a list of names you might like to give to future characters. Draft a letter to your mother or to an imaginary or famous person (see the entry for February 15). Compose a greeting card verse. Just because you're no longer able to continue with the task at hand does not mean you have to stop writing.

Another way to prevent writer's block is to play word games. For example, one might choose ten words at random from the dictionary and use them meaningfully in a paragraph.

FOR FURTHER REFLECTION
Writer's block is preventable. The trick is to find unblocking strategies that work best for you. Most importantly, you need to find out the cause in order to combat it. Often, the simplest solution will work best: a short break to freshen up your perspective or state of mind; a stint of physical exercise to burn off the anxiety that inevitably accumulates from spending too many hours at the keyboard.

..................................TRY THIS...................................

The next time you're blocked, ask someone to select three or more words from the newspaper. Use those words in the first paragraph of a story.

GETTING RID OF BAD WRITING HABITS

While the writing habit itself is intrinsically good, it is all too easy to pick up bad writing habits—bad as in counterproductive; bad as in writing carelessly or uncaringly (indifferently, hastily) about your subject. Some of the more popular bad habits that writers fall prey to include making factual errors (it's all too tempting to trust our faulty memories or even "take a wild guess" and never follow up on its accuracy), not being sufficiently mindful of the way we structure our sentences, using words with less than razor-sharp precision, repeating ourselves, and not making the effort to take a truly fresh, lively approach to our subject matter. All of these bad habits can be overcome simply by being aware of the fact that they can creep into our writing very easily if we get lazy—which, of course, is a bad habit unto itself.

FOR FURTHER REFLECTION

The first step in getting rid of bad writing habits is to recognize them for what they are. The second step is work out a plan to phase them out. If you spend too much time sharpening pencils or fretting over a day's work, then sharpen fewer pencils the next day, spend half the time fretting, and use the time left over to cultivate the good habits, like writing character profiles, working on plot structure, or plunging into your draft and seeing where spontaneity takes you.

..................................TRY THIS....................................

Draw up a list of all the bad writing habits you've succumbed to over the years. If you can't think of any, you'd better reassess your writing habits soon. Better yet, have a friend–someone on whom you can rely for objective criticism–read a few of your drafts with a close critical eye. Over the next several weeks, make a conscious effort to get rid of those bad habits that your friend points out.

CONCERNING RITUALS

Every culture and religion has its rites and rituals—solemn or festive practices that keep traditions alive. Some are tied to long-standing religious practices, such as the Festival of Lights (better known as Hanukkah) in Judaism, or Ramadan in Islam. Of course, there are rituals we now consider barbaric, like animal (let alone human) sacrifices and Satan worship.

However, the barbaric rituals are the ones that can make for compelling fiction, especially in the occult/horror genre. In David Seltzer's novel, *The Omen* (based on his screenplay of the film, starring Gregory Peck and Lee Remick), we learn a great deal—probably more than we care to know—about the kind of ritual needed to stop a devil-child from taking over the world. In *The Exorcist*, William Peter Blatty dramatizes the ancient ritual of exorcism, the casting out of a demon inhabiting a human being.

FOR FURTHER REFLECTION

Rituals deepen one's experience of a religion or cultural tradition. Works by cultural anthropologists, such as Sir James Frazer's *The Golden Bough* or Margaret Mead's *Coming of Age in Samoa*, are excellent sources for learning about ancient and primitive religious rituals.

......................................TRY THIS....................................

1. Outline a horror story that includes one or more rituals. Research the practice of these rituals so that you can convey them realistically.

2. Study the religious or coming-of-age rituals practiced by a non-Western culture, such as Samoa or Tibet; then, outline a story that is set in this culture.

NOVEMBER 2
HENRY FUSELI:
"OEDIPUS CURSING HIS SON, POLYNICES"

The story of Oedipus has captivated artists and writers for millennia, starting with Sophocles, the greatest of the ancient Greek tragic dramatists. In *Oedipus at Colonus*, the sequel to *Oedipus the King*, the blinded Oedipus goes into shameful exile in a village outside of Athens, after being devastated by the realization that he had unwittingly murdered his father and married his mother, Queen Jocasta. Fuseli's painting, with its wraithlike figures, as if out of a nightmare, depicts the blinded king expressing outrage at his son, Polynices, who had usurped his father's throne, and condemns him to die in battle. His sister Antigone tries to effect reconciliation.

Fuseli's painting is both haunting and moving: a family torn apart by wrongdoing, one tragic event leading to another. You may view the painting via the Web site of the National Gallery of Art (www.nga.gov/collection/index.shtm).

FOR FURTHER REFLECTION

From ancient Greek drama to contemporary drama and novels, the most poignant misfortunes that befall human beings are tied to moral blindness (physical blindness being its common symbolic referent). The story of Samson in the Old Testament (Book of Judges) is similar to Oedipus in that Samson's sexual transgression leads to the betrayal of his people as well as to his own betrayal in the hands of the Philistines (who bind him in chains and blind him after Delilah has robbed him of the source of his strength).

...................................TRY THIS....................................

Plan a story in which a character's moral blindness eventually leads to his literal blindness. You might want to retell the story of Oedipus or Samson in a modern context—e.g., your Oedipus counterpart is made the CEO of a giant corporation after marrying the daughter of the company's founder—who had been an intimate friend of your main character's mother. ...

UNPOPULAR OR UNSAVORY VIEWS

At the end of the film, *The Story of Louis Pasteur* (starring Paul Muni in his Oscar-winning role as the eponymous hero), Pasteur tells the young physicians who had come to honor him, "All scientific progress is unpopular at first." He should know, having endured much ridicule for daring to insist that certain microbes (such as those responsible for anthrax and rabies) can kill.

Like scientists, writers also dare to explore ideas that the general public may not find appropriate, that may clash with carefully guarded beliefs. A good writer pays attention to the things that nonwriters tend to turn away from. Why? Because the truth often resides in what is unpleasant, disturbing, and unconventional. The photographs of Annie Leibovitz collected in *Women* offer a good analogy: Leibovitz's photographic eye gazes with an almost defiant warmth at women whose appearances often violate conventions of femininity—and in so doing breaks down our stereotyped notions of beauty. (See also the entry on Diane Arbus for October 2.)

FOR FURTHER REFLECTION

Artists, like scientists, often must weather ridicule—or, even worse, neglect. Innovative or controversial ideas and unconventional manners of new expression will kindle the ire of some, garner the praise of others. Be confident in your convictions; at the same time, consider the possibility that some of your views, or the manner in which you express them, could benefit from a little alteration.

..................................TRY THIS..................................

1. In a journal entry, describe in detail someone whose appearance or behavior unsettled you.

2. What do you instinctively turn away from? Homeless persons? People whose physical appearance or manner of dress you find distasteful? List everything you can think of that you ignore or avoid. Now, write a story in which you make a hitherto unsavory character the hero.

SLANTING YOUR WORK

To best understand how to "slant" a topic for a particular magazine, study carefully the material that the magazine publishes. All magazines strive to build a reader base, and once they have it, they maintain it by publishing articles and stories their readers have come to expect.

Editors almost always advise would-be contributors to "study the magazine before submitting"—but what, exactly, should you be studying? Here is a list of questions you want to be able to answer when studying a magazine for its "slant":

- Does the magazine publish fiction, and, if so, are the stories plot-driven or character-driven? Do the authors focus on romantic relationships? Social injustices? Spiritual concerns? Are some or all of the stories light-hearted? Deeply serious? Satiricial?

- Does the magazine publish essays, poetry, or articles? How does this material differ from that found in other magazines?

- Does the magazine publish poetry?

FOR FURTHER REFLECTION

To stay solvent, periodicals need to build a readership. Success depends on whether the periodical in question succeeds in offering subscribers what they look forward to reading from one issue to the next. That is how a periodical develops a personality over the years. Writers who hope to publish in a particular periodical must be able to produce just this kind of material—in other words, must learn to "slant" their writing to that specific readership.

...................................TRY THIS....................................

Before sending a story or article to a magazine you hope will publish your work, study at least two issues of that magazine thoroughly. First, read every selection, even if that selection represents a genre you don't write in. The reason is that fiction and articles overlap in terms of the subject matter and tone. Then, write or revise the manuscript and submit it.

BUILDING A WRITER'S LIBRARY

Every profession rests upon a steadily growing body of expertise, dissemi-
nated through books and courses of study in which those books are used. The
profession of writing is no different. When it comes to deciding which books
are most useful for writers, one glib answer is any book is useful because it
demonstrates how one writer applied her craft well enough to get published.

Seriously, there are two basic categories of books for writers: books that
demonstrate superb writing—i.e., masterpieces of fiction and nonfiction
through the ages (see the entries for May 5, June 5, July 5, and August 5),
and books about the craft of writing and the experience of being a writer.

Beginning and veteran writers alike benefit greatly from the many books
devoted to the craft of writing (e.g., genre-oriented instruction in novel, short
story, memoir writing; or in particular subgenres such as mysteries, science
fiction, horror), the profession of authorship, and tools of the trade—language,
manuscript preparation, and information about marketing and publishing.

FOR FURTHER REFLECTION

While it is true that any book has a place in a writer's library, you ought to
build your library in a way that suits your interests and needs as a working
writer. Begin with the tools: a style manual, a good dictionary, a guide to writing and publishing, an up-to-date market guide, and how-to books on the kinds
of writing you do. Next, build a collection of basic reference works—world
histories and regional histories, specialized dictionaries (e.g., of biology, geology, psychology, mythology, quotations).

.....................................TRY THIS.....................................

Set up a row of books on your desk (or within arm's reach) that you refer to
most frequently when working on a given project. The aim here is to have books
you can refer to quickly without disrupting the momentum of your writing. Over
the next several weeks, use your journal to keep tabs on how you made use of
those books.

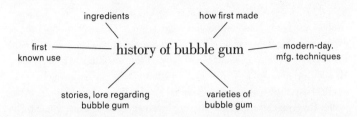

NOVEMBER 6
IDEA MAPPING

One useful brainstorming technique is to map out ideas. Idea mapping (sometimes referred to as "clustering") is a kind of nonlinear outlining whereby
subordinate ideas radiate in all directions from main ideas, like spokes from
the hub of a wagon wheel—something like this:

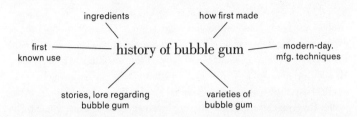

This adds a visual dimension to the abstract process of brainstorming. An idea
"spoke" demonstrates the connection—indeed, a physical connection—between the main idea and its offshoot.

FOR FURTHER REFLECTION
Idea mapping brings abstractions into the sensory limelight. It isn't that abstractions should be avoided, but that translating them visually makes them
easier to work with, and more fun, too.

.....................................TRY THIS....................................

1. Create an idea map for your next writing project. Begin by placing the
   topic in the center of the page, and free-associate to generate subordinate ideas. Use differently colored pencils to draw connections between
   primary, secondary, and tertiary relationships.

2. Transform the idea map you prepared for number one into a first draft,
   inventing new connections as you go along.

"FLAT" VS. "ROUND" CHARACTERS

Some of the characters we encounter in fiction seem more like caricatures in the sense that they are stereotypically villainous or benevolent, tragic or comic. Other characters are more complex, individualistic, realistically portrayed. In his influential 1927 examination of novelistic structure and purpose, *Aspects of the Novel*, E.M. Forster, himself a gifted novelist (*A Passage to India*; *Room With a View*), refers to these types of characters as "flat" and "round" respectively—and both types can inhabit a single work. Characters who "can be expressed in a single sentence" are flat; those who cannot are round, according to Forster. For example, in *David Copperfield*, according to Forster, when Mrs. Micawber says, "I will never desert Mr. Micawber," Charles Dickens has in effect captured that woman's essential nature. However, in William Makepeace Thackeray's *Vanity Fair*, Becky Sharp cannot be so encapsulated. She possesses the complex, inconsistent personality of a traditional heroine and a traditional villain, and so cannot be categorized as one or the other.

FOR FURTHER REFLECTION

In fiction, as in real life, some characters seem more like allegorical embodiments of certain virtues or vices (the seductive type, the self-effacing type, the swashbuckling adventurer type); others cannot be pinned down, except to say that they're inconsistent or unpredictable. Novelists usually understand this aspect of human behavior and so will create characters who are both flat *and* round in E.M. Forster's sense of those terms.

..................................TRY THIS....................................

In your journal, set aside four pages—two of them labeled "Flat Characters," the other two "Round Characters." Now compose two character profiles of each type. Remember that flats will embody a certain type: the con artist; the fanatic. Rounds will not fit into a mold.

DESCRIBING WITH PRECISION

Precise descriptions are as important to storytelling as plot development. Readers love the feeling of being made part of the story world, which is what precise description is able to do. In his novel *The Ambassadors*, in which the American Lambert Strether becomes seduced by the old-world glory of European culture, Henry James describes Strether's hostess's Parisian house with sumptuous and precise detail:

> He found himself making out, as a background of the occupant, some glory, some prosperity of the First Empire, some Napoleonic glamour, some dim luster of the great legend; elements clinging still to all the consular chairs and mythological brasses and sphinxes' heads and faded surfaces of satin striped with alternate silk.
>
> He had never before ... been in the presence of relics ... little old miniatures, medallions, pictures, books, books in leather bindings, pinkish and greenish, with gilt garlands on the back ... under the glass of brass-mounted cabinets. His attention took them all tenderly into account.

FOR FURTHER REFLECTION

Precise description has a cinematic effect: It allows readers to visualize the story, to experience the sensuous delights of a setting. Broad, general descriptions will not do the trick; writers must focus sharply on particulars.

.................................TRY THIS...................................

1. Practice precise description by describing a room in your home in meticulous detail. After finishing your description, test it out by reviewing the details in the room and seeing if you missed anything.

2. Describe a character's appearance in two different ways: in formal dress at a special event such as a concert or wedding; then in casual dress in an informal setting, such as a beach.

MULTIPLE DRAFTING

Who says you can't do more than one thing at a time? When it comes to writing, such multitasking might prove to be the ideal way to proceed. A surefire preventative for writer's block, multiple drafting has a way of recharging the creative batteries. Also, the thinking you put into one draft can trigger ideas for the other draft.

By working on more than one draft at a time, it is only natural to see connections, comparisons. If story number one is about rebellious slaves in the antebellum South and story number two is about an adolescent rebelling against his tyrannical father, the events that take place in the first story can parallel those in the second.

Some writers are able to multitask by working on project A in one room, project B in another, and so on. This is actually an elaboration of a technique of ancient rhetoric whereby segments of an oration were placed inside specific mental compartments or "rooms" called *topoi* (from which the modern word *topic* is derived) to facilitate memorization.

FOR FURTHER REFLECTION

Multitasking may not be for everyone, but it's worth a try anyway. Working on more than one writing project at a time is actually quite suitable to highly creative people, who compulsively make connections between disparate ideas. Multitasking might be seen as a physical manifestation of one who gets bored easily by doing only one thing at a time.

.....................................TRY THIS...................................

Start work on a story or essay; once you are well into it—and at a convenient stopping point—begin work on a second story or essay (it's okay to shift genres). Keep shifting from one project to the other until both are completed. In your journal, describe the experience of working on two projects at once.

DREAMS WITHIN DREAMS

"Is all that we see or seem / But a dream within a dream?" Poe's speaker demands to know in his sonnet, "A Dream Within a Dream." The thought is provocative, and has given rise to many a science-fiction story. Can it be literally true that "life is but a dream"? Certainly, as we grow older and we think back on the years and decades, our experiences seem to acquire the tenuousness of dreams. Is it possible that we are still dreaming? A religious person might say, of course! Soon you will wake up to Eternal Life.

Our technological age has produced a more profane interpretation of that beatific vision: virtual reality. In films like *Total Recall* (based on the Philip K. Dick story, "We Can Remember It for You Wholesale") and *The Matrix*, the very idea of "reality" is ambiguous as a result of the degree to which computers can simulate reality and tap the human mind into that cyber-universe. The story possibilities are endless.

FOR FURTHER REFLECTION

The computer age has changed our understanding of reality. It's frightening, certainly, but it also provides writers (not just science-fiction writers) with a rich fund of story material. A dream world can seem exactly like the real world so long as you are inside it; only when you awaken do you realize the difference. What if your waking world was also a dream?

..................................TRY THIS..................................

1. Write a story in which your viewpoint character discovers that what he assumed was the real world was actually a dream world.

2. As a variation of number one, imagine that your viewpoint character is living inside what we readers can see is a cyber-universe, a simulation that, from your character's perspective, is the real world. Imagine that something disastrous happens in this cyber-universe. How will your protagonist escape, if at all?

EXPERIENCE AS EXPERIMENT

We write essays in order to explore the nuances of a topic or a personal experience, to articulate an emotional state, to grapple with an idea. Montaigne, the father of the essay, coined the term *essai* (from the French word for an attempt, an experiment), in order to stress the exploratory nature of essay writing. "Could my mind find a firm footing," he writes in his essay "On Repentance," "I should not be making essays."

Our experiences, in a sense, are all experiments in living, and, as such, are worth sharing with others. Topics can range from the metaphysical to the mundane. Paging through an anthology such as Philip Lopate's *The Art of the Personal Essay*, one finds an essay on "Death" by Lu Hsun; an essay on "Laughter," by Max Beerbohm; an essay by Carlos Fuentes on "How I Started to Write"; an essay by Joan Didion on being "In Bed" with a migraine. No experience is too trivial to be milked for an underlying lesson that was learned from it.

FOR FURTHER REFLECTION

The art of the essay is the art of prodding and poking at an idea or an experience until it yields the most meaning. Essays, Edward Hoagland writes in his introduction to the *Best American Essays, 1999*, "simulate the mind's own processes in a murky and incongruous world." Every good essay, then, offers us yet another example of how a reasonably intelligent person grapples with the murkiness and the incongruity of life.

..................................TRY THIS..................................

1. Use your journal to list, and briefly describe, all kinds of experiences, large and small. Do not judge them according to "significance." The most seemingly insignificant experience can yield much wisdom.

2. Each week for five weeks, develop one of the experiences you listed for number one into an essay.

NOVEMBER 12
CRITIQUING OBJECTIVELY

Critiquing objectively is not the contradiction in terms that it seems to be. True, critiquing or evaluation of any kind is an expression of one's sense of quality and excellence and taste—criteria that are self-evidently subjective. On the other hand, by following widely adopted standards of story and character development, use of dialogue, backstory, suspense-building, and so on, it is possible to avoid overly subjective feedback.

By being an objective critic, you are in effect telling the writer under scrutiny, "Let me remind you of these tried-and-true criteria; see if they work. If you don't think they do, then ignore them."

FOR FURTHER REFLECTION

Objectivity and subjectivity are relative terms; that is, they exist in degrees of one or the other. (Think of a spectrum: total objectivity at one end, total subjectivity at the other, with each end of the spectrum registering zero.) There is always the risk, when critiquing a fellow writer's work, of working too closely at the subjective end of the spectrum. The ideal is to operate somewhere near the middle, to draw as little as possible from personal taste and more from mainstream standards of good storytelling or idea development, as the case may be.

......................................TRY THIS....................................

Prepare a list of "objective" criteria for evaluating a short story or essay. (This becomes tougher with poetry.) Use this list as a springboard for evaluating a fellow writer's work; it will prevent you from becoming too subjective.

WINE CONOISSEURSHIP

It's all too easy to poke fun at the wine connoisseur and his vocabulary of gustatory variations—*character, full-bodied, complex, meaty, woody, legs*—but these are formal terms used in wine-tasting and determination of quality. Wine has been an integral part of culture since ancient times; the Greeks even had a god of wine—Dionysus (Bacchus for the Romans)—and during the past thirty years it has become an important part of the good life throughout North America, Europe, Australia, and South Africa.

The varieties of wines are so numerous they have filled encyclopedias—for example, Hugh Johnson's *Modern Encyclopedia of Wine*, which also includes information about wine-growing regions around the world, winemaking, wine-tasting, and choosing wines. Because of their symbolic value, the roles they have played in history, and their many social functions, wines and wine lore are well worth the attention of writers of all stripes.

FOR FURTHER REFLECTION
Wine is associated with fine dining and celebrations (especially with that variety of wine known as champagne). In ancient times, wine enabled mortals to feel, however fleetingly, godlike—hence the Dionysian festivals that were regularly held. Wines and wine culture offer writers a wealth of material. It is even the subject of a popular film, *Sideways*, in which a young wine connoisseur who cannot form healthy relationships with women takes his soon-to-be-married friend on a wine-tasting adventure.

......................................TRY THIS......................................

1. Expand your knowledge of wines and wine lore, and plan a story—say, a romance in which the couple's mutual love of wine extends to love for each other, or a fantasy about a winemaker who creates a wine that imparts supernatural abilities to its imbibers.

2. Write an essay on the art of selecting different wines for different kinds of meals or for different occasions.

NOVEMBER 14
HISTORY IN FICTION

History records significant events of the past, but literature brings those events to life; and it does so by giving the long-ago a sense of dramatic immediacy. Notice, for example, how in *Pompeii*, his novel about the eruption of Vesuvius in 79 C.E., Robert Harris captures the experience of being an eyewitness to the event:

> All around them was a fury of noise—the heaving sea, the blizzard of rock, the boom of roofs giving way. ... It was like being stoned by a mob—as if the deities had voted Vulcan a triumph and this painful procession [of Pompeiians struggling to escape], stripped of all human dignity, was how he chose to humiliate his captives. They edged forward slowly, sinking up to their knees in the loose pumice.

Similarly, Robert Graves in *I, Claudius*, instead of merely telling us that his hero visited the future-seeing Sybil, dramatizes the moment:

> I came into the inner cavern, after groping painfully on all fours up the stairs, and saw the Sibyl, more like an ape than a woman, sitting on a chair in a cage that hung from the ceiling, her robes red and her unblinking eyes shining red.

The details enable us to see the Sibyl in our mind's eye so vividly that they seem completely realistic and believable.

FOR FURTHER REFLECTION

History comes to life in fiction through the experiences of the characters. History, then, becomes an intimate human experience. Perhaps teachers should ask their students to read novels set in the times they are studying, to supplement their history textbooks.

...............................TRY THIS....................................

Invent a character who becomes an eyewitness to a historical event, such as the assassination of Julius Caesar or the attempt of those two obscure bicycle mechanics at Kitty Hawk to get a machine to fly, and write a page describing that event in as much minute detail as you can to give readers the impression that they have entered that world.

NOVEMBER 15
CAPTURING THE INNER LOGIC OF DREAMS

Even in our sleep we are storytellers. However, because dream stories possess a bizarre inner logic of their own, they can be difficult to capture—but they're stories nonetheless. Many of them are mosaics, each fragment contributing to an overall design. Incidents usually unfold in a free-associative and spatial rather than rational manner.

The goal of keeping a dream journal is to be able to examine the content and the sequencing of dream stories. Doing so might help you develop the inner compulsions and desires (repressed or otherwise) of your characters.

FOR FURTHER REFLECTION
Keeping a dream journal is a kind of biofeedback phenomenon: The greater your effort to capture your dreams, the more vividly your dreams will become, and the likelier you will be to capture some of them—at least that's the theory. It might work for you, or it might not—but it's worth a try, and perhaps, as a bonus, your dream life will improve and truly serve as a resource for your writing.

......................................TRY THIS......................................

1. Give yourself a full month to get into the knack of recording your dreams. First, you will need a dream journal that you'll keep on the nightstand within easy reach. Every morning (or in the middle of the night as the case may be) upon awakening, immediately jot down as much of your dream(s) as you can recall. Don't take time to edit. Even seemingly wrong or inappropriate usage can be revealing.

2. Over the next few weeks prepare lists of desires, fantasies, compulsions for some of the characters in your short story or novel in progress.

DICTIONARY PLAY

Turning to a dictionary for *play*? Yes, if you're a lover a words (as you should be). Writers often pay attention to words adjacent to the word they're looking up, which is not unlike browsing in libraries: We tend to page through books that surround the one we've come to retrieve.

There's a rich opportunity for serendipity in dictionary browsing: The adjacent words we discover might possibly shed unexpected light on our essay in progress or on the subject of our research. The unexpected light could also conceivably send researchers back to their proverbial drawing boards to rethink their projects from scratch.

Studying the dictionary is probably not the best way to build vocabulary; however, if you do so purely for fun, to satisfy curiosity, then you'll be more likely to retain the new words.

FOR FURTHER REFLECTION

A dictionary is a marvelous tool, when you stop to think of it: There, at your fingertips, are all the words in the language, together with their varied meanings, pronunciation, parts of speech, spelling variations, and etymology. If you consult the *Oxford English Dictionary*—and every writer should, for it is the greatest dictionary of all time—you will find yourself immersed in *twenty* folio-sized volumes containing not only every word in the language but a history of every word in the language, together with examples of usage from earliest times to the present day. Spending a few hours now and then with the *OED* will grandly enrich your knowledge of the English language.

......................................TRY THIS....................................

1. Open your desk dictionary at random and jot down every word and meaning that is unfamiliar to you (in the unlikely event that you know every word on those two pages, turn to the next page). Next, write a paragraph or two in which you put each of your newly learned words to use.

2. Open your dictionary at random and choose a single word that strikes your fancy. Use that word to spark an idea for a poem, an essay, a short story, or a play.

NOVEMBER 17
CITY SOUNDS

We are creatures with one foot rooted in the natural world and the other in the artificial world of our own devising. We may wax idealistic and wish that we could return to nature, to allow ourselves to become more in tune with the rhythms and harmonies of nature—and these are noble ideals, to be sure. But a great many of us would not feel at home in the wilderness; for better or worse, we have become too conditioned by urban life, which has rhythms and sounds of its own. Of course, inching one's way through highway gridlock, rushing to a meeting, listening to horns and sirens and jack-hammering may not be everyone's idea of rhythm or euphony, but they do characterize city life. The rhythms and sounds may resemble jazz more than they do classical orchestral music—but both are examples of music. If you're a student of modern life, you need to pay attention to the jazzy rhythms and sounds of city life.

FOR FURTHER REFLECTION

Cities offer writers a kaleidoscope of sounds and rhythms that communicate a great deal about modern life. Writers tapping into this frenetic energy will, in effect, be tapping into the heart of modern life, with all its harmonies and dissonances.

...................................TRY THIS....................................

Over the next several days become a student of city sounds. Pay close atten-tion to the subtler urban sounds that may be obscured by the more obnoxious ones: sounds emanating from factories, airports, shopping malls; evening and nocturnal sounds; early morning sounds. Visit a city park and record what you hear there. How do those sounds differ from those encountered in wilderness areas? Maintain a written record of the sounds you encounter in these various urban locations.

ON MAKING CONNECTIONS

Part of the pleasure of creative writing, along with transforming story ideas into dramatically fleshed-out stories, is stumbling upon unanticipated or spontaneously discovered connections that add texture and intrigue to your story. To be able to make such imaginative connections, however, you need to give your story plenty of variables, plenty of loose ends to connect.

You also need to let your subconscious mind do some of the work. Turn off (or at least lower the volume of) the logic center of your brain, and allow for a certain degree of free-associating. Your subconscious is very good at making connections among seemingly unconnectable ideas.

FOR FURTHER REFLECTION

Walt Whitman's poem, "A Noiseless, Patient Spider" creates a vivid image of how a writer uses his soul the way a spider spins its web in order to connect things:

> It launch'd filament, filament, filament, out of itself,
> Ever unreeling them, ever tirelessly speeding them.
>
> And you O my soul where you stand,
> Surrounded, detached, in measureless oceans of space,
> Ceaselessly musing, venturing, throwing, seeking the spheres
>   to connect them,
> Till the bridge you will need be form'd, till the ductile anchor
>   hold,
> Till the gossamer thread you fling catch somewhere, O my
>   soul.

......................................TRY THIS....................................

Examine a recently completed essay, poem, or short story and pinpoint the connections you've established in it. Did you compare and contrast one idea or individual with another?

NOVEMBER 19
"NEVER FORGET"

Certain events in the history of a people must never be forgotten: the forced migration of Native American tribes, the shameful racist practices of the pre-Civil Rights era, the Holocausts of genocide and nuclear annihilation of World War II; the list is long and painful.

Perhaps too painful to write about, you might think. Yet they must continue to be written about. Many Holocaust stories have been told; far more have not been. After all, there are six million of them to tell. At Holocaust memorials and museums around the world, the abstract statistics are given faces, and if not faces, then personal effects, like shoes: a mountain of shoes, confiscated from those who were summarily executed or murdered by slower means.

It is difficult to write about barbarity that defies the imagination; one must be careful not to slip into bathos or melodrama. One must not try to cover it all, but rather proceed in the opposite direction: to find the narrowest possible topic and probe it deeply—the story of a watercolor painting from the Warsaw Ghetto, let us say, and of the child who painted it.

FOR FURTHER REFLECTION

We must never forget the atrocities of history, for doing so increases the likelihood that they will recur. But writing about atrocities is difficult—not just because the subject matter defies conventional expression, but because the subject matter can overwhelm any rational thesis the writer wishes to advance. The best strategy is to focus on a minuscule portion of the whole, on something happening out of range, in the shadows, as is the case with Anne Frank's diary.

..................................TRY THIS....................................

Write about a painful moment in history, say, the persecution of Christians in the Roman arenas. Tell the story of the persecution from the point of view of a single person who is about to be thrown to the lions.

NOVEMBER 20
READING TO MOTIVATE WRITING

Successful writers are omnivores—gluttons—when it comes to reading because they are continually fascinated by yet another way of telling a story, of new ways of using language to evoke sensory impressions, to transport us to other times and places. Reading omnivorously means reading outside the boundary of storytelling that is most similar to your own. Do you like writing mysteries à la Sue Grafton and Jonathan Kellerman? Then read Virginia Woolf and Ernest Hemingway. Do you like to write lighthearted fiction? Then read Dostoevsky and Strindberg. If you're a poet with a penchant for composing Wordsworthian pastoral meditations via Petrarchan sonnets, then take the time to read poets with modernist sensibilities like T.S. Eliot and Anne Sexton. You will learn much from reading authors whose modes of storytelling, writing styles, and worldviews are very different from your own.

FOR FURTHER REFLECTION

Reading of any kind can prove to be an excellent way to rekindle the writing flame. That's because when we read, we're indulging ourselves in the primal pleasure that made us want to become writers in the first place: magically shaping language into stories, into other worlds that we can venture into.

......................................TRY THIS....................................

1. Pick up a book or magazine and, with pen and paper within easy reach, begin reading one of its stories or articles. Your aim here is to be on the alert for whatever it is in the piece of writing that triggers an idea, however vague. As soon as it comes, stop reading and jot it down.

2. Go over the notes you've taken for number one, and select one of them to work into a story or essay.

"NOTHING NEW UNDER THE SUN"

If you're striving to be absolutely original, you're engaging in an act of futility. The most original works of art, be they paintings or musical compositions or novels, draw from what has gone before. On the other hand, the way you see the world is your way and yours alone; it is inevitably unlike anyone else's. The trick is to be able to highlight your special angle of vision, to offset it from conventional perceptions. After all, in the words of the distinguished writing teacher Sidney Cox (*Indirections for Those Who Want to Write*), "The only thing that makes you more than a drop in the common bucket ... is the interplay of your specialness with your commonness."

FOR FURTHER REFLECTION

All of us see the world differently. At the same time, our perceptions of reality are similar enough to enable us to communicate our differing angles of vision. In fact, the departures from our own angles of vision are what delight us. Think of it as seeing difference embedded in similarity (or vice versa).

...................................TRY THIS...................................

1. Write a love story that follows, *almost* faithfully, one of the tried-and-true formulas, such as boy wins girl's affection; boy loses girl's affection to rival lover; boy wins girl's affection back after performing some heroic deed. Change just one of the elements of the formula. For example, instead of losing girl's affection to rival lover, make the loss of affection the result of some indiscretion, such as the boy having said or done something stupid.

2. Write a humorous version of a serious classical story, or a serious version of a humorous classical story. Here are a few possibilities:

    The Phantom of the Opera   *Don Quixote*

    Gone With the Wind   *How the Grinch Stole Christmas*

WRITING AND USING SYNOPSES

Think of a synopsis as a jazzed-up summary. In an ordinary summary, only the main abstract ideas are mentioned, but in a jazzed-up summary—a synopsis—choice plot *details* are included so that the summary begins to resemble the actual story, highly compressed. Omitted are mood setting descriptions, character development, pacing, atmosphere.

So what is the point of writing synopses? Why not simply leap into the story itself and let one thing lead to another? Well, some writers do work this way. Usually, it's messy—much trial and error and wadding up false starts. A synopsis can help set a course for your project and help you head toward it. Of course, it's possible to do both: to launch headlong into a draft without any planning and then, once into it, pause to work out a detailed synopsis for the whole work. Usually, the synopsis will lead to revising that initial draft; the new draft will in turn lead to a better developed synopsis. One method helps to refine the other.

FOR FURTHER REFLECTION

Synopses encapsulate the work in progress in a way that enables the writer (and the editor or agent to whom the writer is pitching the work) to get the clearest possible sense, in the most condensed way possible, of what the work as a whole will be like—with minimal distortion. Synopses are more detailed than conventional summaries; the latter includes only the bare bones of the work in progress, relying heavily on abstraction. Synopses lay out the story scene by scene, focusing sharply on key conflict situations.

...................................TRY THIS....................................

1. In your journal, write a one-page summary of a short story you've been planning in your head. The summary should include the basic conflict situation, the key characters, the climax, and the outcome.

2. Develop the summary you've prepared for number one into a five-page synopsis. This time, go into more detail about character background and motivation, setting, and the twists and turns of the plot (see the entry for September 22).

ON EXISTENTIALISM

Existentialism is a fancy word for a simple concept. It is the principle by which human beings must come to recognize that they alone are responsible for what befalls them in life, that they alone control their destinies, not God. The French existentialist Jean-Paul Sartre took it a step further: Human beings were solely responsible for their lives because there *was* no God. To be an existentialist, then, regardless of whether theistic or atheistic, is to accept the burden of fate. Nothing to an existentialist is "meant to be"; nothing "happens for the best." The poles of determinism and freedom are never pre-existent or absolute but are always negotiated with others. The behavioral psychologist B.F. Skinner, in his 1971 treatise, *Beyond Freedom and Dignity*, describes such ideas as free will in terms of stimulus and response. As Skinner writes,

> Man's struggle for freedom is not due to a will to be free but to certain behavioral processes characteristic of the human organism, the chief effect of which is the avoidance of or escape from so-called "aversive" features of the environment.

At the risk of overgeneralization, such is the existentialist's worldview. We writers may accept or reject this view, but we cannot ignore it.

FOR FURTHER REFLECTION

An existential view of life detaches it from any metaphysical or transcendental reality. Human beings "control" their destiny insofar as they are able to manipulate their environment and negotiate their needs with others. If they fail—if their efforts to establish policies that satisfy all parties involved fail—then we are in the world of Sartre's play, *No Exit*, the mantra from which can chill the blood: "Hell is other people."

..................................TRY THIS..................................

Read an introduction to existentialism. (*The Philosophy of Jean-Paul Sartre*, edited by Robert Denoon Cumming, is a good place to start, as it includes key passages from Sartre's most important works.) After absorbing this challenging material, write an essay in which you support or refute Sartre's views, or existentialism itself.

ON SPECULATION

One need not be a futurist to appreciate the role that speculation plays in certain kinds of storytelling. What effect would a near-death experience have on a character? What would happen to ordinary citizens, or foreign visitors, caught in a military coup? How might astronauts trapped in a crippled space vehicle in Earth's orbit be rescued?

Of course, mystery, fantasy and science fiction is based on creative speculation. If angels really existed, what would they be like and how would they interact with mortals? How will your detective hero catch a serial killer who happens to be an undertaker and cremates the victims?

To be adept at plotting, you should cultivate speculation as regular habit of mind. Regularly build everyday events into predicaments: a hot-air balloon ride becomes a frantic survival adventure when the balloon is caught in a windstorm; a couple enters a funhouse and winds up in an alternate universe. Don't be reluctant to play out "what if" scenarios every chance you get.

FOR FURTHER REFLECTION

Speculation is important for effective plotting. Once you imagine a dire situation for your protagonist, you must then speculate on the possible ways to get her out of that dire situation. This will usually result in working out several steps, not just one; you don't want to come up with too easy a solution!

...................................TRY THIS...................................

Use your journal to practice your speculations skills. Draw a line down the center of a page. The left side will be the "What if" side; the right will be the speculation that answers the question.

URBAN SETTINGS

Cities are exciting places because so many different things are happening all at once, generating a plethora of sensory impressions. For writers, cities are showcases of human behavior; the larger the city, the greater the spectrum of human diversity, the greater range of foods, arts and crafts, architecture, fashions. Cities offer writers a cornucopia of story possibilities.

Commenting on the character of modern life and the impact it has on writers, especially when facing the paradoxical problem of finding sufficient tranquility in an urban environment, the Nobel Prize-winning novelist Saul Bellow noted in an interview that "art has something to do with the achievement of stillness in the midst of chaos, a stillness which characterizes … the eye of the storm. I think that art has something to do with an arrest of attention in the midst of distraction."

FOR FURTHER REFLECTION

Paradoxical as it may seem, the noise and distractions of cities can prove to be valuable stimuli for writers—not only for story material, but for raw energy. Because so much of modern life takes place in urban settings, writers will benefit from being astute observers of urban life.

...................................TRY THIS....................................

Practice describing various urban settings in your journal, even if you have no immediate plans for writing stories set in cities. People-watching sites would be ideal. Some suggestions:

- an art gallery during a reception
- a parade or protest march
- the lobby or cocktail lounge of a posh hotel
- a children's museum
- a street arts and crafts fair

MAGIC REALISM

Magic realism is associated with the works of Latin American authors, most notably the Colombian novelist Gabriel Garcia Márquez and the Argentinean short-story writer and poet Jorge Luis Borges; but Italian authors such as Italo Calvino and Umberto Eco, Japanese authors such as Haruki Murakami, and American authors such as Alice Hoffman have also been called magic realists. Basically, the term refers to stories that combine gritty realistic details with supernatural or fantastical ones. Of course, combinations of the real and the fantastical are as old as storytelling itself. Homer's *Iliad* is filled with reality-fantasy juxtapositions—the brutal realism of warfare combined with the intervention of gods. For modern writers, though, it's more of a challenge to make the fantastic seem to fit into reality. In *Practical Magic*, Alice Hoffman tells the story of two orphaned sisters, Sally and Gillian, who seem to have acquired uncanny, and unwanted, powers from their guardian aunts. Sally, for example, places witch-like spells on men who befriend her:

> When Sally swings the door open, Gary looks into her eyes and sees himself upside down. He finds himself in a pool of gray light, drowning, going down for the third time, and there's not a damn thing he can do about it. His grandfather told him once that witches caught you this way …

FOR FURTHER REFLECTION

Who can say where the boundary between the natural and the supernatural lies? In fiction, as in real life, one realm may easily spill into the other. Magic realists, we might say, capitalize on such moments of spillover. Lovers suddenly discover that they can read each other's minds; an archaeologist discovers that he possesses the "genetic memory" of a Babylonian king.

............................TRY THIS....................................

Try your hand at magic realism by describing an incident that take place in a familiar setting—say, an inner-city playground—where, for some strange reason, some of the children begin to levitate, or everything begins to change color.

TELLING STORIES ABOUT TELLING STORIES

Perhaps you know the story of Scheherazade, the heroine of the medieval *1,001 Nights*, whose storytelling skills kept her tyrannical husband, King Shahriyar, sufficiently entertained to dissuade him from beheading her, as he had done with his other wives. In Mary Shelley's *Frankenstein*, the narrator Robert Walton conveys the tale of the scientist Victor Frankenstein and the creature he brought to life, only to be cast out for its defects. The story within a story device has been used throughout the history of storytelling—but for what good reason? Why not simply tell the main story directly? Why "frame" it within a larger narrative?

The reason has to do with the magic of storytelling itself, the intrigue that is instantly generated when someone says, "Let me tell you a story"—especially if that person seems haunted or deranged from the experience embodied by the story to be told.

FOR FURTHER REFLECTION

Storytelling is itself a topic of fascination, which is why novels are sometimes written as stories within stories. Readers are then intrigued by the gradually unfolding connections that are made between what is going on in the stories being told and the present circumstance.

.... TRY THIS ....

Create a story that has a storyteller as its narrator. You might wish to pattern her after Scheherazade or simply present the storyteller as a survivor of a harrowing incident who tells the story as a kind of flashback.

CONVEYING NOSTALGIA

The older we get the greater the occasions for nostalgia, for dwelling on how things used to be. For students beginning their first year of college, the excitement of being on their own for the first time is offset by bouts of homesickness, of finding themselves tossed upon the choppy seas of adulthood. Because nostalgia speaks to everyone on some level, readers easily are moved by it. If you're planning a memoir, you will want to include nostalgic experiences: long-ago moments of early-childhood frolic, happy-sad moments with grandparents, the house in which you grew up, your earliest holiday memories, your first experience with the death of a pet, the day you had to say goodbye to your friends when your family moved to another state …

FOR FURTHER REFLECTION

Nostalgia captures life's transitions. Some of our most emotional experiences are nostalgic ones. Curiously, nostalgia evokes both positive and negative feelings, not unlike the "sweet sorrow" of parting lovers. By capturing the feelings of nostalgia, we are, in fact, giving our readers a rewarding emotional experience.

......................................TRY THIS....................................

1. Take yourself on a nostalgic trip through your past: the homesickness you experienced when you went off to college; memories of your grandparents' home; the close friends you had when growing up; the happy-sad moments you shared at weddings, confirmations, bar/bat mitzvahs, and so on. Write a journal entry for each of these nostalgic memories.

2. Select one of the entries you wrote for number one and turn it into a short story or personal essay.

METAPHORICAL THINKING

Thought consists largely of representing abstract concepts with concrete representations that stick in the mind. We might be able to hold in memory the abstract definition of patriotism ("a devoted love, support, and defense of one's country"—*Random House Webster's College Dictionary*), but it is easier to root that abstraction in a symbolic image—say, of people surrounding a flag, hands over their hearts, or that unforgettable photograph of soldiers hoisting up the flag at Iwo Jima. The art of poetry is largely the art of metaphorical thinking. We gain insight into the nature of things by comparing them with other things …

- My life is *an open book*
- Paul has been growing *like a weed*
- The invaders *swarmed* across the field (the metaphor of insects such as locusts captured by the verb *swarmed*)
- The jellyfish resembled tiny undulating *umbrellas*

FOR FURTHER REFLECTION

Metaphors are pleasing to readers because they stretch the imagination, are playful, and, at the same time, deepen our understanding through comparison. A good poet will startle us with metaphors that are at once highly unusual and weirdly fitting, like Sharon Olds's description, in her poem, "California Swimming Pool," of dead oak leaves lying on the ground "like dried-out turtle shells."

......................................TRY THIS....................................

Spend a few days getting into the habit of thinking in metaphors. Use your journal to describe objects metaphorically. What do the icicles lining your eaves remind you of? Dragon teeth? The interior of a cave? The entrance to a troll's den? Here a few objects that should lend themselves to metaphoric description:

- oil well pumps
- dozens of sunbathers on a beach
- church bells
- lightning
- vegetables, fruits, tubers (bell peppers, melons, squash, ginger root)

NOVEMBER 30
PROJECT CONNECTING

Here's a writer's block zapper that can also help with generating new content for your work in progress. Not only does the mind enjoy a fresh task now and then by shifting from one writing task to another, but the new task can indirectly serve as a resource for the old one. If one project is a novel set in Washington, D.C., for example, and another project is an essay about the history of the Pentagon, you might be able to integrate some of that Pentagon history into the novel.

Regularly making connections among your various works in progress can add new life to works that have lost their momentum. Whenever you make connections like that, you are stimulating your creative juices, which is an excellent way to fend off writer's block.

FOR FURTHER REFLECTION

Integrating writing tasks often replenishes concentration and may even increase the likelihood of serendipity, in that ideas generated from working in one subject area can shed unexpected light on the other one. Some writers, whether blocked or not, will try integrating parts of one work into the other, simply because they want to see what happens to the story dynamics. Every writer works differently.

...................................TRY THIS...................................

Spend the next couple of weeks working on at least two writing projects at once just to see how this method of project connecting affects your productivity. Does it make you more energetic? Does the work you do on one project shed light on the other?

DECEMBER 1
WINTER FESTIVALS

December and January are months of festivity: Waves of frolic and expressions of glad tidings and colorful lights effectively counteract the darkness and barrenness of winter. In fact, the customary images of winter are given positive associations; thus, snow brings with it the festivity of skiing and building snowmen; ice the merriment of the skating rink. The colder it gets outside, the cozier people make themselves inside—"Chestnuts roasting on an open fire," and so on.

For writers, the winter season offers many opportunities to contribute to the good cheer. There can never be enough good cheer either, so never hold back on writing on holiday season topics because it seems as if too many other writers are doing the same. Remember, too, that every writer has a distinctive set of experiences to share.

FOR FURTHER REFLECTION

Through the power of spirit and imagination, we imbue the "dead" months of cold and barrenness with images of birth and renewal. The colors and iconography of the holiday season are a testament to the collective optimism of humanity, the assurance that life and light will prevail over death and darkness.

......................................TRY THIS....................................

1. What is your favorite holiday ritual? Write an essay about it and how you have come to love it.

2. Just for fun (or for satiric purposes) invent a ritual and build a fantasy story around it.

DECEMBER 2
GIOVANNI BATTISTA TIEPOLO: "TIME UNVEILING TRUTH"

In this allegorical painting, Time (represented by the hideous, winged abductor and his scythe, which also equates Time with Death) is exposing Truth to Cupid (i.e., mortal love), which cannot prevail in Time's presence. Only the sun offers promise that Truth will transcend her mortal trappings, including that of Time, and achieve her ultimate revelation in heaven.

Allegorical paintings are like prose allegories, whereby individuals and objects represent complex abstract ideas. Such allegorical representation enables the viewer (or the reader) to apprehend the complex interconnections more readily.

FOR FURTHER REFLECTION

Tiepolo's painting helps us realize the difficulty of truth to prevail in a world of mortality, vanity, carnal desire, and fear. Yet truth does prevail. She may be vulnerable to the temptations and corruptions of the flesh, but there is a divine spirit that shines forth (symbolized by the sun directly above her head), giving her strength and endurance. You may view Tiepolo's painting via the Web site of the Boston Museum of Fine Arts (www.mfa.org/collections/search_art).

..................................TRY THIS...................................

Compose an allegorical poem in which you dramatize Time's struggle to expose Truth to the things of the world that will threaten to undo her. You might use as a model Keats's "Ode on Melancholy," in which Melancholy "dwells with Beauty—Beauty that must die; / And Joy, whose hand is ever at his lips / Bidding adieu …"

DECEMBER 3
BREAKING THE RULES

It is never wise to break the rules for the sake of breaking them; on the other hand, new ideas often come into being only if one breaks the rules.

Just what are "rules" anyway? They're practices that have become standards. For example, it was once a rule—a standard practice—that a poem conform to a particular metrical and/or rhyming format. Imagine if Walt Whitman, T.S. Eliot, Elizabeth Bishop, William Carlos Williams, Allen Ginsberg, Sylvia Plath, Anne Sexton, or Billy Collins had taken that rule seriously. Writing free verse may be like "playing tennis with the net down," as Robert Frost famously quipped, but free-verse poets in effect rejoin: false analogy! Writing poetry is nothing at all like playing tennis.

The essence of art is its daring to penetrate the dark corners of the psyche, of human experience in general. To do that, one cannot be bound by conventional rules.

FOR FURTHER REFLECTION

Rules come into being so that standards may be established. We have rules of grammar that define the way a language functions as well as maintain a standard of usage. But the authority of rules diminishes in artistic contexts. Or rather, old rules are replaced with new ones. If the old rule had been that rhymes must be exact (spring/sing), a new or modified rule might be that rhymes may be either exact or slant (farm/worm).

....................................TRY THIS....................................

Write a story without thinking consciously of the rules of short story writing as you have learned them. (For example, "tell the story from one point of view only"; "keep your tense consistent throughout"; "begin a new paragraph when a different person speaks"). After completing the draft, reread it carefully with the rules in mind, and decide which of them you want to eliminate or reinstate, as the case may be.

DECEMBER 4
AUTHORSHIP AND MARKETING

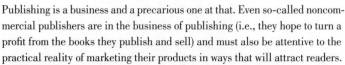

Publishing is a business and a precarious one at that. Even so-called noncommercial publishers are in the business of publishing (i.e., they hope to turn a profit from the books they publish and sell) and must also be attentive to the practical reality of marketing their products in ways that will attract readers.

Some writers feel that marketing their work is beneath them; they're artists, not merchants. In some ways, this sentiment is justified because book publishing *has* become heavily commercialized. Books are becoming increasingly more expensive to publish, which is why even financially secure publishers are reluctant to take a chance with unknown authors.

The best way for an unknown author to break through the competition is to find a reputable agent. "Reputable" means that the agent is listed in *Writer's Market* or *Guide to Literary Agents* (both updated annually) or *Literary Market Place* and is a member of the Association of Authors' Representatives (AAR). Literary agents do what editors used to do thirty years ago: screen through thousands of proposals in search of promising material.

FOR FURTHER REFLECTION

The competition for getting your book published is formidable, but do not let that discourage you. There is always room at the top. Let the reality of tough competition be your constant reminder to do your very best work.

..................................TRY THIS....................................

After you finish the draft of a book, select the best three chapters and send them, together with a proposal, to a reputable literary agent. The proposal should consist of the following:

- a detailed chapter-by-chapter outline or synopsis of the entire book

- a market analysis: why your book should be published; existing books that are similar to it, how your book is different, and who the target readers will be

- an estimated time for completion of the book

- a résumé listing your credentials and previous publications

- a cover letter summarizing your project and a description of the proposal package you're enclosing

- a stamped, self-addressed envelope for the agent's reply

DECEMBER 5
THE GIFT OF READING

Few gifts are as precious as the gift of reading. All children learn to read in school, of course, but unless that skill is continually nurtured, it will atrophy. What better time to reinforce children's intrinsic love of reading than by showering them with books as gifts during this holiday season? Periodicals devoted to books such as *The New York Times Book Review* and *The New York Review of Books* publish special sections of gift books for children as well as for adults every holiday season.

As a writer, you can set a fine example in your family through your advocacy of books and reading. To be sure, you do not want to be heavy-handed about it; that has a way of backfiring. But expressing your own enthusiasm for reading, telling stories about the stories you've read, quoting what great thinkers have said about writing—e.g., Richard Steele's famous words, "Reading is to the mind what exercise is to the body"; or Anna Quindlen's, "In books I have traveled, not only to other worlds, but into my own"—will prove to be more influential than mere proselytizing.

FOR FURTHER REFLECTION

As creators of reading, we writers are best suited to giving reading as a gift, especially to the young people in our lives. Children are naturally voracious readers; yet, sadly, children sometimes are made fun of for reading a lot. The more enthusiastically adults advocate reading, and do so by example, the less likely reading will be an object of ridicule.

..................................TRY THIS....................................

Make a list of all of your family members. Beside each name, name the books you think he or she would likely enjoy. This will be your gift list for the holidays.

FREE-ASSOCIATING

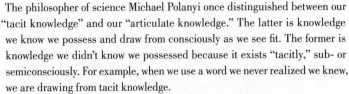

The philosopher of science Michael Polanyi once distinguished between our "tacit knowledge" and our "articulate knowledge." The latter is knowledge we know we possess and draw from consciously as we see fit. The former is knowledge we didn't know we possessed because it exists "tacitly," sub- or semiconsciously. For example, when we use a word we never realized we knew, we are drawing from tacit knowledge.

It is important for writers to be aware of the fact that their tacit knowledge lurks like a surging subterranean sea inside their heads, waiting to be tapped into—but how? Simply by writing freely—that is, by free-associating on paper (or on the screen) without resorting to premature editing. Free-association writing (or simply free-writing) opens the channels to that hidden reservoir of tacit knowledge. Invariably writers surprise themselves when they review what they have churned out in a matter of minutes.

FOR FURTHER REFLECTION

We know a lot more than we think we know. Much of what we learn we in effect place in deep storage because we can find no use for it in our daily lives. But writing requires more dynamic knowledge retrieval than ordinary thinking. The more you write, the thinner will be the boundary between your tacit and articulate knowledge.

......................................TRY THIS....................................

Spend a half hour writing nonstop, free-associating on a broad topic, and writing down whatever comes to mind, no matter how irrational or irrelevant it seems. Shut off the editor in your brain that will want to put a stop to such nonsense. Your goal here is to see how readily you can retrieve tacit knowledge about the subject. Afterward, pluck out the morsels and use them as the basis for a poem or short story.

DECEMBER 7
HEROES, SUPERHEROES, AND ANTIHEROES

The idea of heroism has become fairly complex these days. Heroes can be flawed, unreliable, unpredictable—in short, downright unheroic. There are even "antiheroes"—protagonists who violate (often comically) the very idea of heroism, or who satirize stereotypically heroic behavior as do comedians like Charlie Chaplin, the Marx Brothers, or Carol Burnett. We find antiheroic types in that mode of drama known as theater of the absurd, a term used to describe the plays of Samuel Beckett, Eugène Ionesco, Jean-Paul Sartre, Harold Pinter, Edward Albee, and others—plays that tragic-comically call attention to life's sound and fury signifying nothing. However, underneath the absurdist actions or inactions (the tramps in Beckett's *Waiting for Godot* spend much of their time sitting around talking about what they're *going* to do), we sense a deeper commentary on the moral or spiritual crises into which our seemingly sacrosanct institutions (church, family, governments) have fallen.

FOR FURTHER REFLECTION

It is not surprising that in the modern age (roughly ever since the mid-nineteenth century) heroism has been under artistic scrutiny. We haven't lost our appreciation of heroism, but we have made our heroes less predicable, less "flat" (see the entry for November 7). We have, in effect, largely (but not totally) stripped them of their superhuman, mythic powers, to make them more compatible with our understanding of human nature.

.....................................TRY THIS....................................

1. Write a story about a flawed hero—say, a Superman-like crime fighter who gets mixed up with a group of Robin Hood types who decide to help the poor in unconventional ways.

2. Write an absurdist comedy in which your main character is a coward or suffers from paranoid delusions or who decides to live out a childhood fantasy, sacrificing his career as an accountant in the process.

SENSORY IMPRESSIONS

Writers sometimes forget that there are five senses from which to draw when writing description, not just the sense of sight. By invoking some or all of the other senses, writers are better able to create the illusion of being there, of experiencing everything that the viewpoint character is experiencing. Here is how Howard Fast makes use of the senses of touch and smell in his novel *Spartacus*:

> From the baths they [the gladiators] went to the rubbing tables. As always, Spartacus closed his eyes as the fragrant olive oil was poured onto his skin and each separate muscle of his body was loosened under the facile and knowing fingers of the masseur.

And here is John Steinbeck, in *The Grapes of Wrath*, capturing a moment during a campfire dinner of jackrabbit:

> [Joad] sat back and clamped his long teeth on the meat and tore out a great bite and chewed it. "Jesus Christ! Hear her crunch!" And he tore out another bite ravenously.

FOR FURTHER REFLECTION

Using more than one sensory impression in your descriptions add depth and realism to your storytelling. Readers take great pleasure in vicariously experiencing everything your characters experience.

......................................TRY THIS...................................

1. Write a scene depicting a family at the dinner table. Describe not only the appearance of the food but its smell, its different tastes, its textures. Be generous in your sensory imagery. See if you can get your readers' mouths to water!

2. Write a short-short story from the point of view of a blind man who must rely on his other senses.

DECEMBER 9
CINEMATIC DRAFTING

Imagine that you are looking at a scene from one of your stories, or your memoir, through a motion-picture camera lens. Let's say your story is about a group of prospectors during the California gold rush. What do you see? Write down everything you notice through the lens: Two prospectors are pouring slurry from the river mill through a giant sieve; another prospector is upstream panning for gold; another is getting a campfire ready. Now, move the camera around, taking in the surrounding mountain wilderness. Next, zoom in for close-up shots—of the mill, the faces of the prospectors, the rushing water, the pan with flakes of gold flashing amid the gravel.

Such cinematic drafting helps writers, at least at the earliest stage of composition, to develop realistic, vividly perceived characters.

FOR FURTHER REFLECTION

Seeing your stories through a camera eye can be a powerful heuristic device—that is, a means of generating story material. The more we see in our mind's eye, the more effectively we can transcribe those images into their verbal counterparts.

...................................TRY THIS....................................

Write a short play or story as if you were watching it unfold behind a motion-picture camera. If you wish, divide the play or story into discreet scenes. Include stage or camera directions for close-ups, panorama shots, boom shots, and the like, to reinforce the camera-eye device.

EXPLORING THE PSYCHOLOGY OF DREAMS

Sigmund Freud and Carl Jung are the first names one thinks of when thinking about dream psychology and dream interpretation. Both have written extensively on dreams: Freud in the context of psychopathology; Jung in the context of mythology and world cultures. Both approaches to dreams are important for writers. Many writers, from Sophocles to Shakespeare to Kafka, have directly or indirectly explored the ways in which dreams intertwine with reality. After all, writers are explores of the psyche, of the deepest longings of the heart; they pay close attention to the ways in which dream symbolism illuminates not only individual personalities, but the Universal Mind of civilization itself.

Dreams, then, are like the tips of icebergs: What they reveal represents a small portion of what lies submerged.

FOR FURTHER REFLECTION

It's not surprising that dreams have intrigued humanity from earliest times. In the ancient world, soothsayers, priests, and oracles were all in the business of dream interpretation. Modern psychology, especially Jungian psychology, continues the tradition. We writers can learn a great deal about human nature from dreams.

......................................TRY THIS...................................

1. Write a story about a modern-day psychologist who travels back in time (to Old or New Testament times, to ancient Greece or Rome, or to the Middle Ages). What kind of influence might he have on history?

2. In the Old Testament, Daniel is seen interpreting King Nebuchadnezzar's dreams (see Daniel 2:31-35). Write a story about an ancient dream-interpreter like Daniel who is obliged to interpret his king's dreams, perhaps to determine if they are prophetic.

FLYING BY THE SEAT OF YOUR PANTS

Why is it that we often can do our best work under pressure? Here is a simple answer: The mind works more efficiently when the heat is on. Because we know more than we think we know (see the entry for December 6), because our experiences and our ideas are so embedded that we sometimes forget we had them, we forget how much in the way of substantive writing we can generate on the spur of the moment—provided we're given sufficient external pressure to do so. Students have an extraordinary knack for churning out papers at the last minute, and while most of the time it shows (because they're inexperienced writers) in terms of faulty diction and poorly constructed sentences and paragraphs, the content they generate is often surprisingly good. Because of the time pressure, they were able to tap into their reservoir of near-forgotten knowledge.

Older, more experienced writers have a deeper reservoir from which to draw. Facing deadlines, meeting quotas, making promises to friends and family members—these are all useful sources of external pressure to help writers get words on paper.

FOR FURTHER REFLECTION

Flying by the seat of your pants—that is, drawing efficiently and quickly from the resources you already possess inside your head—is not a bad way to fly. At least, one should not feel guilty about eleventh-hour composing. We often surprise ourselves by how much we can generate in relatively little time.

......................................TRY THIS......................................

Spend a writing day flying by the seat of your pants at the keyboard. First, you need to give yourself a good excuse for getting *x* number of pages completed. Invite a friend or colleague to come up with an idea. Don't worry; she will quite likely be most resourceful.

DECEMBER 12
CRITIQUING AS COACHING

Coaching is a fine metaphor for critiquing creative work. It suggests that the person doing the critiquing is standing on the sidelines, always mindful that the writer whose work is being critiqued is the object of the game, the star player. A good coach, then, to use a metaphor within a metaphor, is a catalyst—a presence that gets a desired action underway without interfering with that action. This ideal is implicit in the word *feedback* as well: Critiquing benefits writers most when it feeds the writer's own sense of how the draft under scrutiny could be improved.

Critiquing is nearly as beneficial to the critic as it is to the recipient. We learn from our own insights into another's efforts to tell a story. A problem in another writer's narrative pacing, for example, can illuminate the critic's own problems from a different angle. The more facilitative rather than directive or judgmental your feedback, the likelier you can adapt it to your own work in progress.

FOR FURTHER REFLECTION

Revising, like initial drafting, needs to come from within. Suggestions should facilitate rather than direct ("Have you considered doing *x*, *y*, or *z*" instead of "You need to do *x*")—otherwise the revision will in effect become a collaboration. Facilitative criticism (i.e., coaching instead of manipulating) also benefits the facilitator by generating a choice of revision strategies.

...................................TRY THIS....................................

In preparation for your next workshop, change the following directive or judgmental criticisms into facilitative (coaching) ones:

- Make your heroine less aggressive.

- This paragraph is boring.

- A talking mouse doesn't work for me, even though you're writing a fantasy.

DECEMBER 13
HOLIDAY FOODS FOR HOLIDAY STORIES

What would the holiday season be without its myriad culinary delights? Virtually any kind of cuisine can serve as holiday food, so long as it is served in a festive context, with themed dinnerware and glassware, table settings, candles, and ambient lighting. If you're going to write a story with a holiday season setting, you'll want to think about holiday-related foods and drinks.

How about a holiday party? Many holiday-themed cookbooks and party organizing books are on the market. Martha Stewart leaps to mind. For example, *The Martha Stewart Cookbook* includes a cassoulet recipe for one hundred persons: 14 quarts chicken stock, 16 pounds white beans, 6 five-pound ducks, 2 ten-pound geese, 3 six-pound legs of lamb, 12 pounds pork loin, 6 pounds garlic sausage, plus a zillion different vegetables and spices ... One could almost set that recipe to music. Ham also comes to mind for the holidays—all kinds of hams: country ham, Virginia ham, Eastern ham, hams that are glazed, hams that are smoked.

As for holiday-related confections and desserts, there's a near-infinite variety from which to choose. Cookies often top the list, mainly because they can be so easily shaped, a great source of delight for children. Once again, Martha Stewart, in her cookbook, includes several cookie cutout patterns. But it would be more fun to create your own.

FOR FURTHER REFLECTION

Festivity is often linked to food. Eat, drink, and be merry! The very word *carnival* comes from *carne*, the Latin word for meat (because traditional carnivals were staged the day before the beginning of Lent). Religious holidays like Passover involve food—in this case, minimally. Unleavened bread, or *matzo*, the survival food of the Israelites as they migrated out of bondage into the Holy Land, is eaten as part of Passover meals today.

................................TRY THIS....................................

1. Make a list of foods that have religious or festive significance. Write an essay describing the history of some of them.

2. Write a short story in which rival family members have been brought together for a holiday feast. Make the different foods and beverages a prominent part of the story.

HOLIDAY HISTORIES

The holiday season offers the enterprising freelance writer a wealth of ideas for articles about the history of holiday traditions. Where and how did the legend of Santa Claus originate, or the practice of decorating fir trees? What does Hanukkah celebrate, and what do the menorah candles represent? Where and when did the tradition of hanging wreaths originate? These topics have all been written about, but new approaches are always welcome. For example, in tracing the origins of Santa Claus, you might pay special attention to the way Santas are depicted in certain countries, how they have been represented in arts and crafts, or you might just limit your scope to the custom of department store Santas through the ages, or Santa Claus as a subject in stories and films (*Miracle on 34th Street*, for example).

FOR FURTHER REFLECTION

No matter what the subject, it has a history that may prove fascinating enough to tap into for short stories and essays. Also—and this is especially true of holiday-related histories—it may be possible to link the topic with one's family history. What is most meaningful, in your family, about the history and traditional practices of Hanukkah or of Eid? What customs in your holiday are most similar to those in other holidays? Think of the holiday season as a time for learning the history of other celebrations.

....TRY THIS....................................

Brainstorm for unusual story or essay ideas on the history of Christmas, Hanukkah, or Eid. How, for example, did Jews celebrate Hanukkah in Victorian times or during the Renaissance? How many versions of the story of the Three Wise Men (or Magi) can you discover? How did each one originate? What role do children play during Eid?

WISH LISTS

Even if you consider yourself a nonmaterialist, it's tempting to daydream about gifts you might receive during the holiday season. Listing of any kind is a fun and painless way to get your thoughts on paper; wish lists enhance the fun, and just about any list can be turned into a wish list. For example, a list of your favorite comic book heroes can easily be turned into a wish list for the kinds of heroic adventures you would like to embark on.

Wish lists can be sublime, practical, and maybe even a bit loony—such as a list of all the places you would like to visit if you could become invisible or shrink yourself down to the size of an ant. (Crazy a wish as that might be, something similar was used as the premise for the film *Fantastic Voyage*, later novelized by Isaac Asimov, in which a science team and their vessel are reduced to the size of a bacterium and injected into the bloodstream of an unconscious man. Moral: Never discard a wish because you think it's too wild or irrational.)

FOR FURTHER REFLECTION

Wishing and wish-listing are good activities for writers to indulge in. You've heard the warning, "Be careful what you wish for …" Well, as a writer, turn that warning upside down: Allow yourself to wish uninhibitedly!

................................TRY THIS....................................

1. Start keeping a list of fanciful, fantastical, fabulous wishes. Challenge yourself to conjure up the most outlandish wishes you can imagine.

2. After a week or so, review your fantastic wish list and choose one or more of them as the basis for a children's fairy tale or an adult fantasy story.

DECEMBER 16
THE ART OF CONCISION, OR LESS IS MORE

Novice writers tend to overwrite. In one sense, it's not such a bad thing: It stems from the desire to make language do all it can to yield up meaning.

There are three kinds of overwriting: diction- and syntax-level wordiness (using more words than are necessary for conveying the intended thought); faulty sentence construction that results in extraneous wording, or redundant phrasing; and excessive description, explanation, or narration. Why say "I wish to answer in the affirmative" when "Yes" conveys the answer much more concisely and forcefully? Less is more.

But that is not always the case, of course. Writers need to develop an eye for passages that would benefit from concision and those that would not. We can condense Molly Bloom's fifty-page virtually unpunctuated interior monologue to a few pages, but to do so would diminish the feeling of intimacy we have with the character, not to mention the extraordinary experience with James Joyce's masterful handling of stream-of-consciousness language.

FOR FURTHER REFLECTION
Writing concisely, both senses of the word, takes practice, like everything else about writing. One good way to learn concision is to study its principles in a grammar handbook, and then apply those principles to your own verbose sentences and paragraphs.

.....................................TRY THIS....................................

Practice condensing paragraphs in drafts of essays and stories—yours or a fellow writer's—being careful not to destroy the drama or essential meaning of the passage in question. Look for bloated phrases ("I find myself wondering whether or not my dependency on computer technology is increasing"), and condense them so that their essential meaning comes through more clearly ("I think I'm becoming too dependent on computers").

DECEMBER 17
INNER LISTENING

Sometimes we have to listen with more than our ears. That is, we need to open our whole selves, all senses deployed. Sensations sometimes need to be absorbed holistically, not just listened to or felt or tasted. This kind of inner listening heightens our capacity for assimilating what we hear into our own worldview. Every occasion for listening, then, is a learning opportunity, an opportunity for personal growth. By seeking out the wisdom in others, we grow wiser ourselves.

In *The Tao of Peace*, a guide to acquiring and promoting peace (including inner peace) through the lessons of Taoism, Diane Dreher addresses the need to resolve conflicts that produce divisiveness and enmity and derail us from what is truly important in life. The first step is to admit to ourselves when we are ignorant of certain matters: "Many people feel it's a sign of weakness to admit they don't know something. The Tao says it's a sign of strength, an opportunity to learn." And keep in mind that just as we learn from others, others in turn learn from us. Learning and teaching are reciprocal; both are greatly enabled through inner listening.

FOR FURTHER REFLECTION

Becoming a successful writer involves opening ourselves to the ideas and experiences of others. When listening to what others have to say, listen with your whole being, not just with your ears, even if you find yourself disagreeing with them. We learn most from those whose views are most alien to our own.

......................................TRY THIS....................................

Here is a suggestion for an experiment in inner listening: Engage a friend in conversation about a particular topic—something controversial in the news, perhaps. Listen carefully to each other's opinions on the issue. After the conversation, write down what you consider to be your friend's unvoiced assumptions about the issue, reflected in her gestures and tone of voice. Ask your friend to write down your opinions about the issue and do likewise. Finally, compare notes to see how accurately each of you has captured the other's unvoiced thoughts.

DECEMBER 18
VISIONS OF SUGARPLUMS

Holidays are an ideal time for letting your imagination roam free, but "free" doesn't mean "aimless." On the contrary, it means exploring, unfettered by rules and regulations, following wishes and desires you may not even be conscious of. Children have visions of sugarplums during these festive days, and so should you—only your sugarplums will take the form of bold new story ideas, whimsical characters, and whimsical situations in which to embroil your whimsical characters.

Use the holidays throughout the year, not just in December, as an opportunity for essays, stories, poems, and stage plays, that would kindle the imaginations as well as heighten the social consciousness of young people. Martin Luther King Day, Presidents' Day, Mother's Day, Memorial Day, Father's Day, Independence Day, Labor Day, Halloween, Veterans Day, Thanksgiving—every holiday is an occasion for simultaneously educating and entertaining young readers.

FOR FURTHER REFLECTION

Every holiday during the year is a potential sugarplum for enterprising writers interested in reaching young audiences. If you wish to write for children and young adults, not only revisit topics that fascinated you in your youth, but reflect on modern day topics from a young person's perspective.

...................................TRY THIS....................................

1. Take several sheets of notebook paper, and at the top of each sheet, write the name of a holiday. Over the next few days, maintain a list of topics you can imagine yourself writing, either for young people or adults, for each holiday.

2. Take one of the topics for one of the holidays you've listed in number one and compose a rough draft in one or two sittings. Set it aside for a few days and then revise it.

DECEMBER 19
COLLECTIVE EXPERIENCES

Just as single individuals possess experiences, so do groups of people, from nuclear families to extended families to tight-knit friends to professional groups (musicians, actors, soldiers, and so on), even whole communities. Anthropologists like Franz Boas, Ruth Benedict, Margaret Mead and Claude Lévi-Strauss have examined the collective practices of so-called "primitive" cultures to discover new insights into social relationships, courtship, and education that not only expand our knowledge of civilization, but offers us insights into our own seemingly "advanced" customs. Mead, for example, who spent years in Samoa (an island group in the South Pacific) studying adolescent behavior, made this observation in her 1928 study, *Coming of Age in Samoa*:

> The Samoan child who participates intimately in the lives of a host of relatives has many and varied experiences upon which to base its emotional attitudes. Our children, confined within one family circle …, often owe their only experience with birth or death to the birth of a younger brother or sister or the death of a parent or grandparent. Their knowledge of sex, aside from children's gossip, comes from an accidental glimpse of parental activity. This has several … disadvantages. … A host of ill-digested fragmentary conceptions of life and death will fester in the ignorant, inexperienced mind and provide a fertile field for the later growth of unfortunate attitudes. …

By comparing parent-child interaction in two different cultures, Mead enables us to better understand human relationships.

FOR FURTHER REFLECTION
Different societies, like individuals, possess a wide range of different experiences. Writers in a sense are anthropologists whose knowledge of different societies and customs can foster peace and good will. The better we understand the governing principles of other societies, the likelier we can live harmoniously with them.

.... TRY THIS ....

Learn all you can about a little known society, say, in the South Pacific, Southeast Asia, the Alaskan and Canadian arctic, or Sub-Saharan Africa. After you have assimilated ethnographic studies of their social, religious, and artistic customs, write an essay about the society, targeted for young adults.

REACHING THE FINISH LINE

Finish line is a popular metaphor for completing a project, of course, but it also can be a metaphor for completing one stage of the project, such as the first draft of an outline synopsis, or a discovery draft. These, too, ought to be regarded as finish lines.

You know the ancient Chinese proverb, "A long journey begins with a single step." Implicit in that nugget of wisdom is that that initial step is its own finish line. Translated into writers' work, a single step can be the opening sentence of a draft that sets the wheels in motion. Setting up a daily writing regimen is also a step, and so is finishing the first page, the first chapter. Tossing it all away because you realized that the story or thesis simply wasn't panning out—yes, that is also a finish-line step.

FOR FURTHER REFLECTION

Writers' work includes many finish lines that ought to be acknowledged as such along the way to the grand finish line. It's a simple psychological strategy that keeps one's energy and motivation levels at optimum performance. Using this scheme is also a good reminder of the fact that writing is a multistage endeavor.

...................................TRY THIS....................................

The next time you plan a writing project, regard each step as a finish line. Don't just think it, record it as the heading for each stage—initial one-paragraph overview; initial outline/synopsis; revised outline/synopsis; opening sentence; first paragraph; first page of the discovery draft; and so on.

HOLIDAY TRADITIONS AND INNOVATIONS

Today marks the beginning of winter in the northern hemisphere, and holiday festivities are underway everywhere. This is a time when traditions are treasured. The old Christmas carols are once again being sung; it doesn't matter how many hundreds of times one has heard "Jingle Bells" or "The Little Drummer Boy"—it's part of the holiday tradition, along with Hanukkah bushes, Christmas trees and wreaths, menorah candles, Santa Clauses, Salvation Army pots, ribbons, bows, and multicolored lights.

But even during this time of traditional festivities, there's plenty of room for innovation: new toys, new games (especially video games with a holiday motif), and, most importantly for writers, new spins on stories like Charles Dickens's *A Christmas Carol*, and plenty of brand new stories with a holiday theme.

As you prepare to enjoy this holiday season, think also of contributing to its legacy by writing a poem, a song, a children's story, a parable that invokes the beauty and solemnity of Christmas, Eid, Hanukkah, or Kwanzaa.

FOR FURTHER REFLECTION

The winter holiday season is a time for festivity, for honoring tradition and a time to create new stories, poems, and songs that draw from those time-honored traditions. The winter solstice (which is today) is also a time for festivity: Although it marks the shortest day/longest night of the year, it also begins the slow return to spring and summer.

..................................TRY THIS..................................

1. Write a poem in the manner of "'Twas the Night Before Christmas"—only give it a somewhat contemporary spin.

2. Compose the lyrics for a song, perhaps in the manner of "Rudolph the Red-Nosed Reindeer," or "The Chipmunk Song," but use different animals instead.

3. Write a new version of the Kwanzaa folktale "Anansi and His Sons" (read the original at www.folktales.net/umoja.html), or of Dickens's *A Christmas Carol* (you might want to draw inspiration from the Bill Murray film *Scrooged*).

CLIMAXES AND RESOLUTIONS

Stories have to lead somewhere and that somewhere is usually known as the climax, epiphany, or moment of reckoning. This is the moment in the story that grips the reader the hardest. Will the viewpoint character's efforts to accomplish his goal pay off? The simplest kind of climax is what we might call the "shootout" climax: As in many Westerns, hero and villain face each other in a duel. They open fire. One lives, one dies—or, both die or both live. Regardless of the outcome, something has changed profoundly and permanently—and the impact of that change determines the story's resolution. The hero may have killed the villain, but the trauma of the duel has made him want to give up being sheriff, or filled him with disdain toward those who encouraged him to agree to the duel in the first place. A thousand variations might stream through a writer's mind when working out the climax of a story; only one can be selected.

FOR FURTHER REFLECTION

Being mirrors of reality, stories heighten the patterns we experience in our own lives, although not as pronounced most of the time. Courtroom dramas come closest, which is why they're used so often in fiction. Verdicts are climaxes. Medical dramas also come close to the way we experience climaxes in real life; the surgeon emerging from the operating room is the climactic moment.

.....................................TRY THIS.....................................

1. Study the way two or three novelists construct their respective climaxes; then outline a short story that includes two or more possible climaxes—each one, perhaps, mirroring those of the respective novels you've been studying.

2. Write a climax scene to a story that is still in its planning stage. Working out the climax first will give you a better idea of how to dramatically render the steps that lead up to it.

REVELATION

Revelation is one of those words that conjures up natural and supernatural visions and visions that fall somewhere in-between, as is the case with artistic revelation, or epiphany, which in a sense is what the author of the Book of Revelation, St. John the Divine, also gives us.

Revelation presents a vision of events that would befall civilization to pave the way for the Day of Judgment, the defeat of the forces of Satan, the Second Coming of Christ, and the establishment of the City of God: "And I John [St. John the Divine, or John of Patmos] saw the holy city, new Jerusalem, coming down from God, out of Heaven" (Revelation 21:2). The influence of the book of Revelation on world literature is pervasive and profound, which is why writers need to be familiar with it.

FOR FURTHER REFLECTION
Prophetic visions permeate sacred texts of all religions and have influenced contemporary prophetic works, including fantasy and science fiction. It is no accident that the biblical Armageddon, the site of the final battle in which the forces of good triumph over the forces of evil, has become a synonym for nuclear holocaust, for the end of the world.

....TRY THIS....................................

Write a story in which two armies from two radically different cultures (or, if you like to write science fiction, two different planets) confront each other with the fate of a carefully guarded secret at stake. What is the precious secret? Why are two mighty armies about to go to war over it? What will be the outcome? That is for you to decide.

DECEMBER 24
THE ETHICS OF AUTHORSHIP

The word *ethics* comes from the Greek *ethos*, meaning proper conduct, integrity, or character. The term is applied to civic policies, to environmental steward-ship (a land ethic), and to professions, such as business and medicine. It also applies to the profession of authorship, and in several ways: (1) The work is your own; any use of words and ideas not your own is properly acknowledged; (2) The facts you present are accurate; (3) When writing autobiographically, you convey personal experiences as they actually happened without distortion. Of course, memory being what it is, and language being what it is, some distortion is inevitable, but that does not excuse fictionalizing or inventing experiences. If you wish to do so, then call your work a novel, not a memoir.

FOR FURTHER REFLECTION

Readers have faith that a work of nonfiction will be exactly that: no invented stories being passed off as true. Of course, a lived experience has to be shaped by words; inevitably, distortion creeps in, just as one's memory of an experi-ence is inevitably a distortion of what "really" happened. But these are givens. Nonfiction writers must do all they can to ensure that the experiences they present are authentic; i.e., they ought to be verifiable.

..................................TRY THIS....................................

After you finish a draft of your next essay, article, biography, or autobiographical project, check it for accuracy, using the following checklist:

- Are dates and names of places and persons accurate?
- Are incidents accurately described? Can they be verified by others?
- Are facts and explanations accurate?
- Is the sequence of events accurate?

DECEMBER 25
MERRY CHRISTMAS

Holidays have a way of magically transforming even the most mundane settings, and Christmas has been able to do this supremely well over the ages. Neighborhoods become ablaze in multicolored lights, Santa Clauses, reindeer, snowmen, and Magi throughout the month of December. Department store windows come to life with storybook characters to delight children and adults. Pine trees are swathed in gold and silver garland; wreathes appear on doors. People of all faiths become more animated; they dress more colorfully and are friendlier. Their eyes reflect the lights surrounding them.

Writers are trained to look for story material anywhere; the holidays make it almost too easy. "'Tis the season to be jolly," the carol goes; indeed, the season seems to bring out the best in people. But sometimes behind the gaiety are lonely people who long to be touched by the holiday magic. They have stories to tell.

FOR FURTHER REFLECTION

A reflection for Christmas day: The spreading of good will and the promise to work toward making a better world; the blessings of joy and peace—these are gifts that we writers can offer the world through our storytelling magic. There can never be too many stories of this kind, and there are countless stories that need to be told. Merry Chirstmas.

...............................TRY THIS...................................

On this Christmas day, compose a poem or a short-short story that will instill love or hope or compassion (preferably all three) in the hearts of others. Write it with the intention of reading it aloud to family and friends.

DECEMBER 26
EPIPHANIES AND AFTERGLOWS

An epiphany is the manifestation of the supernatural or divine into the real. It can also be an aesthetic revelation—a kind of Eureka moment when a problem you've worked on for years suddenly, magically falls into place, either in a dream or while awake; think of the cliché image of a light bulb flashing over a cartoon character's head. Epiphanies also have a way of leaving behind an afterglow that colors one's perceptions of the world. Wordsworth, in his Preface to *Lyrical Ballads*, speaks of emotion recollected in tranquility: "The emotion is contemplated till ... the tranquility gradually disappears, and an emotion, kindred to that which was before the subject of contemplation, is gradually produced ... In this mood successful composition generally begins."

In the novel by Diane Schoemperlen, *Our Lady of the Lost and Found*, a woman is visited by the Virgin Mary who, exhausted after two thousand years of making appearances and being adored, is in need of a long rest. The woman invites her in, and so begins a story that gives new understanding to the experience of faith and divine intervention.

FOR FURTHER REFLECTION

Epiphanies, whether spiritual or artistic (assuming there's any significant difference between them), can change us profoundly. We look for the magical, the miracles (large or small) that allow us to glimpse behind the surface of everyday life, reminding us that an unfathomable mystery lies beyond.

······························ TRY THIS ·····························

1. Write a story in which an angel or saint pays you a visit—not as an apparition but as a flesh-and-blood person—no haloes, no wings (unless they can be somehow strapped down and covered up). What would be the compelling reason for such a visit? What would you have happen in the story?

2. Write an essay in which you relive a Eureka moment or some other kind of epiphany in your life.

NEW STORIES FROM OLD

Literature is filled with stories that are based on myths, legends, fairy tales, and Bible stories, both oral and written. Retellings (or adaptations) attract a wide readership and thus prove to be a delightful alternative to conjuring up stories from scratch.

West Side Story is a mid-twentieth century retelling of Shakespeare's *Romeo and Juliet*. Instead of Capulets vs. Montagues, we have Jets vs. Sharks—a white gang vs. a Puerto Rican gang. In James Joyce's *Ulysses*, Leopold Bloom embarks upon a twenty-four-hour odyssey through labyrinthine Dublin just as his counterpart Odysseus spends twenty years at sea in an effort to find his way home to Ithaca. In his National Book Award-winning novel, *The Centaur*, John Updike creates modern-day characters from mythological counterparts. In *Wicked* (and its sequel, *Son of a Witch*), Gregory Maguire takes us back to L. Frank Baum's land of Oz, only this time we get the story from the point of view of the Wicked Witch of the West.*

FOR FURTHER REFLECTION

Readers love to revisit venerable old stories from a fresh new perspective. Great stories like *Cinderella* and *The Wizard of Oz* are filled with such colorful minor characters that they succeed at becoming major ones in retellings. In the play *Rosencrantz and Guildenstern are Dead*, Tom Stoppard makes the two minor envoys from *Hamlet* the principal characters and brilliantly re-presents Shakespeare's masterpiece from their point of view.

. . . . TRY THIS . . . .

Choose one of your favorite myths or fairy tales and retell it from the point of view of its villain or a minor character. Also consider changing the mood of the story from tragedy to comedy or from fantasy to gritty reality.

---

* Maguire has also written *Confessions of an Ugly Stepsister*, a retelling of *Cinderella*, and *Mirror Mirror*, a retelling of *Snow White*, set in Tuscany during the Renaissance.

DECEMBER 28
JUBILATION

Year's end is a time to feel jubilant, to share our jubilation with friends and loved ones—and for writers, to spread the jubilation through our writing. We can do so in several ways:

- composing New Year themed verse for greeting cards

- creating festive food dishes and sharing the recipes with friends

- writing and illustrating winter wonderland fantasy stories for the children in your family (and if you don't do illustrations, have one of the children do so)

- writing holiday-themed skits and asking family members and friends to act them out

- devising vocalizing games along the lines of "The minister's cat is a(n) _____ cat," whereby each player must utter a suitable adjective in alphabetical order; thus if one player says "… an angry cat," the next player must instantly utter an adjective that starts with the letter b.

FOR FURTHER REFLECTION

The closing days of December are a time for jubilation, and for closure. Reflect back on all that you have accomplished this past year, and celebrate your accomplishments. Next year you will accomplish even more.

............................TRY THIS....................................

1. Create a parlor game that involves the use of the voice—singing, naming, declaiming—for several persons.

2. Compose a poem that celebrates the end of the year and that is meant to be read aloud. Include colorful words with lots of alliteration.

3. Write the lyrics for a year's-end or New Year's song, then set it to music, or ask a musician friend to do so.

SYMBOLS OF BIRTH AND REBIRTH

Fertility, birth, and rebirth symbols abound in the world's religions and have their roots in pagan rituals, myths, and legends. Of course, fertility, birth, and rebirth symbolism can have natural referents. Grain grows from seeds; trees and plants die in the winter and return to life in the fall. In many religions, human beings also may experience rebirth. In Christianity, the miraculous birth and rebirth both parallel and transcend the natural. Jesus becomes the means by which humanity, fallen because of the fall from grace in the Garden of Eden, may be redeemed, given a second chance to achieve eternal life—in that sense, reborn.

Both the dynamics of life, death, and rebirth in nature and their supernatural counterparts in religion, provide writers with a vast reservoir of cultural riches from which to build stories, poems, and dramas. It matters not whether a writer is "religious"; the point is to become deeply familiar with the books, the art, the music that comprises these cultural legacies and which bind humanity together.

FOR FURTHER REFLECTION

Some of the most powerful symbols are those that convey fertility, regeneration. Every society throughout history has produced a body of stories having to do with birth and rebirth.

..................................TRY THIS...................................

1. Locate stories from different mythologies (Greek, Roman, Norse, Germanic, Native American, African, Asian) and retell some of them in your own words.

2. Take one of the stories you've come upon for number one and turn it into a full-fledged short story set either in ancient times or in the modern world.

DECEMBER 30
REACHING FOR CLOSURE

Writers are sometimes blocked because they are uncertain about how to bring a story or an essay to an end. It can be a major cause of anxiety because the writer may have been laboring on the project for months or years. Hit a brick wall *now*? Intolerable!

The first order of business is to defuse the anxiety. One way to do this is to compose multiple endings and see which one works best—easier said than done, perhaps, because an "ending" can turn out to be several dozen pages long. Writing two or three of them could be like writing another book.

Some writers work out their endings before anything else. It might spoil the fun, but it reduces the anxiety and gives one a coherent sense of direction. Even with an ending already worked out, though, the likelihood remains that incidents and their sequences will have to be rearranged, and this can affect closure. In other words, an important aspect of closure is determined intuitively. One simply acquires a sixth sense of how best to wrap things up.

FOR FURTHER REFLECTION
Closure in writing may be comparable to closure in music. A symphony will often end with a distinct "coda" in which all the motifs expressed earlier return for synthesis. Perhaps that's the most important word of all to keep in mind when wrestling with closure: *synthesis*—how it all comes together as a powerful, harmonious unity.

..................................TRY THIS....................................

Outline a short story in which the ending represents a culmination of motifs introduced throughout the work. Use the word *coda* to remind you of the musical analogue.

QUOTAS

When asked how he would react if his doctor told him he had but six months left to live, one of the twentieth century's most prolific writers, Isaac Asimov, glibly replied he would just type a little faster. Asimov didn't make quotas for himself—he didn't need them! "Are you a morning writer or a nighttime writer?" an interviewer once asked him. "I'm an all-day writer," he promptly replied.

Well, since very few writers can endure the stamina of writing all day, establishing a quota can be useful. But be careful: Too demanding a quota may easily backfire; too light a quota will not get big projects completed in any reasonable amount of time. Experiment with different quotas to find one that works best for you in the long run.

FOR FURTHER REFLECTION

Quotas help us get large writing projects completed in a reasonable amount of time; quotas also help to inculcate the habit of writing on a regular basis. This is important because, as with any skill, efficiency is maintained through steady application. But quotas can have a negative effect on productivity as well. It's better to fall short of your quota for a given day than to plunge ahead doing less than your best work.

......................................TRY THIS......................................

Give yourself a modest quota to follow for the next ten days, and follow it as rigorously as you can without sacrificing quality. Give yourself a little bit of a margin. Even though missing your quota just once can disrupt the habit you are trying to form, it's better than producing poor quality work.

Start off with a quota you feel confident you can adhere to—say, two pages per day. By the end of those ten days, you'll have a draft of an essay or short story completed.

11 Experience

12 Feedback and Criticism

13 Food and Drink

18   Meditating, Thinking, Questioning

19   Memories and Memorabilia

20   Motivation, Inspiration

about the author

Fred White, an associate professor of English at Santa Clara University in Northern California, received his Ph.D. in English (emphasis on rhetoric and the teaching of writing) from the University of Iowa. In 1997, he received Santa Clara University's Louis and Dorina Brutocao Award for Teaching Excellence. He is the author of four textbooks on writing, the latest of which, *The Well-Crafted Argument*, co-authored with Simone Billings, is in its third edition (Houghton Mifflin, 2008). Other recent books include *LifeWriting: Drawing from Personal Experience to Create Features You Can Publish* (Quill Driver Books, 2004; a Writer's Digest Book Club Selection); *Essential Muir: A Selection of John Muir's Best Writings* (Heyday Books, 2006); and *Approaching Emily Dickinson: Critical Currents and Crosscurrents Since 1960* (Camden House, 2008). He has also published numerous shorter works—most recently a one-act children's play, *Beowulf & Grendel*—an adaptation of the great Anglo-Saxon epic (Big Dog Plays, 2007); a full-length play, *Bones*, based on the life of the poet John Berryman (*Oregon Literary Review*, 2005); plus essays, short fiction, and poetry in *The Cambridge Companion to Emily Dickinson*, edited by Wendy Martin (Cambridge University Press, 2002); *The Chronicle of Higher Education*; *College Literature*; *Confrontation*; *Pleiades*; *Rattle*; *The San Jose Mercury News*; and *South Carolina Review*. He lives in San Mateo, California, with his wife, Therese (an attorney), and their insubordinate cat, Cordelia.